But Enough About Me

But Enough About Me

A Memoir

Burt Reynolds

and Jon Winokur

G. P. PUTNAM'S SONS | *New York*

PUTNAM

G. P. PUTNAM'S SONS
Publishers Since 1838
An imprint of Penguin Random House LLC
375 Hudson Street
New York, New York 10014

Frontispiece photograph: © The Palm Beach Post/Zuma Wire

ISBN 978-0-399-17354-7

Printed in the United States of America
1   3   5   7   9   10   8   6   4   2

BOOK DESIGN BY NICOLE LAROCHE

*Penguin is committed to publishing works of quality and integrity.
In that spirit, we are proud to offer this book to our readers;
however, the story, the experiences, and the words
are the author's alone.*

For Nancy Lee

A movie star runs into an old friend on Rodeo Drive. The friend can't get a word in edgewise as the star goes on and on about her glamorous life: the A-list parties, the Bel-Air mansion, the Bentley convertible. After what seems like an eternity she finally takes a breath and says, "But enough about me. How did you like my last picture?"

Contents

Author's Note

This book is about the people who've shaped me, for better or worse. In chapters named for specific individuals, or for groups of people, I pay homage to those I love and respect, from my family and friends to the athletes, actors, directors, teachers, and students who've enriched my life. You'll find mostly love letters here, but a few poison-pen notes, too, because my bullshit detector has improved with age. I don't hesitate to call out the assholes I can't forgive, like the Hollywood "friends" who came and went in herds. But I also try to make amends for being an asshole myself on too many occasions. I've always made fun of myself, and I don't stop now. And I think I've learned a few things about acting, about filmmaking, about love, about life . . . but enough about me. I hope you enjoy my book.

—B.R.

Foreword

by Jon Voight

It's the second day of filming *Deliverance*. Burt Reynolds is playing Lewis Medlock, a macho survivalist, and I'm Ed Gentry, a mild-mannered suburbanite. Our characters have arranged for a couple of backwoods guys to lead us down to the river in their truck. We're to follow them in our Scout SUV, with Burt behind the wheel and me riding shotgun. With no seat belt. As I would learn, that's the way it often feels with Burt: no seat belt.

In the script, Lewis decides he wants to lead, not follow, so he cuts onto the road in front of the truck, and it makes Ed nervous. That's the script.

So the plan is to give the truck a small head start, then cut through a grassy area and beat it to the road. Now we're rolling film, and the assistant director calls through a bullhorn, "Number one car!" and the truck takes off. A few seconds later we hear, "Number two car!" but Burt waits. And waits. I'm wondering what the hell's going on. When he finally takes off, I know we have no chance to keep close to the truck, never mind beat it to the road. Burt floors it and we almost go airborne. I'm certain now we're going to crash into the truck and I brace against the dashboard. But somehow we land on the road about a foot ahead of the truck, throw up some dust and stones, and head on down the road, and I hear Burt's whoop of a laugh that I would come to learn signals another happy brush with danger. It's at about this time that I learn that this world-class athlete, this all-star halfback back at Florida State, is in the stuntmen's union.

We're not done. A few scenes later the two of us are still in the SUV facing what looks like an overgrown cow path in the middle of the woods. There are tiny trees growing on it and we don't have much visibility. We're in a tight spot on both sides with no room for technicians or camera crew. A couple of crew members have fastened a gyroscope camera on the hood of the SUV, which is supposed to keep steady no matter how rough the ride is. It's an early use of this technology and everyone is hoping it will work. With the camera secured, the director and all of the crew leave us to take over the filming ourselves.

I switch on the camera and jump into the SUV, pick up the clapboard, and, for some reason, maybe because I know I'm crazy putting myself in Burt's hands again, I announce in a German accent, "Und now ve happily go forvard into who the hell knows vhat. Take one!" As soon as I clap the thing, Burt floors it.

We don't know what's in front of us (apparently no one's checked out the terrain). Burt doesn't care. He's going flat out. Trees are raking the side of the vehicle and slapping at the camera, which seems to be holding. Suddenly we hit what feels like a crater: BAM! It rocks the vehicle down to its frame. We somehow bounce out of it, although we may have been inches away from going through the windshield. I think even Burt is shocked at how close we came to disaster, but his reaction is to giggle and soon the two of us are laughing, the kind of deep laughter little kids get. Yet even in our hysteria we remember to play it into our characters and finish out the scene. A bit of a miracle.

All this is in the final film. It's one of my favorite sequences in all of the filming I've done, and it is this portrait of our laughter that comes to mind when I think of my friendship with Burt Reynolds.

When we began shooting *Deliverance,* Burt was in a place where the depth of his talent hadn't been truly recognized. Our director, John Boorman, must be given all the credit for seeing his greatness and for insisting on Burt for the plum role of Lewis Medlock. Ned Beatty, Ronny Cox, and I, his costars, became his great fans, and Burt knew what we all came to know: that his performance would expose his enormous talent to the world and change his career forever.

Look at the scene where Lewis saves the team from the mountain men. He takes total command of a dangerous situation and delivers a powerful aria in the middle of those woods. It's a sensational piece of acting. I think we all did our parts well, but it was Burt who rose up and showed his full stature in that central great moment. The success of the film has everything to do with his performance. The story is compelling and the filmmaking is superior, but the key ingredient in *Deliverance* is Burt Reynolds.

Burt and I had different approaches to acting in *Deliverance.* Some of it certainly had to do with the difference in our characters. Like my character, Ed, I'm questioning everything and wanting to stay on solid ground. I'm thinking about all the different motivations, building my character piece by piece, always refining. But there's Burt saying, "Let's go!" He already knows exactly what to do and he can't wait to do it.

Of course a lot of this is just us. I'm naturally reflective and Burt is a man of action. This is evident, too, in our approaches to celebrity. I was wary of it, thinking it would erode my artistic aspirations. Burt loved signing autographs. He knew how happy it made people. Today, when I sign autographs or take photos with fans I think about that time and Burt's lesson to me.

Whenever Burt and I get together, it's a happy occasion. We've both had our ups and downs in life, but we can step back and laugh at ourselves. Again: it's the laughter. The laughter has become the signature of our friendship. Burt has it in abundance. And it's in this funny, honest book, too. As Burt shares his memories of the people in his life, you get a true sense of the man. It's like sitting down and talking with him. You'll learn things you might not know, like the fact that Burt built a theater in Florida at great personal expense because he wanted to give back to the community, and that he's dedicated himself to teaching in order to keep faith with the drama professor who changed his life.

Burt loves people and has always liked to keep his friends close. During that incredible five-year period when he was number one at the box office, he based a lot of his career decisions on friendship, like when he helped his stuntman buddy Hal Needham get a film made called *Smokey and the Bandit*. When Burt did his TV show *Evening Shade*, he brought his pals along with him: Marilu Henner, Ossie Davis, and Charles Durning.

I've known some of the beautiful, talented women in Burt's life. I've sat with Quinton, Burt's son with Loni Anderson, enjoying evenings when Burt would host gatherings of artists like Dom DeLuise, Charles Nelson Reilly, Angie Dickinson, and Charley Durning. Quinton is a wonderful young man pursuing a career in film editing. I see him every so often in a deli we both frequent and I catch up on his father's adventures. I know he'd want me to finish this up with a statement by Charles Durning.

Charley represented many things to Burt. He was a consummate artist. It was not by accident that he was nominated for two Academy Awards. He had a marvelous sense of humor and was as quick a wit as any of the brilliant company he kept, Burt included. But Charley was also a war hero. He enlisted in the army during World War II when he was seventeen and was part of the Normandy Invasion that was the turning point in the war. He fought in the Battle of the Bulge and was awarded the Silver Star for valor. Through all this experience, he certainly came to know the measure of a man. Charley once told me he loved Burt Reynolds because he knew that Burt would have his back if he was ever in trouble. I think his words to me about Burt are the highest praise a man can pay another man. I concur with Charley. That's the kind of guy Burt is, and I'm proud to be his friend.

Big Burt

Growing up in Palm Beach County, Florida, I went by the name Buddy. I remained Buddy in high school and through college, and my old friends still call me that. I was billed as Buddy Reynolds early in my acting career until my agent said, "You know, you're twenty-three years old and we can't keep calling you Buddy."

"Why not?" I said. "There's Buddy Rogers, Buddy Hackett . . ."

"See what I mean?" she said.

So I took my dad's name. He was Burton Milo Reynolds Sr.—Big Burt—and I was Burton Milo Reynolds Jr. I think he was pleased, but he never said so.

I come from a time and place where boys and then men try to please their fathers. It's the most important thing in a man's life. My dad was my hero, but he never acknowledged any of my achievements. I've always felt that no amount of success would make me a man in his eyes. I never lacked confidence, but I always felt the need to prove myself to him.

Big Burt was a cop and a war hero. He was tough on me, but looking back I think that was a good thing, because I was a hellraiser. If he hadn't gotten my attention, I probably would have wound up in prison or worse. My mom was wonderful to me and

I loved her very much. She was a head nurse at a hospital in Michigan, so she really knew her stuff whenever I got hurt—which was often. She had a lot on her shoulders when my father was overseas, and she handled it with grace and good humor. I couldn't have asked for a better mother.

Mom and Dad were both born on farms in northern Michigan. When Dad was twenty, he had a job shoveling coal in a factory and became friends there with Wade Miller. Wade introduced Burt to his sister Fern, who was in nursing school. It didn't take him long to pop the question. Their marriage lasted sixty-five years and I never heard them fight. (They must have done it quietly.)

Dad always had a job, even during the Great Depression. He worked in an auto factory and in a steel mill; he dug ditches— anything to put food on the table for my mom and my sister, Nancy Ann, who was born in 1930. I came along in 1936. Nancy Ann was a lot like Mom in many ways: very quiet, very strong. She was a terrific gal, but we never got to know each other well, I guess because of the age difference.

BIG BURT JOINED the army at the start of World War II and went into the cavalry, but it was soon disbanded and he transferred to the field artillery. He'd made lieutenant by the time he shipped overseas, where he earned a chestful of medals for taking part in the Normandy Invasion and the Battle of the Bulge. Like most veterans who were in the thick of things, he never talked about it. After V-E Day he was stationed in Germany. After V-J Day, when all the troops came home, he stayed in the army for three more years as part of the occupation of Japan. He was a colonel by then and they promised to make him a general if he stayed in for another three years.

When my mom heard that, she said, "You may be a general, but you won't be my husband."

When he came home, it was right out of *The Best Years of Our Lives*. We were all at my uncle's house in Michigan. I stayed in the kitchen with Nancy Ann while Mom waited on the front lawn. Dad drove up in a taxi and I started to run out, but Nancy Ann stopped me and said, "No, let them be alone."

I saw him through the window. He was six-two, and when he got out of the taxi he looked smashing in his uniform. The two of them stood there in an embrace for a long time. When they finally came inside, he kissed my sister on the cheek. I wanted to jump up and hug him, but we didn't do that sort of thing in our family, so I just stood there. He stuck his hand out and I shook it.

"You look good, son," he said.

"Thank you, sir."

He handed me a ten-dollar bill and said, "Here, go buy yourself something." Then he and my mom disappeared into the bedroom until the next morning.

My dad was strong, but my mom was the boss. Not long after he came home, they went south on a second honeymoon. When they got back she announced, "We're moving to Florida." It was all her idea. He didn't want to go, but she put her foot down. I didn't want to go either. I pictured us living in the jungle with alligators and snakes.

As soon as we were settled in Florida, Dad got a job in construction. I don't think he'd ever done that sort of work, but his boss was taken with him and made him the foreman of the project. They built prefab houses that everybody said would blow away in the first hurricane, but those houses are still standing today. That summer I went to work with him. One day a wire caught on his finger and sliced it off from the knuckle to the tip. He didn't even say "Ouch!" He just picked it up, wrapped it in a handkerchief, and stuck it in his pocket.

"When we get home tonight," he said, "remind me to give this to your mother."

When we got home, Mom was only a little surprised. She knew how he was.

I WAS a wild kid and got my share of whippings from my dad. It would be the same thing every time: He'd take his belt off, I'd bend over, and he wouldn't spare the horses when he hit me. I wanted to yell, but I didn't. I never cried, either. I'm glad he did it. It was a real deterrent. I didn't want to get hit again, so I never committed the same offense twice. My mom never intervened when Dad disciplined me, though I know she wanted to. I think she was glad that she didn't have the responsibility. It tore her up to see me get a whipping, but she knew that I needed discipline badly in those days. I once made the mistake of sassing her in front of Big Burt. I think I said something flip like "Oh, yeah?" Without saying a word, he picked me up and deposited me in the hall closet. Unfortunately, the door to the closet was closed at the time.

Despite the corporal punishment, I still managed to get in trouble. There was a canal next to the Skydrome Drive-in in Lake Worth with a kind of homemade zip line across it consisting of a cargo box on a wire. People would put bottles and things in the box and push it across the water. It was just big enough for us to cram ourselves into and ride across. It was our own little amusement ride. It didn't occur to us that there might be a reason everybody called it "the kid killer." One day I got in the box and the guys pushed me, but not hard enough. I went halfway out and got stuck. I was hanging there over the water and didn't know what to do. I grabbed the wire and started pulling myself across, inch by inch, but each time I made headway it rolled back over my hands and cut them all to hell. I was still swaying in the wind when someone said, "Hey, Buddy, here comes your dad!"

Big Burt, who by that time was chief of police, pulled up in his patrol car and got out. "Get back here!" he said.

"How'm I gonna do that, Pop?"

"I don't know, but you'd better get back here *now*!"

"Pop, I can't move. Are you gonna help me?"

"No!" he said, and he got back in the car and left.

I sat in that damn box for an hour before my buddies found a rope and reeled me in.

One Saturday night a bunch of us were arrested for fighting, and they put us in a big holding cell. My dad came in and told the other kids one by one: "Your father's here, you can go home. *Your* father's here, *you* can go home." Then he looked at me and said, "*Your* father didn't show up."

I was in that cell all night. By morning I figured that any minute he'd come and take me home for a whippin' and a good breakfast, but I stayed there all day, with every drunk and vagrant in town. I stayed in that damn cell for two days! I know it sounds harsh, but it straightened me out. I never got in trouble after that. I think that lesson saved me, along with the fact that there were very few illegal drugs floating around back then.

MY DAD was a great man, but sometimes he did things that were hard to swallow if you didn't know who he really was. He was judgmental, if not downright prejudiced, and it could be cruel. There was a wonderful girl in my high school named Sally; she was half Seminole. The guys called her "Sally Seminole," which made me mad. Her whole family worked as migrant laborers, and she'd miss school when they had to pick tomatoes. When she wasn't working we'd ride the bus together and talk all the way to school. I had a crush on her and tried to get her to go out with me, but she said, "No, I'd better not."

But one day around Christmas she came and knocked on the door. I wanted to ask her in, but my dad was standing there. He didn't say anything, but I could tell he didn't want her to come in the house. Sally got the message, too, and she left.

I was ashamed of him, but more ashamed of myself. I wanted to tell him how hurtful he'd been, but I didn't have the courage. It's one of the biggest sorrows of my life, because I looked up to my dad. To this day it's hard for me to understand how he could have such a blind spot.

After we graduated, I never saw Sally again, though I tried to find her. Told she lived in a trailer in the middle of nowhere, I drove out to the address I'd been given, but the trailer was gone. I wish I knew what happened to her.

Yet Big Burt could be generous and compassionate. I had a friend in junior high named Jimmy Hooks. He had an alcoholic mother and an absent father, and it was tough on him. I went home with him one day after school and saw him fight a grown man. Damn near whipped the guy, too. I felt sorry for Jimmy and admired his guts. I felt he deserved better. "Hooksey," I said, "you're coming home with me."

When we got to the house, I said to my mom, "Jimmy's gonna live with us from now on."

"We'll talk about it when Big Burt gets home," she said.

My dad knew about Jimmy's situation, him being the police chief and it being a small town. "Yes, son, he can live here," he said. "But we've got rules in this house, and you'll both have to abide by them. Come upstairs." He opened my closet, put his hand in the middle of the clothes, and went *pffft*, dividing them in half. "Jimmy,

these are your clothes over here, and those are Buddy's over
he said.

Gee, I didn't even get a chance to pick 'em out or anything.

My parents legally adopted Jimmy and treated him like a son
from then on.

Jimmy has a winning personality and everybody likes him. He
was a pretty good football player, too. He wasn't big, but he made
up in desire for what he lacked in athletic ability. He became a high
school football coach, and when my dad talked about the two of
us, he considered Jimmy the bigger success.

Unfortunately, Jimmy and I haven't stayed close over the years.
It isn't his fault. The gal he married wasn't crazy about me. She
thought I should have been more attentive to Jim and helped him
more financially, but I'd already helped him a lot, and there came
a time when I thought he should strike out on his own. As it was,
he had every break anybody could ask for, and I was disappointed
with him in that sense. I thought he could have done better if he'd
tried harder.

RIVIERA BEACH—growing up, I thought it was pronounced
"Riveera"—was a tough town on the wrong side of the river, but
the people there respected Big Burt. He'd take me with him sometimes to places I had no business going, and Mom wasn't thrilled
about the idea. One night when I was sixteen, he said, "C'mon,
we're going down to the Blue Heron." It was a bar that was scary
to drive by in your car. He had to go in and arrest a couple of hard
guys. There were already two cops there, but the guys said, "We
ain't goin' nowhere until the chief comes."

I went in with my dad, but I stopped at the end of the bar to
watch. Both guys had knives. Dad said, "Put the knives on the

bar," and they did. He picked one up. "This is a nice knife," he said as he jammed it into the bar, causing the blade to break off. "But a lousy blade," he quickly added. Then he threw the handle at him. I thought we'd have to fight our way out, but everybody in the place seemed to think that was terrific, including the two guys!

We all went out and got in the car. They were in the backseat and I was in front with my dad. "Your dad's a hell of a man," one of them said, and the other nodded. I was amazed that they were praising him while he was taking them to jail.

Big Burt was tough, all right. He thought acting was for sissies. When I was in junior college taking theater classes, whenever he was pissed off at me he'd say, "Is that an acting thing you're doing?" And whenever I mentioned the name of one of my friends, he'd say, "Is he an actor or does he *work*?" He thought it was a candy-ass profession. I hoped he'd get over it, but years later, after I'd done a television series, he said, "When are you going to get a *real* job?"

"I think this is it, Dad."

"It's not a real job. You're just playacting."

He never acknowledged that I was any good at it. He was of course the police chief, and all the officers under him were proud of me. I asked them, "Does he ever talk about me?"

"Nope."

IN 1960, just before I went to Germany to do a picture called *Armored Command*, Dad gave me the name of a woman there and asked me to look her up.

"She may not be alive," I said.

"She's alive," he said.

"How do you know her?"

"She's a friend."

I phoned the lady when I got there. I sound like my father on the phone, and when she heard my voice she said, "Burt?"

"Yes."

"Oh, Burt . . ."

Uh-oh, I thought. "Not Burt senior, Burt *junior*," I said.

There was a long pause before she said, "Please come visit me."

The house was more like a castle. It was on top of a mountain, at the end of a winding road. When I got out of the car a woman who looked like Grace Kelly was standing there to greet me. She gave me a great big hug.

We went inside and made a tour of the house. There were huge paintings of her relatives on the walls, all highly decorated soldiers. And then we came to a portrait of my dad.

"Do you like it?" she said.

"Yes, it's beautiful."

"Would you take a photograph home and show it to your father?"

I said I would, so she snapped a picture. Then she took one of me and said, "I'd like to put your picture on the wall, too." By this time I was a little numb, but I told her I was flattered.

We spent the rest of the afternoon talking about my father.

The next morning on the set, a German reporter came up to me and said, "I understand you looked up your father's sweetheart."

"Not his sweetheart," I said, "his *friend*."

I did everything I could to prevent it, but the story broke in the European tabloids. I felt responsible for the invasion of the lady's privacy, and I was so embarrassed, I never called her again.

When I got home, I told my dad that I met her and that she was beautiful and sweet. When I told him about the portrait, he seemed touched.

"She wanted my picture, too," I said, "so I guess we'll both be on the wall."

"That's nice," he said. "But please don't tell your mother or your sister about it."

THE FIRST TIME my dad came to visit me in Hollywood, the only actor he wanted to meet was Charles Durning. Charley was, without a doubt, the best actor I ever worked with. Everything he did was completely real. It was never like he was reciting lines, it was like he was talking to you. He was loved and respected by his fellow actors, but at the same time they were scared to death of him, because they knew his war record. What they didn't know was that in his youth, Charley had been a hell of a boxer. Here's a trivia question: Which two actors were on the same fight card at Madison Square Garden? Charles Durning and Jack Warden, who fought under the name Red Costello. Two of our best character actors fought on the same fight card!

I'd heard that Charley earned a Silver Star and three Purple Hearts during World War II, but I never knew the details because, like my dad, he wouldn't talk about it. I found out on my own that he was temporarily blinded and spent three years in military hospitals being treated for shrapnel wounds. After he got out of the hospital, he enrolled in the American Academy of Dramatic Arts in New York on the GI Bill, but they kicked him out. They said he didn't have the talent to be an actor. But he kept at it, doing bit parts while working as a doorman, night watchman, cabdriver, dishwasher, and ballroom dancing instructor at an Arthur Murray studio.

Charley got his big break when Joseph Papp asked him to audition for the New York Shakespeare Festival and cast him in dozens of plays. He made a big impression in *That Championship Season* (1972) on Broadway, then did a long string of standout roles in films like *The Sting* (1973), *Dog Day Afternoon* (1975), *Tootsie*

(1982), *To Be or Not to Be* (1983), and *O Brother, Where Art Thou?* (2000).

Over the years Charley and I made four or five films and did *Evening Shade* on television together. For as long as I knew him, he was always working. Yet he was insecure. He doubted his ability as an actor, and between roles he thought he'd never work again.

When Big Burt and Charley got together and began comparing notes, they realized that they'd been on the same beach in Normandy together. They'd sit for hours talking about the war. Charley was one of the few actors my dad had any use for, and it wasn't because he was an actor.

Big Burt was strict while I was growing up, but he never mistreated me, at least not on purpose. He taught me to accept the consequences of my actions like a man and to be the last one standing in a fight. Sure, there were times where he couldn't rise above his prejudices, but I forgave him for it. My mom died in 1992, when she was ninety. After that he was very dear to me. He died in his sleep exactly ten years later, at ninety-five. He never said he loved me, but he did finally say that he was proud of me. And that was enough.

Mo Mustaine

Kreig "Mo" Mustaine has been my best friend since junior high. Everyone called him Mo because he's part Mohawk. We played football, baseball, and basketball together through high school. He was a terrific athlete. Mo didn't have it easy growing up. His father wasn't around and his mother struggled. He wanted to go to college and play football, but he had to work, so after high school he got a job with an electrical company. All the guys with football scholarships felt sorry for "poor Mo." Well, poor Mo is retired now, but at one point he had 150 electricians working for him and all you saw around West Palm Beach was *Mo Mustaine Electric* billboards and trucks.

Mo was always one of the "neat" fellas. His trademark was taping his socks up. He said he did it because he couldn't stand it when they flopped down. What he didn't point out was that he had the skinniest legs in the world. Tall socks and skinny legs. (I hope he won't mind me telling this, but he *still* tapes his socks up!) He also bleached his hair blond in front. Like I said, one of the neat fellas.

Most of the boys in junior high came to school barefoot, and I didn't want anybody to think I was a candy-ass, so I'd leave the house with my shoes on, hide them in a palmetto bush, and pray it didn't rain. Mo and I both played football barefoot. He even kicked extra points that way. When we got to high school, they made us wear football shoes and we were convinced it slowed us down.

We had occasional whippings in school, for talking or laughing or whatever. One day Mo and I were both getting it at the same time. We grabbed our balls and bent over. Mo would get five slaps and then I'd get five and so on. I wasn't about to cry and neither was Mo. It always makes 'em mad when they can't make you cry.

South Florida was a wonderful place to grow up in. I spent many an afternoon diving off the bridge over the Boynton Beach Inlet. It was a high span, and what made the dive more interesting were the turrets on either side of the deck. I'd climb on top of one and be fifty feet above the water. The tourists would pull over to watch, and Mo and the guys would run around taking up a collection. We learned to get the money in advance, because the audience wouldn't always be there when I came back. I could make five or six bucks on a good day.

The Everglades were our backyard, and we'd go out on air-boats and bulldog deer. The boat would come up behind one and you'd jump out and grab the deer around the neck. Not only was it cruel to the deer, it was stupid: their hooves were like knives and you had to watch out for the horns, too. Plus there were gators everywhere. I didn't bulldog *them,* but I did swim in their vicinity. I'd see their little eyes and think, This could be trouble. Brilliant! That's when I learned to swim *really* fast, and how to board a boat without hopping in, just shooting right onto it from the water in one swimming motion.

Mo and I would go deep into the 'Glades to visit this amazing character, an American original who has become a legend in South

Florida. His name was Vincent Nostokovich. During the Great Depression he left his home in Trenton, New Jersey, to ride the rails as a hobo. He wound up in Jupiter, Florida, changed his name to Trapper Nelson, and dropped out of society. With borrowed money he bought eight hundred acres deep in the jungle on the Loxahatchee River, and lived off the land by hunting, fishing, and trapping. At six-foot-four and 240 pounds, Trapper Nelson was known as the Tarzan of the Loxahatchee River.

Mo and I would skip school to go see him. The first time we went he put us through a rite of passage: We had to swing on a rope over a lagoon he said was filled with alligators, though we never saw one. We swung across praying the gators wouldn't chomp our legs off. Trapper thought that was hysterical. He showed us how to set traps and skin small game. He could tell I wasn't crazy about snakes, so he made me handle rattlers to conquer my fear. I'd grab it by the head and hold on for dear life.

"Isn't that great?" he'd say.

"Yeah, just wonderful."

We talked about everything, including politics. He had a hard-on for the government and he hated what the country was coming to. He said it was stupid for the United States to be the world's policeman.

Though Trapper was a handsome man, he was a hermit, and everyone was surprised when he married a woman from Palm Beach and went to live with her. For one night. He couldn't stand it, so he brought her back with him to the jungle. She stayed for one night and went back to Palm Beach, and that was the end of the marriage.

He kept buying acreage and eventually opened a zoo that became a tourist attraction. During the winter, Yankees would go there on a "jungle cruise" and walk around thinking they were in danger. When the state health department closed down the zoo in

1960, he couldn't keep up the tax payments and lost most of his precious land, which made him even more of a hermit.

His death in 1968 from a shotgun blast to the stomach was ruled a suicide, but it was suspicious. The official story is that he was sick with cancer and depressed over losing most of his property, but I don't believe it. He wasn't the kind of man to kill himself. Developers wanted his remaining land, but he wouldn't sell. Mo says that if Trapper had killed himself, he wouldn't have used a shotgun, he would've let a rattlesnake do it. But I don't think he would have done it at all. I think he was caught up in something he couldn't control.

Mo and I stayed close, but on one occasion we didn't let friendship get in the way of money. When we were sixteen I bought a motorbike from Mo. He'd paid twenty dollars for it and I drove a hard bargain: "It's been used now!" So we agreed on seven bucks. I intended to ride it to school every day, but my dad didn't approve. He said it was too far to take that little thing, but I was determined. I'd go out every day before school and it wouldn't turn over. But it would start up miraculously on Saturday mornings. Dad was disconnecting the spark plug wires on weekdays and reconnecting them on weekends. I didn't discover this until I was fifty years old. Dad didn't tell *me*, he told Mo.

Like all teenage boys in those days, Mo and I were obsessed with cars. There was a nearby town called Kelsey City that was nothing but streets. No houses, no traffic signals, just streets. It was a casualty of the real estate booms and busts in Florida and a perfect place to take your girl to park. It's where I taught Mo how to drive, in my dad's Buick. Including how to parallel-park! As I look back, it warms me to know that I was able to do that for him, because we were like brothers.

In more ways than one. We had fraternities in high school, even though they were officially banned. All the neat guys belonged to one, so Mo and I joined Alpha Sigma Pi. Our frat colors were green and yellow. There was an advertising blimp the size of a car that hung over a local garage. They kept it inside during the day but brought it out at night and tied it to the building with ropes. One night at about midnight, Mo and I and a couple of fraternity brothers decided to take the blimp, paint it green and yellow, put a big ASP on it, and let it float over the high school. We untied the blimp and were each holding one of the ropes. It was fine until one guy let go. The blimp started to rise and another guy let go and then it really started going up. When Mo dropped off, he must have fallen ten feet.

Mo was screaming: "Let go, Buddy, let go!"

I must have been twenty-five feet in the air when I finally did.

Luckily I landed in tall grass and not on concrete. If I'd waited another second or two, I'd probably have broken both my legs. The blimp kept going up until it disappeared.

The next day we made the front page of the newspaper: VAN-DALS CUT LOOSE ADVERTISING BLIMP. The paper estimated that the blimp would come down somewhere in Texas, and said it was worth four thousand dollars, which was a *lot* of money back then. We would've had to work years to pay it back. We were scared for a month that they'd find out who did it.

Recently over lunch, Mo said, "Listen, Bud, maybe you shouldn't tell that story in your book. Somebody might read it and come after us." But then he smiled and said, "Well, I guess we're safe after sixty years."

Mo and I have stayed friends all these years. When he lost his wife, Linda, it was a blow to me, but it just about killed him. She was a wonderful woman and they were a great couple. People said that every widow in town would be after Mo and that he'd marry again right away, but I knew he wouldn't. He's that kind of guy. He lives nearby now and we get together for lunch every week. Mo comes to watch me teach on Fridays whenever he can. He has a way about him that I admire. He couldn't care less about Hollywood, which is another thing I love about him. We've been friends since junior high and never had a cross word between us. It's not easy to go a lifetime without finding fault with your pal, but we never have.

Buddy

A lot of the residents of Riviera Beach came from the Bahamas and supposedly had mixed blood, which made them undesirable to a lot of people in those days. I was lumped into that group, probably because some of them were friends of mine. I've never forgotten how it felt to be excluded.

I got the nickname Mullet in junior high. After the fish, not the haircut. It's what they called people from Riviera Beach. We were "fish heads" and "greaseballs" and "mullets." I got in fights about it, but like anybody else, I wanted to be accepted. The cool guys were the lettermen, and though I'd never participated in organized sports, I dreamed of being one of them. Football gave me my chance.

My career started with a footrace against one of the best athletes in the school, Vernon "Flash" Rollison. I wasn't the brightest kid in the world, but I knew it couldn't be a good idea to race anyone named Flash. I also knew that if I lost the race, I'd remain Mullet for the rest of my life.

We walked down to the football field with a crowd behind us. We would run the hundred yards between the goalposts. Flash took out a pair of track shoes. I'd never seen track shoes before, and I was amazed at how sharp the spikes were. He got down in what I later learned was a four-point stance, and suddenly we were running. I can still hear the sound of those spikes biting into the turf, and my bare feet making no sound.

He got off to a quicker start and took the lead. I reached down inside myself for more strength or more guts or whatever it would take, and somehow found the extra speed. I passed him at the five-yard line and crossed the goal line first.

Nobody cheered. They were stunned that anyone could beat Flash Rollison.

Peanut Howser came over, shook my hand, and said, "Great race, Buddy. We could use you on the football team."

From then on I was Buddy Reynolds.

The next day the student body had a whole different attitude. They knew I'd beaten the fastest kid in the school, and I was suddenly everybody's best friend. I didn't fully enjoy my sudden popularity, because I hadn't forgotten all the crap they'd given me. But I smiled and kept my mouth shut.

When I joined the team I was clueless about how to put on the pads. I remember sitting on the bench, running my hands over the number on my jersey—I'd never had a jersey with a number on it. I looked up and Peanut was standing there, smiling.

"You need help?" he said.

"Yeah," I said. "Does the big number go in the back?"

I chose number 22 and kept it all through high school and college. I'd thought it was a great number ever since Bobby Layne wore it to bring the Detroit Lions back from the dead in the 1950s. I liked Bobby because he was a rebel and I wanted to be just like him.

I'd never played tackle football before, at least not in full uniform. We played tackle without pads or helmets on an open field near my house, and it was rough. But it is a different game with pads on. I couldn't see how anyone could possibly get hurt.

I played mostly on instinct. I hadn't had any real experience or instruction in the fundamentals. So I watched and imitated everybody else. We'd have a chalk talk before a game and I knew what I was supposed to do on certain plays. Otherwise, I hid behind cockiness. I'd tell the linemen in the huddle, "Just give me a crack and I'll go through it," and I usually did. I made the team at Palm Beach High and started every game at running back.

Richard Dalton "Peanut" Howser was small in stature, but he was the best athlete I ever saw. We played on the ninth-grade football team together and then all through high school. He was too small to play college football, so he concentrated on baseball and made All American in his sophomore, junior, and senior years. He was drafted by the Kansas City Athletics and was American League Rookie of the Year and captain of the team. He went on to manage the New York Yankees and then the Kansas City Royals, who won the World Series three times with Peanut at the helm.

We stayed the best of friends over the years. Besides being a great athlete, he was a magnificent man. He died of cancer in 1987 at fifty-one. When he got sick, I went to see him and he handled himself the way I hope I would. Not a day goes by that I don't miss him something terrible. There's a structure at Florida State University called the Dick Howser Stadium. Across the street, the football dorm is called Burt Reynolds Hall. So I guess old Peanut and Buddy are still together.

WHEN I WAS FIFTEEN, I was fascinated by the window display in an antique shop on Worth Avenue in Palm Beach. I'd stop whenever I could to peer in at the exotic objects on display. One day I looked up and there was a beautiful woman looking back at me. She was probably in her early forties, which seemed ancient to me at the time.

She smiled at me and I smiled back. She asked me to come in. "What do you like?" she said.

"I like everything in the store!"

"That's perfect: You like old good things. You fit right in."

That made me laugh, and then I said something that made her laugh, and it went on like that for about an hour.

In those days I'd go down to the old wooden pier, which has long since blown away. I'd walk out to the end and do a jackknife or a half gainer, shinny up one of the pilings, get back on the pier, and then do it again. I'd gather small crowds of tourists who'd give me fifty cents a dive.

One day I looked over and she was there, watching. I didn't acknowledge her, but I could feel her eyes on me, and I loved showing off for her.

At the antique shop the next day she said, "You ought to come to the house sometime."

She lived on the beach. We had drinks, we laughed, and one thing led to another.

It was my first time, and I was smitten.

After that, I'd go there once a week. We'd have dinner, tell stories, and make love. It went on for several months, until the night she said it was time to call it quits. I protested, almost pleaded, but she just smiled.

And that was it. She left me bewildered and frustrated, but she'd also made me very, very happy. Not a week goes by that I don't think about her.

After that, I began dating Betty Lou, a rich girl from Palm Beach. I'd drive there on the North Bridge over the Intracoastal Waterway, thinking it was a big deal. Boys from Riviera Beach didn't date girls from Palm Beach. In those days Jewish people didn't live in Palm Beach and you'd never even *see* an African-American there. The residents were proud of the fact that the Everglades Club had blackballed Joe Kennedy because his money wasn't old enough. And the town had the silliest laws, like a man couldn't ride a bicycle with his shirt off.

If you went to a party in Palm Beach, it was right out of a movie. You'd see old men dancing with young beauties, and older women dancing with young studs, usually Latin Americans, who were great dancers. They weren't their nieces and nephews.

Betty Lou was more than a young beauty, she was a knockout. She had the most incredible body I'd ever seen, and a sweet personality to go with it. Plus she was wild, a genuine free spirit. I'd never met a girl who was so uninhibited. She had only one flaw: two deformed fingers on her left hand. She turned that little imperfection into an asset by always holding a hankie in that hand like a Southern belle.

After sixth period, Betty Lou would come running down the hill to the football field. She never wore a bra, so everything would be bouncing all over the place. Everyone on the field would stop dead, including the coach.

When I rang the bell to pick up Betty Lou on our first date, her mother came to the door and said, "From now on, Buddy, when you come to pick up my daughter, please use the service entrance."

"Okay," I said, "that's what I'm here for anyway."

Her mother laughed, and when I got to know her better, I liked her. Not only was she gorgeous, she had an earthy sense of humor. When Betty Lou and I would be leaving the house, she'd say to me, "Buddy, I know what you're going to do, and I want you to be kind to her. She hasn't been around a man like you."

The inevitable happened and kept happening until one night Betty Lou told me she was pregnant. It was at the junior prom. We'd been crowned king and queen and were dancing to "Harbor Lights" when she broke the news. After I got over the initial shock, I resolved to do the right thing and marry her. I figured I'd get a football scholarship and then play pro ball and we'd live happily ever after. I made arrangements to go to Georgia, where you could get married at sixteen. When I went to the service entrance to pick Betty Lou up for the trip, her mother stopped me at the door.

"Betty Lou isn't here," she said. "We took care of the problem, so you don't have to worry, but she doesn't want to see you again."

I could hear the faint sound of Betty Lou weeping in the background, but I didn't fight it. I got back in the car and went home. I found out later that her mother had taken her to Cuba for an abortion. From then on when I saw her in school we were polite, but it was never the same between us.

Twenty years later I was on a show called *Take Me Home Again*, produced by Merv Griffin. It was the pilot for a series where celebrities go back to their hometowns. (The pilot didn't sell, I think because it became obvious that most celebrities don't give a damn about their hometowns.) I told Merv, "Let's not make it like *This Is Your Life*. Let's find people who *don't* like me—though you'll probably have to search." But they found *hundreds* of people, including Betty Lou.

Merv went to her Palm Beach mansion to interview her. They set up the cameras at the pool and she came out in a string bikini. She was pushing forty, but had the same measurements she had in high school.

"Betty Lou, I understand that you and Burt dated in high school," Merv said.

"Yes, Merv, we did," Betty Lou said. "And you know what? I was a virgin until about five minutes after I met him."

"We can't say that on television, Betty Lou," Merv said. "You'll have to rephrase it. Let's keep rolling and we'll start over. Betty Lou, I understand that you dated Burt in high school."

"That's right, Merv. See that curved palm tree over there? He used to lay me against it and bang my brains out."

Teammates

I made First Team All State and All Southern Honorable Mention at Palm Beach High and I was recruited by a bunch of college coaches, including Alabama's legendary Bear Bryant. I sat there in awe of him.

"I hear you like to hit," he said.

"Yes, sir, I do."

"That's good, because we like to hit here."

I think I would have done well at Alabama, but I'd always dreamed of going to the University of Miami, which had a great team in those days, and I signed a grant-in-aid.

Peanut Howser was going up to Florida State on a recruiting trip and he asked me to go with him. They fell all over themselves to get him, and they did.

The FSU football coach, Tom Nugent, called me into his office.

"What's Miami giving you?" he said.

"A *lot*, coach," I said.

"Can they give you this?" he asked, pointing to a chart on the wall showing a seven-to-one ratio of women to men on campus. The number was so high because FSU had been a girls' school until only a few years before. He let that sink in for a while and then he pulled down a blackboard and drew a chalk figure 7 and then a 1. He pointed to the 7 and said, "This represents the girls. Then he pointed to the 1 and said, "This is you. Think about that!"

I thought about it. And about the fact that if I went to FSU, Peanut and I would still be together.

"Coach," I said, "I think I know where I can get a hell of an education."

Tom Nugent was an innovator. He invented both the "typewriter" huddle and the I formation. Most teams had never seen the I before, and when we set up on the line of scrimmage, the defense would be scrambling all over the place.

Coach Nugent was quite a character. He belonged in show business. We had a team choir that we all had to join, whether we could sing or not. We actually performed at campus events. But his training was brutal. There must have been twenty-five guys on the team with full scholarships, but they couldn't take the practices and they all ran off. Most of them wound up as starters on other teams.

The year before I got there, FSU was playing schools like Stetson. By the time I arrived they'd begun playing up, trying to elevate the program by scheduling better teams. My freshman year we played Alabama and Georgia, which was a big rise in class.

Coach brought in some real bad dudes. I swear he got them out of the penitentiary. Others were fresh out of the 'Glades. They weren't great athletes, but they were tough. And they'd *hit* you. Even when we lost, the other team would be carrying players off the field. I thought, If I can hang in with *these* guys, I can do anything.

One of my best pals on the team was Bobby Renn. He was one of the most gifted and versatile football players I've ever seen. He was a brilliant rusher, receiver, and defensive back, and an incredibly accurate punter. I ran around with Bobby a lot. He wasn't super good-looking, but he was a ladies' man. For one thing, he was older. He'd been in the army and seen action in Korea. He had a mystique that women were crazy about, a real James Dean quality.

Bobby was dating a Pi Phi, which was considered a big deal. I looked up to him, so I started going with a Pi Phi, too, and we'd double-date. I tried to be as slick as Bobby. I watched him and tried to do whatever he did, and once in a while a girl would ask, "Aren't you going a little fast?" We'd go to this awful joint in Tallahassee called the Oasis and drink beer and tomato juice, which we thought was the height of cool. Bobby introduced me to it and I picked it up. I ordered it once with a girl, thinking I'd score points, but she thought I was an idiot.

Bobby fell in love with a rich girl whose family thought he wasn't good enough for her and did everything they could to break them up. The girl married him anyway and then tried to force him into a mold. She wanted him to be a lawyer, but he wanted to be an actor and dreamed of making it in Hollywood. As the years went by, he took acting lessons and went on auditions in his spare time without making much headway. Then one night he was fixing a flat tire and a car hit and killed him.

I've always tried to help ex–Florida State ballplayers break into acting. I've advised them and helped them get parts. But not Bobby. I don't know why, because of all the guys, I thought he could have been good. But for some reason I didn't reach out to help him, even though we were the best of friends. I've always regretted it.

THERE WAS ONLY ONE whirlpool in the FSU locker room and we had to stand in line to use it. And there was no weight room. I had to do push-ups and sit-ups to stay in shape. We had players who were strong as bulls, but without weight training, they were just "farm strong." And there was no sense of proper nutrition. They fed us mashed potatoes and gravy to pork us up. I guess they thought the more weight, the better, even if it was fat.

We had some real characters. Ray Staab was an animal and most of the other guys on the team were afraid of him, including me. One night in the dining hall I saw him pick up a cockroach and eat it. I had a buddy, Tommy Thompson, from Boston. Talk about street tough—he was the only one Ray was afraid of. Tommy used to say, "Why don't you let me beat the shit out of him?" I should have said, "Be my guest," but I couldn't do that to a teammate.

Big Al Mackowicky was tough as hell and a great ballplayer. His dorm room was across from mine. One day I got a "Dear John" letter from my girlfriend back in West Palm, and I ran out of my room hopping mad. I punched the first thing I saw, which was Big Al's door. My fist went through it and I couldn't get it out. Big Al opened the door and said, "What's the problem?"

"I just got a Dear John letter," I said.

"That's tough," he said, and he closed the door with my hand still stuck in it.

At six-seven, 270, Tom Feamster was the tallest man in college football back then. He was a terrific ballplayer and the nicest guy in the world. He played both sides of the ball, at defensive and offensive end. He was so large, he intimidated everybody. Tom married a gal who was large, too, thank God. After football he became a preacher, and when he called people to come down, they came down!

Gene Cox at fullback was a great ball carrier. He was only about five-eight, but he weighed more than 200 pounds. He was hard to bring down, like trying to tackle a bowling ball. Gene was blind in one eye, and sometimes you'd be talking to him and he'd stop you and point to his good eye because you'd been looking at the bad one.

We played against some real characters, too. Dick Christie was an All American receiver for North Carolina State, which was ranked second in the nation. On one play I was covering him on defense and he ran off the field, so I dropped off him. But he came back on the field behind me, which is illegal. (If they'd had instant replay in those days the play would have been called back.) The next thing I knew, they'd passed the ball to him and he was carrying it toward our end zone. I finally ran him down at the one-yard line.

Coach Nugent never let me—or anybody else—forget it. At half time he said, "We'd be leading right now if Reynolds hadn't fucked up!" I tried to tell him that Christie ran out of bounds, but he was having none of it.

Auburn had a defensive back named Fob James, who later in life was the governor of Alabama. We found out later that he was their hundred-meter champion, but we didn't know it at the time. Early in the game I ran fifty-four yards from scrimmage until Fob ran me down and tackled me on the one-yard line. We failed to score and it cost us the game. I caught a huge bunch of shit from Coach Nugent about that, too. Had I known then that Fob was a world-class sprinter, I would've had an answer.

The last time I saw Coach Nugent, I was sitting next to him at a dinner.

"Buddy," he said, "I thought you hated me."

"You were a little rough on me, Coach, but I never hated you. I thought of you like a father."

And I did. I'm glad I got the chance to say that to him.

By the way, my run against Auburn gets longer at every reunion. It was fifty-four yards, but the last time I told the story it was ninety-eight yards and I got tackled in the parking lot next to the hot dog stand.

VIC PRINZI was a wonderful guy and a great quarterback for FSU. Vic and I would go out and carouse around the night before a game, and on the first play, he'd look at me and smile and I'd think, Oh, shit, he's gonna give me the ball. The later we were out the night before, the more he ran me. If we hadn't been to bed at all, he'd run me until I almost fainted. But Vic was my goombah. He was the reason I always wanted to be Italian. He had a wonderful philosophy of friendship. But Vic wasn't perfect. Like my dad, he had a terrible blind spot.

"You have a problem with black people!" he'd say.

"No," I'd say, "I don't have a problem with black people, I have a problem with white people who have a problem with black people."

But we were able to get past it and remain lifelong friends.

LEE CORSO wasn't big, but he was a sensational athlete. He was a standout at Miami-Jackson High at quarterback in football, guard in basketball, and shortstop in baseball. The Brooklyn Dodgers offered him a $5,000 signing bonus, but his father made him go to college. Lee wound up at Florida State, where he played both offense and defense: As starting quarterback he broke all kinds of passing records, and at defensive back he set a career interception mark that stood until Deion Sanders came along thirty years later. And Lee was so quick as a punt and kick returner they nicknamed him Sunshine Scooter.

Lee and I were roommates our sophomore year. He had an old

Chevy that he painted metallic green. We named it the Green Hornet, and we were a dynamic duo in that car.

When Florida State played Texas in the 1955 Sun Bowl in El Paso, Lee and I went down to Juárez the night before the game. We were having such a good time that we almost forgot to come back. Lee broke his fibula on the fourth play of the game and they took him to the hospital. I was his backup on defense, but I hadn't expected to play both sides of the ball. We'd gone to a few parties in Juárez and been up all night. That Texas team was tough and fast. They beat us 47–20. By the end of the game I was totally wasted. When Lee heard, he found a good deal of humor in that.

Lee was way too small for the pros, and after graduation he went into coaching. At the University of Maryland he became the first coach in the Atlantic Coast Conference to recruit an African-American player. He was head coach at Indiana for ten years before he moved into broadcasting. He's had a fabulous career as a TV commentator, and he's been the mainstay of ESPN's *College GameDay* since it started in 1987. Lee always had something funny to say in the huddle, and he's hysterical on television. He's a natural showman, and the highlight of the show every week is when he dons the headgear of the team he's picking to win the featured game. He calls everybody "sweetheart," and his "Not so fast, my friend!" has become a national catchphrase.

Though Lee and I were teammates at Florida State, we played against each other in high school when I was at Palm Beach High and he was at Miami-Jackson. In a pileup during one of those games, somebody tried to gouge open a previous wound on Lee's cheek. He still has the scar. I keep telling him that it makes him look tough, but he's not amused and still swears I did it. He's been going around accusing me of trying to rip his face off, and I'm sick of it. So, for the record, I have only one thing to say to that slanderous charge: *Not so fast, my friend!*

I STARTED three games at running back as a freshman. I began my sophomore year starting at left halfback and had a good opening game. On the first play from scrimmage of the second game, I ran off tackle, and when I made a cut, there was a sound like a gun going off. I looked down and there was a lump in my right knee. They had to help me off the field.

We had a wonderful trainer named Don Fauls, whom we called Rooster.

"Rooster," I said, "am I finished?"

"You're finished tonight," he said. "We've got to get this thing in place, and it's gonna hurt."

"Okay, just do it."

He had a big tackle come over, and when the two of them snapped it back in, it made that sound again.

"Great," I said when I caught my breath. "Now I can play."

"No, you can't," he said. "It'll come back out again. Let me tape it up at half time and we'll see how you feel then."

So at half time he put a ton of tape on it and it felt like it couldn't possibly come out again. I started the second half and it went out on the first play. They sent me to a doctor, who performed surgery.

Afterward he came into my room and said, "What the hell did you do?"

"I didn't do anything," I said. "I was running and it popped."

"Well," he said, "it must have been bad for a long time, because it looks like ground meat in there."

After the operation I tried to play, but nothing worked. I was a step slower and couldn't cut left or right. I realized I couldn't play football like that, but I was hoping for a miracle.

Watson Duncan III

A few months after the operation, before midnight on Christmas Eve, I was barreling down the Beeline Highway in my dad's Buick when I saw red lights flashing in my mirror. The cop who pulled me over was John Kirk, and he knew my dad.

"Did you know you were going almost a hundred miles an hour?" he said.

"No, sir, I didn't," I lied.

He was kind and gave me a ticket for doing only sixty. I headed home, making sure I stayed under the speed limit. I was already in big trouble and didn't want to rack up two tickets in one night. I was worrying about how to explain it to my dad when I slammed into the truck.

A bunch of geniuses were stealing concrete blocks from Rinker Cement and loading them onto a big flatbed truck parked across the road. I didn't see it until it was too late. I went right underneath the bed of the truck. I was canny enough to roll up into a ball and dive under the dash just before the entire bed full of concrete came down on me. If I'd been going much faster—if John Kirk hadn't given me that ticket—I'd have been crushed to death.

I don't know how long I was trapped in what was left of the car, but at one point I felt somebody reach in and take the ring I got for playing on the All Southern High School football team. Pulled it right off my finger. I never found out who it was or what happened to the ring.

The first cop on the scene was Clark Bibler, a lieutenant on the force with my dad.

He was yelling, "Anybody in there, anybody in there?"

"Clark, it's me, Buddy."

"Jesus Christ, Buddy, what are you doin' in there?"

All I could say was "Don't tell my dad!"

"I've got a feeling he's gonna know," Clark said.

My dad's big ol' Buick was now the size of a Mini Cooper. It looked like there was no way in the world someone could come out of it alive. They didn't have the Jaws of Life in those days, so they used pry bars to get me out. They gently set me down on the pavement, put a blanket over me, and said there was an ambulance on the way. I felt okay lying there and thought, This is ridiculous, I don't need an ambulance. But when I got to my feet I coughed up blood and blacked out.

I woke up in the ambulance and recognized the attendant as Tommy Price, a classmate of mine at Palm Beach High. I remembered that Tommy was religious and asked him to pray for me. As I went in and out of consciousness, he held my hand and prayed, all the way to the hospital.

By coincidence, my high school doctor, Lynn Fort, was on duty that night and admitted me to our local hospital. When he checked my blood pressure he turned to the nurse and said, "Prep him, this boy is dying."

Dr. Fort performed emergency surgery to remove my spleen. During the operation I heard the nurse say, "We're losing him!" and in fact I did flatline. I clearly remember going down a tunnel toward a white light and heard myself saying, "Fuck this! I'm going back!" Doc Fort climbed on top of me and began giving me CPR. It wasn't common practice in those days, but it saved my life.

I woke up on Christmas Day with fifty-nine stitches in my stomach, lucky to have lost only my spleen. I felt I'd been on the receiving end of a miracle, though not the one I'd hoped would allow me to play football again.

While I was recuperating, somebody told me that the ancient Greeks cut out the spleens of athletes to make them run faster, and I wanted to believe that it might revive my football prospects. But that would have taken a really big miracle. People ask me how having no spleen affects my life, and the answer is, not much. Except that my body temperature is weird. I can't take cold weather, no matter how much I bundle up. But warm weather doesn't bother me, which is a good thing if you live in Florida.

It happened that the man who owned the cement company was Marshall Edison "Doc" Rinker, a local philanthropist and the biggest high school football fan in Palm Beach County. After the accident he put money in a bank account to pay for my college education or whatever else I wanted to do with it. I'd never even met the man, but he'd heard about the accident and wanted to help me.

I've often wondered what kind of four years I would have had at FSU if I hadn't been injured. I'll never know, of course, but I think I could have made it to the NFL. I had the speed and the moves, and there were things I did that a lot of running backs have no stomach for. I loved to run over people and I actually enjoyed blocking because I loved knocking guys on their ass. And after that, I almost certainly would have been a coach.

Everything had fallen in place: I'd had a great career in high school and I'd started strong at Florida State, which was becoming a national powerhouse. The pros were even sniffing around me. Football was my reason for being, my great passion in life. And it was over, just like that. It would take a long time to get through my thick skull that there could be more to life than playing football and chasing sorority girls. I had no idea what to do. But what's that old saying? When one door closes, another door opens. I didn't find another door, I found another *building.*

Coach Nugent had been kind. He said I could keep my scholarship if I worked as the team manager. My dad said, "Well, you'll still get a free education."

"Dad," I said, "they want me to hand out jockstraps."

"I don't care what they want you to do," he said, "you'll get your degree." So I went back to Florida State in the fall to be a manager. It took about an hour to realize I couldn't do it, and I left FSU for good. Now I *really* had no idea what to do with my life. I thought about a career in law enforcement. I didn't want to be a cop, but I thought it might be interesting to work in the criminal justice system, and I eventually enrolled in Palm Beach Junior College as a sophomore, intending to become a parole officer. It was there that I met a teacher who changed my life.

Watson B. Duncan III, an English literature professor and the school's theater director, was my first and greatest mentor. He was a gentle soul and a master teacher. He stood at the lectern and didn't just recite the words of Milton and Shakespeare; he breathed life into them with his booming voice. Every class was a performance. No wonder they called him the "Pied Piper of English literature." The son of a Methodist minister, he answered a calling to be a teacher. He often said that the greatest sin a teacher can commit is to bore his students. He was never in danger of that, because we hung on his every word.

I wasn't interested in drama or literature. I took the class to fulfill a requirement, and like all good football players, I sat in the back row. But as Professor Duncan read Byron, Shelley, and Keats, I was amazed at how *he* was Byron and *he* was Shelley and *he* was Keats. He especially loved Shakespeare—"the Big S," he called him. Students lined up to get into his Shakespeare classes, where he wore Shakespeare T-shirts and brought in a cake to celebrate Shakespeare's birthday. And every summer he went to the Stratford, Ontario, Shakespeare Festival to act in the plays.

He was such a good actor, I started moving closer and closer to the front of the room. By the time he got to *Paradise Lost* I was in the first row and totally hooked on English literature. It was a whole new world I'd never dreamed of. To this day I'm a ravenous reader . . . because of Watson Duncan.

Professor Duncan's passion for literature was second only to his love for his wife. Honey Harper Duncan is as Southern as a peach orchard. She was one of his students. We were in his English literature class together, and like me, she moved from the back row to the front row; only he *married* her. They were devoted to each other for the rest of his life.

Professor Duncan encouraged us to be everything we wanted to be. He touched the lives of countless students over his forty-year career. He helped many of them get financial aid to get through college, and he even went into his own pocket if they didn't qualify.

One day he said, "Buddy, you're going to be an actor."

"Professor Duncan," I said, "you're a smart man, but I have no talent and no interest in being an actor."

"Tomorrow we're reading for a play," he said. "Be in my office at three o'clock."

I had no intention of going, but the next day at three I found myself sitting across from him in his office. He pushed a play over to me. I picked it up and read one word—I think it was *the*—and he said, "You've got the part!"

"You're kidding," I said.

"You've got the part," he said.

"You mousetrapped me!" I said. "I'm stuck now and I can't get out of it!"

"Do you *want* to get out of it?"

"Well, no, I guess I don't," I was surprised to hear myself say.

The play was *Outward Bound*, about people on an ocean liner who discover that they've died and are about to face the final judgment. I was cast in the lead as Tom Prior, a tragic figure played by John Garfield in the 1944 movie version, *Between Two Worlds*. I felt at home from the first rehearsal. I thought, I can do this! Maybe I've found something that can take the place of football.

As rehearsals went on, Mr. Duncan gave blocking to everyone but me. I thought it was odd, but didn't question it. I figured I could move wherever I wanted. So I wandered all over the stage. While the other actors were talking, I'd be at the bar fixing myself a drink. I'm lucky they didn't strangle me. The performance went well and the audience seemed to like it. We took scenes from the play to local hospitals and veterans' homes and they loved it. And it was great for me, too, because I felt I was being useful.

At the end of my sophomore year I won a Florida State Drama Award scholarship to summer stock. So instead of spending eight weeks working on a fishing boat, I went to Hyde Park Playhouse in New York. The theater was actually a big barn, the most glorious barn in the world. The first week I had a walk-on part in *Affairs of State* by Louis Verneuil, directed by Wynn Handman. I was listed in the program as an apprentice.

There were two older women in the company—they must have been in their early thirties—and they seemed very sophisticated to a nineteen-year-old from Riviera Beach. I went out with them every night, and it got to be, Holy cow! If this is show business, count me in! But the language! I'd been so sheltered, I'd never heard women talk like that before, and it turned me off at first. But then I realized that it didn't change the fact that they were wonderful in every other way, and I stopped judging them. It was the least I could do.

Rip Torn

The first time I saw New York, it was like Oz. It was the mid-fifties and I was fresh and innocent and unsophisticated. Walking down Broadway, I looked up, and there was a giant neon waterfall advertising Pepsi-Cola. I stood there gawking for ten minutes, my mouth open. I couldn't believe it. It was a block long, that waterfall. Around the corner was a huge sign with a man smoking Camels. I spent an hour watching him blow smoke rings. At that moment I fell in love with New York. Unfortunately, New York didn't fall in love with me.

I didn't know anyone in town except Joanne Woodward, whom I'd met at Hyde Park Playhouse doing *Tea and Sympathy*. She played the teacher and was wonderful. I played Al, an athlete who shows the young gay man how to walk like a jock. I was positive that Joanne had a crush on me, and I thought, This is great, we'll have a drink after work and we'll talk about the theater and one thing will lead to another . . .

"I'd like you to meet my boyfriend, Paul Newman," she said.

"I can't wait," I said.

I was disappointed but not discouraged. I thought, I'll blow this guy right out of the tub.

The next weekend he came up to see her and she introduced us, and I don't know which one was prettier. He had the bluest eyes I'd ever seen. And he was one of the nicest guys I'd ever met.

Monday morning she said, "What did you think of Paul?"

"I think I'm in love," I said.

In Manhattan a couple of months later, Joanne invited me to a party at Gore Vidal's. (Paul was off working somewhere.) I wanted to meet the great writer, of course, but I also looked forward to seeing Joanne because I was still under her spell.

It was Gore, his companion Howard Austen, Joanne, and me. The dinner started out fine, but as the evening wore on, Gore got drunker and bitchier. For some reason he didn't like me, and he really sliced me up. I'd always thought I was semi-clever, but I couldn't handle him. He was saying things like "What do you plan to do, drive a truck or what?"

"Excuse me?"

"Well," he said, "you're not an *actor*. Paul's an actor, but *you're* not."

I was wounded and angry and almost speechless. All I could manage was to call him an asshole. Brilliant! And I remember thinking, This man is smart. What if he's right?

Looking back, I realize that Paul was Gore's friend, and Gore was annoyed because I was obviously chasing Joanne. He was trying to provoke me into behaving like an idiot in front of her, and he did a wonderful job.

I got up and went to the kitchen to gather myself. I was standing at the sink running the water when all of a sudden Howard's arms were around me. I knew it was Howard by the fringed cowboy jacket he was wearing. I'd complimented him on it earlier.

"I think I love you," he said.

"Are you *nuts*?" I said.

"You can have the jacket!" he said.

I picked him up and threw him into the living room. He landed at Gore's feet. I told Joanne I was leaving and she offered to drive me home.

In the car, after a long silence, I started to apologize, but she wouldn't let me.

"Gore's a brilliant man," she said, "but he was very drunk and I think he was testing you."

"Well, I flunked," I said.

"Oh, you passed," she said. "Just in a different way."

I ATE MOST of my meals at the Horn & Hardart Automat on 42nd Street. One whole wall was basically a big chrome vending machine, with a bunch of little windows, each with an item of prepared food and a coin slot. You'd get change from a woman in a hairnet with rubber tips on her fingers. It was a great place to eat if you were on a budget: It was self-service, so you didn't have to leave a tip, and nobody tried to hustle you out. A cup of coffee was a dime, and if you were really broke, you could make yourself "tomato soup" out of hot water and ketchup or "lemonade" with the free lemons and ice water.

To survive in New York, I had the usual actor jobs: washing dishes, waiting tables, making deliveries. I got a job as a bartender, but they fired me on the second night because I poured too heavy. I worked on the docks unloading cargo ships. It was a great job because it kept me in shape. And I liked the guys down there. They were all men's men, but they never put me down for wanting to be an actor.

It was an exciting time, and New York was full of surprises for me, some of them pleasant. Elvis Presley came to town for the premiere of his first movie, *Love Me Tender* (1956). Over the marquee of the Paramount Theatre in Times Square there was a cutout of him that must have been fifty feet tall. People lined up around the block to see the picture and there were barricades to hold back the girls who'd been waiting since early morning to catch a glimpse of the King. I didn't know Elvis, but we had a mutual friend, so I ended up playing poker with Elvis the day before the opening.

At one point he asked one of his gofers, "When's the new Chrysler coming out?"

"I think today."

Elvis handed him a wad of cash and said, "Go get one."

"Any special color?"

"Nah," Elvis said. "I don't care."

IN 1957, I was in a Broadway revival of *Mister Roberts*. William Inge, who'd written *Picnic* and *Bus Stop* and other plays that I only dreamed of being in, came backstage one night after the show.

"I'm giving a party later. Why don't you come by?" he said.

It was one of those buildings on Riverside Drive where the elevator doors open and you're in the apartment. I arrived early and there were only two people there: Mr. Inge and this absolutely stunning lady. He introduced us, but I didn't pay attention to her name. She looked familiar, though I couldn't remember where I'd seen her.

She was a mature woman and very beautiful. She had a low, kind of whiskey voice, but she didn't look old and had this youthful energy about her. And she was funny. By that I mean she not only laughed at my jokes but made me laugh, too. She seemed terribly interested in everything I had to say. I was bowled over by her.

Other guests arrived, but I didn't know any of them. They all tried to engage with her, but she wasn't interested. Whenever I moved away to allow her to talk to someone else, she followed me. At one point I was mixing a cocktail and asked if she'd like one.

"Yes," she said.

"What would you like?"

"Anything you fix."

She was wearing a bright yellow silk blouse with nothing underneath. It would be interesting now, but this was 1957, and it was frightening. I couldn't stop staring at her beautiful breasts, and she caught me.

She smiled and said, "My eyes are up here."

"Yes, ma'am," I said. I was twenty-one and about as sophisticated as, oh, I don't know . . . *Mel Tillis's cow.*

After the others left, Mr. Inge, the lady, and I sat down on the couch.

"Why don't you tell us your life story," she said.

I began blabbering. I heard myself talking total nonsense and knew I was boring them to death. It was like I was outside my body, watching this idiot make a complete mess of things. I jumped up and said, "I'm gonna go home now, Mr. Inge. It was nice to see you, and nice to meet *you*, ma'am."

I started for the door and she touched my arm and said, "Why don't you come home with me?"

I started to giggle! And then I blurted out, "I'm just down the street at the hotel and I'll just go on home by myself, but thank you, though."

Ten years later I was walking down the street at MGM and there came Mr. Inge and the actor Ralph Meeker.

Mr. Inge said, "Ralph, you should have been there the night Burt said no to Greta Garbo."

Ralph's eyes widened.

"Yeah, it's true," I said. "I didn't realize until the next day that it was Garbo!" And Mr. Inge said, "That's because you never looked at her face."

IN THOSE DAYS the Actors Studio was just emerging as a mecca for aspiring actors, but it was so hard to get in, I didn't have the guts to try. But I started frequenting places where Actors Studio people hung out. Some of them used to go to Childs Restaurant on Broadway. A kind of white-tiled McDonald's of the day, with actual waitresses and pancake griddles in the window, Childs was a step up from the Automat. A small step.

I never had the courage to talk to any of the actors, I just watched them. I don't know what I expected to see. I guess I hoped something would rub off on me.

There was another guy who always ate alone, and for some reason I felt comfortable approaching him.

"Hi," I said, "I'm Buddy Reynolds."

He introduced himself as Rip Torn. He asked, "Why do you give a shit about these assholes in black turtlenecks?"

"I don't know," I said. "I want to be an actor and thought I might learn something."

"Buddy, you ain't gon' learn nothin' from these silly motherfuckers."

Rip had already been in Hollywood and done film work. He told me that the only reason he became an actor in the first place was to earn enough money to buy a ranch. After studying animal husbandry and drama at the University of Texas, he went to Hollywood in the belief that he'd be an instant star. After kicking around town without much success, he forgot about the ranch and moved to New York to learn his craft.

Before long, Rip and I were roommates in a cold-water flat in a building on 44th Street we called "Gorpy Towers." We both enrolled in a voice class to get rid of our Southern accents. We'd take the subway up to 128th Street to see a teacher who gave us diction exercises.

We'd repeat: "Oh-too-lah-me-da-meeni, oh-too-lah-me-da-meeni, oh-too-lah-me-da-meeni." Except in Rip's drawl it came out, "Oh-too-lah-may-dah-may-nay, oh-too-lah-may-dah-may-nay, oh-too-lah-may-dah-may-nay."

Well, it sounds a *little* Texas, I thought, but I'm not gonna say anything. On the subway back downtown, Rip would still be going, "Oh-too-lah-may-dah-may-nay," and people would be staring. I'd move to the other end of the car and pretend not to know him.

"Goddamn it," he'd say, "you ain't never gon' be an actor if you're embarrassed! What the hell's the matter with you?"

I didn't answer him, I just moved to another car.

New York opened up a whole new world. I discovered *The Catcher in the Rye* and thought it was the greatest book ever written. At first I couldn't get Rip interested in it—he was kind of lazy about reading. So I started reading it to him, and pretty soon *he* was reading it to *me*. That book affected me in so many ways. It told me I wasn't alone in thinking how screwed up the world was, it gave me the courage to be myself, and it inspired me to write. I wanted to be able to do what J. D. Salinger did. I knew I couldn't, but I was having a ball. I still have some very badly written pages tucked away somewhere. Over the years I've given the book to a lot of people. If they like it, I like *them*.

Rip and I spent hours talking about what we hoped to do in the theater. I thought he was the best actor in New York and kept telling him to audition for the Actors Studio. For a long time he didn't want to hear about it, but I wore him down and he finally said, "If I go, will you go with me?"

Rip got up to do a scene for Elia Kazan, Lee Strasberg, and three or four top-of-the-line actors, and he was electrifying. But right in the middle of the speech he yelled, "Motherfucker!" and ran out the door.

Strasberg and Kazan jumped out of their chairs and said, "Get him! We want him!"

I caught up with him two blocks away. "What the hell's the matter with you?" I said. "They *like* you!"

"They do?"

"Yes! And they want me to bring you back."

"Well, fuck 'em if they don't want you too."

"Fuck *me*," I said, and persuaded him to go back.

Rip finished the scene and they said, "Okay, you're in."

"What about Buddy?" Rip said.

"Buddy who?" they said.

"Buddy Reynolds, goddamn it! I wouldn't be here if it wasn't for him, you elitist prick assholes."

I took him aside and said, "Rip, don't push your luck. It's okay. I'll get in eventually."

But Rip was stubborn. He held out, and they finally took me, but only to get him. And I didn't last long.

There's a famous story about Laurence Olivier and Dustin Hoffman making *Marathon Man* (1976). Dustin stayed up all night to be physically and emotionally exhausted for the scene where Olivier tortures him with a dental drill. The classically trained Brit couldn't believe how much trouble the young American took to make it look real, and after the third take, he said, "Why don't you try acting, dear boy?"

I'm with Lord Olivier: Just act!

Frank Capra said something about acting that makes sense to me: "Drama isn't when the actor cries, it's when the audience cries." Amen. I can't stand to watch actors painfully staring at the rug. And I don't go in for jargon. One of the things I didn't get about the Actors Studio was the lingo. Whenever I heard terms like "justification" and "affective memory," I thought, I wonder how many more classes I'll have to go to before *I* can talk like that.

But I don't reject that stuff completely. I find myself somewhere in the middle between Method actors and the great movie actors I admire, people like Spencer Tracy, James Stewart, and Gary Cooper. They seemed to be playing not for the back row, but just nice and easy. And fun. And most of all, truthful. That's what impressed me, and that's the path I've tried to follow. Sure, the Method is there, if the Method is where you reach back and call upon something in your own life, but you shouldn't abuse it. Hal Needham will always be in my heart, and I'll use that to reach a certain emotion, but I use it respectfully. Otherwise you're dishonoring a love.

After I dropped out of the Actors Studio, I went to see the acting teacher Sanford Meisner. He was gruff with me and I didn't like it. But he had an assistant named Wynn Handman who was a gentleman. Wynn had directed me at Hyde Park, so I went to him and said, "If you ever go off on your own, I'm going with you." Before long he had his own students, and I was one of them.

We practiced all kinds of exercises in Wynn's class. One day he asked me to go outside and come back in on cue. "You're coming home from Korea and they surprise you," he said. I went downstairs and waited a long time before he called me back. When I came in, Wynn was sitting in the dark, smoking his pipe. I didn't see anybody else. Then the whole class jumped out and yelled, "SURPRISE!" They were laughing and patting me on the back, saying how glad they were to see me, and I got angry. I felt they were not respecting what I'd been through in the war. I went so over the top that I chased everybody out, including Wynn! I had no control over it.

In another class Wynn complimented me on my laugh, saying it was "organic" and that it came from my heart rather than my head. The other students wanted to know how I turn it on. I told them that I don't know how to turn it *off*!

"But where does it come from?" they persisted.

I told them that it comes from someplace deep down, and that there were times in my life when I shouldn't have been laughing— at a funeral or some such—and I had to push it down and tell myself, You can't laugh now. So when it came out, it *really* came out.

To this day, whenever a student of mine goes to New York, I tell them to go see Wynn, who's in his nineties and still teaching. They take classes with him and come back singing his praises.

BEFORE LONG, Rip was the hottest young actor in New York. Everybody was talking about him. Whenever anyone told him how wonderful he was, he'd say, "Now don' bullshit me, man!"

He made his Broadway debut as Tom Junior in the original cast of *Sweet Bird of Youth*, directed by Kazan, with Paul Newman and Rip's then future wife, Geraldine Page. I'd sit in the back row at rehearsals and Rip was *amazing*. When he took the stage, he *took* the stage.

At that time there were probably a dozen dramas running on Broadway and the acting was dazzling. I was lucky that older, established actors let me hang around with them, people like Jack Lemmon and Mildred Dunnock. Sometimes they even let me eavesdrop on their conversations about acting. I watched them work and observed how they handled themselves in public.

It was magical. You could go into a rehearsal of any play on Broadway and see great things. Having been a jock, I'd learned to keep my mouth shut and watch, but at the same time I was a pretty good mimic. One day I'd be Jack Lemmon and the next day I'd be somebody else. I tried to take the best from the actors I saw. I would constantly ask myself, "Why is this person so damned good?" I finally realized it was because they worked so damned hard.

Tennessee Williams was around the theater in those days and was always friendly. He once asked me what I was doing and why I wasn't in *Sweet Bird of Youth*.

"Well," I said, "my roommate's in the play."

"Who's your roommate?"

"Rip Torn."

"Oh, my God!"

Rip went on to do interesting work on the stage, in films, and on television, but I don't think he fulfilled his early promise. He never got the one part that would have made everybody go, "My God, *look* at this guy!" For that I am truly sorry, because Rip is a loyal friend who believed in me when nobody else did. He kept saying, "You gon' be great, Buddy, you gon' be just *great*."

I'd be so happy to see him if he walked through the door right now.

IN 1961, I auditioned for *Look, We've Come Through* by Hugh Wheeler, produced by Saint-Subber and directed by José Quintero. I walked onstage and began reading. Quintero was in the back row, saying, "Read it again." I read it again and heard him say, "Read it again." I did it three more times and then walked down to the front of the stage and yelled into the darkness, "WHAT THE FUCK DO YOU WANT?"

"THAT!" he said. "You've got the part!"

The cast was full of good young actors. I hadn't met any of them before, but I'd seen Zohra Lampert in *Splendor in the Grass* (1961) and thought she was terrific. Collin Wilcox went on to play the girl who falsely claims she was raped in *To Kill a Mockingbird* (1962).

I played a sailor named Skip. It's a showy part. There's a scene where I tell the kid, who doesn't know if he's gay or not, to come over, and I unzip my fly. And the audience gasped. I'm sure they thought I was about to flop something out. And the kid, who was played by a brilliant young actor named Ralph Williams, comes toward me and then stops and breaks down. I zip my pants back up and laugh at him.

Like I said, a showy part.

The second act opens with me alone on the stage, laughing. When the curtain rose my eyes came up and I did what you're never supposed to do: I looked into the audience. This action is called breaking the fourth wall, and it reminds them that what they're watching isn't real. But I did it. I looked out and thought, Oh my God, there's Tennessee Williams! There's Elia Kazan! There's Natalie Wood and Warren Beatty! What the hell's my line?

I couldn't remember the line! So I kept laughing. I laughed and laughed . . . and laughed . . . and laughed some more. Then God said, "Okay, he's suffered enough, I'll let him remember the line."

AFTERWARD I WAS in my dressing room (if you could call it that: it was a tiny cubbyhole at the top of a winding staircase), and Tennessee Williams came back and said, "Young man, I never saw anybody hold a laugh that long in my whole life! I'm going to write a play for you." Then William Inge came in and said, "I loved what you did with that laugh! I'm going to write a play for you." And then there was a knock on the door and it was Ben Gazzara. I'd never met Ben, but he was the hottest actor on Broadway and I liked his work.

"What *guts*!" he said. "What fuckin' guts to laugh like that, and to keep it going that long!"

"Well, *you* know, Ben," I said. "I thought about it and figured, if you're gonna do it, really *do* it!"

Look, We've Come Through closed after three performances. In his review of the play, the *New York Times* critic said, "Please don't let these young actors go to Hollywood." I left the next day.

Spencer Tracy

Lew Wasserman, the head of MCA, brought me to Hollywood and said I'd be a big star. Wasserman was a powerful man. If he predicted rain, everyone put up umbrellas, so Universal signed me to a seven-year contract. It was at the tail end of the studio system and there were only a few of us. Clint Eastwood was there doing *Rawhide*, Doug McClure was in *The Virginian*, and Bob Fuller was in *Laramie*.

They tried to give us acting classes, but we wouldn't go. People with clipboards would come around to warn us that if we didn't attend class we'd be suspended, but we never went and we were never suspended. If you were in a hit show, you had that leeway.

I was in a series called *Riverboat*, which was set on the Mississippi before the Civil War. It was one of the worst shows on television, but it had more viewers than any of the top ten shows today. Darren McGavin played the captain and I was the pilot, Ben Frazer, but I thought of him as Dum-Dum the Whistleblower, because that's all I did. Every so often they'd cut to me up in the wheelhouse and I'd toot the whistle. When they did give me a line it was something like "Do you think the Indians will attack?" And there must be a warehouse full of my close-ups somewhere, because none of them ever got on the screen.

Stanley Kramer was on the Universal lot directing *Inherit the Wind* (1960), the film version of Jerome Lawrence and Robert E. Lee's play about the Scopes "Monkey Trial," with Spencer Tracy as Henry Drummond, a character based on Clarence Darrow, and Fredric March as Matthew Brady, modeled on William Jennings Bryan. By then I'd seen all of Tracy's films and he was—and still is—my idol. He could play any part, from a simple Portuguese fisherman in *Captains Courageous* (1937), to a shady sports agent in *Pat and Mike* (1952), to the head of a war crimes tribunal in *Judgment at Nuremberg* (1961).

I didn't have much to do on *Riverboat* except pull that whistle, so I had plenty of free time. I knew all the guards, and they'd let me sneak onto the sound stage where Tracy was shooting. I stood in the back watching them film the climactic courtroom scene where Drummond cross-examines Brady. Fredric March was a great actor, but he did things one way. Spencer Tracy surprised you on every take.

Tracy quit every day at five p.m. It was in his contract. It didn't matter if he was in the middle of a scene, at five sharp he'd go to his trailer. I'd follow him from a distance, hoping he'd notice me.

After a few days he took pity on me and said, "Are you an actor, kid?"

"The jury's still out on that, sir," I said.

"Well," he said, "I'm gonna give you some advice."

I thought he might repeat his famous words "Know your lines and don't trip over the furniture," but he said, "It's a great profession, as long as nobody catches you at it."

That's still the best acting advice I've ever had: *Don't let anyone catch you acting.*

I could never catch Tracy acting. He made it look so easy. Everything he did on-camera was completely natural. He just behaved. When he ate, he ate. He chewed fast and talked with his mouth full. Most actors take small bites so they can speak their lines clearly and make it easier for the film editor to duplicate the action over several takes. But Tracy ate like he was starving, no matter how many takes he did.

When I asked how he did it, he said, "I just eat."

And when I questioned how they matched shots, he said, "That's not my job."

For a few weeks we met every day at five o'clock and talked, mostly about sports, but occasionally about acting. I always called him Mr. Tracy because he never said, "You can call me Spence, kid."

One day he said, "Did you learn anything today, kid?"

"Yes, sir. That I'll never be as good as you."

He laughed.

It was a thrill to make him laugh, and I began to relax in his presence. But I still called him Mr. Tracy.

One day he said, "What's the matter, kid? You look pissed off."

I told him that a director on *Riverboat* wasn't allowing me any freedom as an actor.

"Fuck 'im, just do it," Tracy said.

"I don't think he'd like that."

"Fuck him!" he yelled. "What's he gonna do, fire you?"

"He just might."

"Well, find out!"

I spoke up to the director, and not only did he not fire me, we became friends.

LEE MARVIN told me that he and Tracy worked up some business for the scene in *Bad Day at Black Rock* (1955) where Tracy gets off the train. In rehearsals Lee had a pencil in his mouth and he was moving it from side to side. When Tracy didn't complain, Lee thought, Wow, this is *my* scene. But when the camera rolled, Tracy, in character, pulled the pencil out of Lee's mouth and threw it on the ground. Tracy's character in that picture was missing an arm, but you bought that he was a tough customer. How many actors could pull *that* off? In another scene, Lee was futzing around with Tracy's tie. In the third take, Lee reached up and grabbed the knot of the tie and Tracy said, "Don't do that, kid. I'm too old and too rich."

Tracy's personal life was full of demons. He battled depression and alcoholism, disappearing on binges for days on end. He was embarrassed about being an actor even though he was a master, and once told me that he considered plumbing a more honorable profession. He was Catholic and I think he felt guilty about his extramarital relationship with Kate Hepburn. And God knows why, but he blamed himself when his son was born deaf.

But I didn't know all that then, and one day I said, "Mr. Tracy, you make everything you do on the screen look so easy. Is *anything* hard for you?"

"Yeah, kid," he said. "Life."

Riverboat was a big, expensive show with wonderful guest actors like Eddie Albert, Dan Duryea, Paul Fix, John Ireland, Raymond Massey, John Hoyt, and William Bendix. I'd grown up watching them on the screen, and I tried to soak up as much as I could from them. They all went out of their way to encourage me, and most of them gave me the same advice: "Don't let the bastards get you down." There was something very tender about it. They seemed to know that I was vulnerable behind the wiseass front, and they didn't want me to get hurt.

But not Darren McGavin. He was the star of the show and never let me forget it. He went out of his way to make me look bad on-camera. I knew very little about film acting, and nothing about the dirty tricks actors play on one another. The viewer's eye goes to movement, so Darren was always fiddling with something. He was so good at it, I found myself watching him in fascination. Another trick he'd use to keep me off balance was to rehearse a scene one way and do it differently in the take.

The funny thing is, he was a good actor who didn't have to resort to all that crap. He was interesting in *The Rainmaker* on Broadway, as Mike Hammer on TV, and as a dope dealer in *The Man with the Golden Arm* (1955). People probably remember him best as the goofy father in *A Christmas Story* (1983).

I don't know why he thought I was a threat. I guess it was because I was younger. Or maybe what I said to *TV Guide* had something to do with it. When they asked me what I thought of Darren, I said, "He's going to be very disappointed the first Easter after his death."

He was an ornery son of a bitch and he threw his weight around. He abused the crew and mistreated the women who guest-starred on the show. He took a run at all of them, and he was the opposite of suave. He'd back them up against the wall so they couldn't move. That would be called sexual harassment now, and I didn't like it. I finally said something to him one day.

"You've got to understand that you're not Mike Hammer," I said.

He didn't appreciate that and we almost came to blows.

At the end of the first season I realized I was on a dead-end street and I asked Universal to release me from the show. When they refused, I got cranky and threatened to blow up the damned boat. They got nervous and called my agent, Monique James, who told them, "If he says he's going to blow it up, that's exactly what he'll do."

They decided I wasn't worth the trouble.

Bette Davis

I always had a thing for Bette Davis. Watching her on the screen as a kid, I knew she was special. When I first came to Hollywood and met her, she was everything I thought she'd be and more: tough and strong, but in her own strange way very sexy. Fortunately, Bette liked me. She had said nice things about me in the press, and the first time I saw her in person, I was amazed that she was only *that* tall. But I wouldn't have fought her with an axe. I'd rather have Ray Nitschke tackle me. And if I was in a dark alley, I'd want her right behind me.

At the start of our friendship, Bette couldn't quite figure me out, but when she did, or thought she did, we got along great. She was always kind to me, very generous and encouraging, saying she thought I would do well in films. In the last years of her life, we became great pals. On occasion she allowed me to be her escort, and let me tell you, taking Bette Davis to an event—the seas parted.

Bette loved to gossip about the people she'd worked with, and one of the first things she ever told me was that she couldn't stand Errol Flynn. They were both under contract at Warner Bros. and made several films together, including *The Private Lives of Elizabeth and Essex* (1939), in which she plays Queen Elizabeth I in that funny makeup. She had her eyebrows removed and her hairline lifted two inches to give the illusion of baldness under a red wig. The eyebrows never grew back and she had to pencil them in for the rest of her life.

Bette had wanted Laurence Olivier for the part of Lord Essex and was unhappy with Flynn. She thought he was arrogant and unprofessional, and she didn't bother to hide it. She would insult him in front of the crew, and in one rehearsal she slapped him so hard it made his eyes water.

I never formally met Flynn, but I thought he was a terrific athlete who moved beautifully. I used to see him around the Warner Bros. lot, but never had the courage to talk to him. A stuntman friend of mine knew him, and one day Flynn asked him to come by his dressing room for a drink. My friend took me with him. We knocked on the door, and after Flynn invited us in, we opened the door to see a girl on her knees giving him head.

Flynn grinned at us and said, "I don't fuck anymore because it interferes with my drinking."

Bette disliked Flynn, but she hated Joan Crawford. When I met Crawford, I didn't care for her either. I didn't like that she was mean to people in the crew, and I wasn't crazy about her work. I caught her acting too many times. *Way* over the top. And the men she worked with—Zachary Scott and that kind of weak-kneed actor—she ate them up and spat them out. I don't think Crawford liked me, either, probably because she knew I had a crush on Bette and it pissed her off.

Crawford was all about *image*. She played the movie star thing to the hilt. She never left the house unless she was made up to the nines and never missed a chance to ingratiate herself with a fan. She'd sign autographs in the pouring rain; she'd sign people's whatever. She acted the way she thought a big star was supposed to act. Bette would certainly sign an autograph if somebody asked her under the right circumstances, but she didn't go crazy and thought Crawford was a big phony about it. Only a saint could truly have that much patience, and Crawford was no saint.

Bette was of Yankee stock from Lowell, Massachusetts. She was born Ruth Elizabeth, but gave herself a new name as a kid, taken from a Balzac novel. Her father was a patent lawyer who left when Bette was seven, leaving her mother, Ruthie, to support Bette and her younger sister, Bobby.

Bette loved to talk about her four husbands. At twenty-four, she married her high school sweetheart, Harmon "Ham" Nelson. She said she was a virgin on her wedding day and "it was hell waiting." They were together six years. Her second husband, Arthur Farnsworth, died suddenly after four years. Her third, William Sherry, sent her flowers every week until Bette discovered that she was paying for them. Her last husband was Gary Merrill, who plays Bette's love interest in *All About Eve* (1950). Bette had just separated from Sherry, and Merrill was in a ten-year marriage. They fell in love on the set, divorced their spouses, and got married. It lasted ten years.

One of the three children from Bette's marriages, Barbara "B.D." Sherry, got married and became a born-again Christian. She tried unsuccessfully to convert Bette, then published a tell-all memoir like Christina Crawford's *Mommie Dearest* that claimed Bette was an alcoholic and an abusive mother. It came as a total shock to Bette, who had no idea that B.D. felt that way about her, especially since she'd been supporting B.D. and her family for years. Bette's son, Michael, and ex-husband Gary Merrill came to Bette's defense, claiming that B.D. was motivated by the $100,000 advance for the book. Bette disinherited her and never spoke to her again.

We used to talk about it a lot. Bette told me that she never fully recovered from B.D.'s book, but said she was glad that it wasn't as badly written as the Crawford book! "I failed to reach B.D.," she said. "I think she had a lot of me in her, and that made it hard. I wish we could have had a better relationship."

I told Bette, "I'm sorry, too. But it was her loss, because you're very special."

Bette would always smile when I said that. "You're one of the few men who think that," she'd say.

"Well," I'd say, "that may not be entirely the men's fault."

And we'd both laugh.

Betty had the reputation of being tough to work with, but only if you were an actor or a director. She always got along with the crew. She wanted them all to like her, and they did, because she behaved like one of the guys. Every Friday night she threw a party for the crew and they all had a few drinks. And Bette could tip 'em back. She was wound so tight, I think alcohol relaxed her and eased her shyness. But I never saw her get drunk. I'm not a big drinker, but when we went out, I would try to match her.

Finally she said, "You know, you don't have to try to keep up with me."

What a relief *that* was!

The best thing about having drinks with Bette was that at some point she'd start in on certain people and destroy them. Including Flynn. I felt bad about that and always wished she liked him be-cause I liked him so much. One day, though, she'd finally had enough to allow her to admit, "By the end of the picture, I'd grown rather fond of him."

Bette was the first to win ten Best Actress Academy Award nom-inations, and she took home two Oscars, for *Dangerous* (1935) and *Jezebel* (1938). At the peak of her career, her pictures were so profitable she was called "the fourth Warner brother," and even her nemesis Jack Warner said she was "a great artist." And as Bette herself would always point out, she did it all without the benefit of beauty.

Bette had the ability to make you believe in the character she was playing while never forgetting you were watching Bette Davis. She was always interesting on the screen, even if she was pushing a peanut up a hill with her nose. She wasn't afraid to play unattractive characters, parts other actresses wouldn't touch, parts that were dangerous and hard to bring off: killers, connivers, ugly ducklings. She always chose realism over glamour and wasn't afraid to change her appearance to suit a role or to play characters older than herself. This was a big help later on, when she was able to shift easily into character parts. I once asked her whether she considered any other actress her equal, and without hesitation she said, "Anna Magnani. There's only one of us in each country."

We didn't talk about acting much, but whenever she was asked about her approach, Bette would invoke Spencer Tracy's no-nonsense advice, "Learn the lines and don't trip over the furniture." Or she'd quote Claude Rains: "Know your words and pray to God." When I pushed her for her own advice she said, "Trust your intuition and just go in and do it."

I feel a little better about my own career blunders when I remember that Bette committed the mother of all passes. Twice! To persuade her not to leave the studio after the end of her contract, Jack Warner promised her the leading role in the movie version of a novel he'd just optioned.

"I'll bet it's a pip," she said, and walked out. She hadn't heard of Margaret Mitchell's bestseller, *Gone with the Wind*. David O. Selznick acquired it from Warner and asked her to do the picture, but it was with Errol Flynn, so she turned it down again. Bette told me it was the worst mistake of her career, and she always bristled at the mention of the film. (*GWTW*'s director, Victor Fleming, declined a percentage of the profits, predicting that it would be "one of the biggest white elephants of all time.") But Bette got a consolation prize: She made *Jezebel* instead and won the Oscar for it. People said the part was inferior to the great Southern heroine Scarlett O'Hara, but I'm not so sure when I look at what Bette did with it.

Bette had a dark, gritty sense of humor, and once you found it, she had a great laugh. She had eccentric, endearing little gestures like striking kitchen matches on the furniture. At the mention of a bad movie she'd say, "If you didn't see it, congratulations." Yes, she was cantankerous, and yes, she had a short fuse.

I heard the stories: that she would cuss like a sailor and call people terrible names when she was angry, that she took out her frustrations on whomever she was with.

She admitted it: "When I was most unhappy, I lashed out rather than whined," she said.

She couldn't stand actors who weren't as professional as she was. She bemoaned their lack of voice training and complained that you couldn't hear half of them across the set. Was it unprofessional of Bette to lash out at other actors and directors? I never asked her that, but if I had, she probably would have said, "No, I only corrected them when they deserved it." She disliked people who opposed her, but despised anyone who gave in to her. And if a director was incompetent or indecisive—a "weak sister"—she'd roll right over him.

She wore the "difficult" label like a badge of honor. "Until you're known in my business as a monster," she said, "you're not a star." She believed that if you didn't dare to make enemies, you'd never be a success. She understood that the audience cares only about the finished product, and if she fought the director, it was for the good of the film.

Bob Aldrich said that Bette had objected to the casting of Victor Buono in *Whatever Happened to Baby Jane?* and tried to get him fired. It wasn't personal, she just thought Victor was too "grotesque" for the film. But halfway into shooting she changed her mind and was big enough to tell the actor: "I want you to know that at the beginning I thought you weren't right for the picture and I did everything I could to convince Bob not to use you, but now I want to apologize because you're wonderful."

As a workingwoman in a man's world, Bette learned to protect herself because nobody else would. One of the things she had to overcome was the double standard that still exists. "When a man gives his opinion, he's a man," she said. "But when a woman gives her opinion, she's a bitch."

I liked being with Bette and we always had a good time together. I think part of the reason that we got along was that I wasn't intimidated by her. Someone once asked me whether we would have had the same rapport if we'd known each other in her prime. In her prime . . . I would have taken a run at her.

ONE NIGHT Bette and I arranged to meet at a party. I got there first, and everyone was talking about Joan Crawford, who had died that afternoon. When Bette arrived she made a beeline for me.

"Well, the cunt died today!" she said.

I was talking with the movie critic Arthur Knight, and concerned about Bette's candor in front of a journalist, I said, "Bette, I don't believe you know this gentleman. He writes the 'Sex in Cinema' column for *Playboy*."

Bette quickly added, "But she was *always* on time."

She was only slightly less blunt for publication, telling reporters: "You should never say bad things about the dead, only good. Joan Crawford is dead. Good!" and "The best time I ever had with Joan was when I pushed her down the stairs in *What Ever Happened to Baby Jane?* I only regret that I didn't get to slap her around more."

Bette told me that Aldrich couldn't get the money to make *Baby Jane* because he insisted on starring "two old bags." So they had to shoot the whole picture in three weeks on a rock-bottom budget, with tiny salaries for Bette and Joan, who took percentages. *Baby Jane* was a big hit and the old bags made a fortune.

Bette would smile when she recalled how she tortured Crawford, like the time she and Joan were sitting on the set between takes, Joan knitting quietly and Bette methodically crossing out huge chunks of the script.

"Whose lines are you cutting?" asked Joan.

"Yours!" said Bette, making Joan burst into tears.

When Joan sent a single rose as a peace offering, Bette told her: "If you're going to send roses, for God's sake, send a dozen or more."

And when Joan asked for a signed copy of Bette's book, *The Lonely Life*, Bette wrote: "Joan, Thanks for wanting my autograph. Bette."

"I tried to like her, but I couldn't," Bette said.

By the time they made *Baby Jane* in 1962, they'd been feuding for decades, and it was no publicity stunt. They truly despised each other. In one scene, Bette was supposed to simulate kicking Joan in the head but "accidentally" made contact, tearing a gash in Joan's scalp that needed stitches.

Joan was married to the chairman of Pepsi-Cola at the time, so Bette had a Coke machine installed on the set.

The famous beach scene had to be shot on a sound stage because Crawford's contract required that everything be kept at fifty degrees. "Vodka was Joan Crawford's life support system," Bette explained. "And when your body is saturated with booze, you perspire in the heat."

I once asked Bob Aldrich, "You know, you're great with men—*The Dirty Dozen*, *The Longest Yard*. What the hell was it like working with Crawford and Davis together?"

"Same thing," he said. "Two men."

Bob told me a story. There's a scene where Bette serves Joan a rat for breakfast. It's the most powerful scene in the picture, all because of Bette. She told the prop man, "Get me a *real* rat. I don't want a rat from the house. I want a New York City river rat. I want a rat the size of a dog!"

They used a prop rat in rehearsal and slipped the real one in for the take. Joan's reaction is electrifying, and in my opinion it's her greatest moment on the screen . . . because she wasn't acting!

The feud started when Bette rebuffed advances from Crawford, who, Bette swore, had had affairs with Greta Garbo, Barbara Stanwyck, Marlene Dietrich, "and every other female star at MGM except Lassie."

Even so, I'd always assumed that it was just the natural rivalry between two great movie stars. Hadn't Bette dismissed Crawford as a no-talent "glamour puss" whose success depended on her looks? Hadn't she said that Crawford *"hay-ayted"* being number two? And hadn't she told me of her own resentment when Crawford finally eclipsed her by signing a seven-year, $200,000-a-picture contract with Warner Bros., Bette's home studio?

Then one night Bette told me the real reason: Crawford had kept her from marrying "the love of my life," she said.

In 1935, while shooting *Dangerous* at Warner's, Bette fell hard for her leading man, Franchot Tone. I was never able to figure out what Franchot had, but he sure had a way with the ladies. It may have been that he was such a gentleman, because most men thought Bette wanted to be talked to like a truck driver.

She loved everything about Franchot: his looks, his name, his elegance. But he was already engaged to Crawford and madly in love with her.

"They met every day for lunch, and he'd return to the set with lipstick all over his face," Bette said. "He made sure we all knew it was Crawford's lipstick. He was honored that this great star was in love with him. I was jealous, of course."

Crawford married him soon after the picture wrapped.

Bette failed to see her presumption in blaming Crawford for taking her own fiancé away: "She took him from me," she said. "She did it coldly, deliberately, and with complete ruthlessness. I've never forgiven her for that and never will."

Not long after *Baby Jane* wrapped, Bette placed a "situation wanted" ad in *Variety*:

ADVERTISEMENT

MOTHER OF THREE—10, 11 & 15—DIVORCEE. AMERICAN. THIRTY YEARS EXPERIENCE AS AN ACTRESS IN MOTION PICTURES. MOBILE STILL AND MORE AFFABLE THAN RUMOR WOULD HAVE IT. WANTS STEADY EMPLOYMENT IN HOL-LYWOOD. (HAS HAD BROADWAY.)

BETTE DAVIS
c/o MARTIN BAUM
G.A.C. REFERENCES UPON REQUEST

She later claimed that the ad was a "rib" on the Hollywood system. She said she was kidding the stuffed shirts who financed movies, the men in New York who had a list of "bankable" actors. But I'm not so sure. Though Bette never stopped working throughout her long career, I think she was afraid that the parts would dry up. Every actor has that fear.

In their heyday, big studios like MGM and Warner Bros. ran the industry. They were like small cities, each with its own sound stages, prop and wardrobe departments, commissaries, and even hospitals. They kept screenwriters and directors on their payrolls. They controlled actors through exclusive long-term contracts, using them not just for films but also for advertising and publicity, putting them in ads without their consent and sending them on dates with other actors.

If you were a big star like Bette and the studio didn't have a decent script for you, they'd send over a piece of crap that you'd have to turn down for fear of ruining your career. The studio would then suspend you without pay and add the time to the end of your contract. You had no control over the use of your own name and likeness, no script approval, no say about directors, costars, costumes, makeup . . . or anything else.

Very few stars had the guts to buck the system. Olivia de Havilland sued Warner's to prevent them from adding suspension time to the seven-year contract. She won the suit, and the seven-year limit became a part of the California Labor Code known as the De Havilland Law.

Bette told me that she was in a constant state of war with Jack Warner, who put her in a series of terrible pictures. Desperate to break the contract, she accepted two films in England. The studio sued her in an English court and won, but Jack Warner—maybe admiring her guts, maybe seeing the value of all the trial publicity and her new image as a feisty, independent woman—paid her legal bills and began sending her scripts with better parts: Judith Traherne in *Dark Victory* (1939), the public's favorite of all her pictures and Bette's favorite, too; Leslie Crosbie in *The Letter* (1940); Charlotte Vale in *Now, Voyager* (1942), which includes that famous piece of business where Paul Henreid lights two cigarettes and hands one to Bette while gazing into her eyes, in those days a tipoff to the audience that they'd slept together.

Bette played Regina Giddens in *The Little Foxes* (1941) only because Jack Warner owed Samuel Goldwyn a $400,000 gambling debt and gave him the use of Bette in the film in payment.

But her most famous role is probably Margo Channing in *All About Eve* (1950), Joe Mankiewicz's biting satire about an aging

Broadway star and the scheming young actress who tries to steal her life. *Eve* was a critical and commercial smash and maybe the greatest film about the theater ever made.

Claudette Colbert had signed to star as Margo Channing but injured her back two weeks before the cameras rolled. Gertrude Lawrence was Mankiewicz's second choice, but she refused to smoke or drink on-camera and insisted on singing in the picture. Marlene Dietrich was briefly considered, but when Bette suddenly became available, Mankiewicz jumped at the chance, despite warnings from fellow directors that it would be suicide to work with her. The only encouragement came from Willy Wyler, who had directed Bette in three pictures *(Jezebel, The Letter, and The Little Foxes)*. He predicted Mankiewicz would enjoy the experience, and in fact the diva and the writer-director got on beautifully. He praised her as "a director's dream: the prepared actress," and she thanked him for giving her the key to the character when he said that Margo Channing is "a woman who treats a mink coat like a poncho."

WHEN SHE WAS SEVENTY-FIVE, Bette had a mastectomy, and then a stroke a week later. The doctors told her she'd never work again, but they didn't know Bette. She wasn't a quitter. "Old age ain't no place for sissies," she liked to say.

She kept working and smoking. She did a one-woman show that opened with clips from her films. After the "fasten your seat belts" scene from *All About Eve*, the lights would come up, Bette would come onstage, puff on a cigarette, scan the auditorium, and say, *"What . . . a . . . dump!"* I don't think I ever saw Bette without a cigarette. It was her trademark at a time when just about everyone smoked, a constant prop that gave her a whole arsenal of gestures. She even smoked in the dentist's chair.

The cancer eventually came back, and she died in 1989 at eighty-one. It says on her gravestone: "She did it the hard way." That's true.

Bette's greatest romance was with her work, and she sacrificed her family life for the sake of her career. But she was a lot more sensitive than people imagined.

Jim Brown

The minute I met Jim Brown, on the set of *100 Rifles* (1969), I felt competitive toward him, and he sensed it. He told me that he got that a lot. It's the gunfighter thing, the same crap that champion boxers have to deal with.

I asked the director, Tommy Gries, God bless him, if I could choreograph the stunts, and he said okay. "But how the hell are you gonna fight Jim Brown?" he said.

"I'm not sure yet," I said, "but I'll get to know him."

One day I asked, "Jim, are you afraid of anything?"

"Only two things," he said, "horses and heights."

I fought him on horseback. At the edge of a cliff.

In the course of the shoot, I learned Jim's story. He was born on St. Simons Island, Georgia. At age eight he moved to Great Neck, Long Island, where his mother worked as a domestic for a Jewish couple who encouraged Jim to develop his athletic abilities. He went to the mostly white Manhasset High School, where he earned thirteen letters in five different sports, then to Syracuse University, where he was All American in football and lacrosse. To this day people say he's the greatest lacrosse player who ever lived.

Jim was drafted number one by the Cleveland Browns and was

their star fullback from his first game as a rookie. At six-two, 230 pounds, with a 32-inch waist, he had a combination of speed and power in one package that made him an elusive and punishing runner and a brilliant receiver out of the backfield. He led the NFL in rushing eight of his nine seasons, averaging 5.2 yards a carry. He's the only rusher in history to average more than a hundred yards per game over an entire career, and he still holds the record for consecutive games without a fumble (twelve). And he never missed a start.

Jim always did that thing of standing up slowly and dragging himself back to the huddle after a carry. He called it "getting up with leisure." People think he did it to make the defense think he was injured, so that the next time he got the ball he could *really* run over them. But Jim told me it was for the opposite reason. He said he did it whether he was hurt or not, so the defense wouldn't notice when he really *was* hurt.

He always made sure that anyone who tackled him never forgot how much it hurt. When they tried to grab him, he'd swing his free arm like a steel hammer. Before we did our first fight scene, I said, "Let me see that thing you throw," and he used it to put me on my ass. I looked up at him and we both laughed.

"That's quite an axe you've got there," I said.

"Yeah," he said, "I used it to keep them from killing me. And it fed me very well."

IN 1966, while working on *The Dirty Dozen* in London during the off-season, Jim retired from professional football. He was only thirty and at the peak of his career, but he decided to quit on top, with his legacy intact.

Always an intimidating figure, Jim was proud and uncompromising at a time when African-Americans were supposed to know their place, and I get the sense that for a long time he was treated unfairly by the powers that be because he was considered "uppity."

WE WERE IN WASHINGTON, D.C., at a party for the cast of *100 Rifles*, and Jim said, "I can tell you what's about to happen. The politicians will get drunk and put their arms around Jim Brown and tell him how liberal they are. Jim Brown will say to Burt Reynolds, 'Let's get the hell out of here,' and we *will* get the hell out of here."

"Why wait?" I said.

We drove to the Lincoln Memorial. At night, deserted and lit from behind, it had an eerie, awe-inspiring quality to it. We stepped over the ropes and walked up the steps. Suddenly there were policemen everywhere. They ran up the stairs and grabbed us, Jim a little more roughly, I thought, but he kept his cool.

One cop had him by the arm and, realizing that it felt more like a leg, said, "Hey, wait a minute. You're Jim Brown!"

"What if I wasn't?" Jim said.

The officer had no answer for that, except to apologize and politely escort us to our car.

For as long as I've known him, Jim has worked for the betterment of the African-American community through his Amer-I-Can Program, which counsels prison inmates and teaches life skills to inner-city kids. He's an honest man and a man of conscience. He doesn't care what people think of him, and he doesn't bite his tongue. He tells you exactly what's on his mind, so if you don't want to hear it, don't ask him.

On the set of *100 Rifles*, Jim and I talked a lot about the differences between the North and the South, and he once told me that he'd rather have a Southern white man put his arm around him than a black man, because the Southern white man knows the consequences. I was with Jim on many occasions when he would say those exact words to people in a discussion. (When Jim Brown has a discussion, it gets real quiet.)

Jim is the least bigoted person I've ever known. He judges people on their own merits. Despite the discrimination he experienced, he's managed to keep a sense of fairness. But if he's challenged or insulted in any way, he reacts the way you would in the same situation . . . if you had the courage.

In 1999, Jim's wife accused him of smashing the windshield of her Jaguar. She took it all back the next day, but the D.A. wanted to prosecute, and Jim was sentenced to one hundred hours of community service and three years' probation.

"No thanks," he said. "I'll take jail. I'm not about to wear an orange suit and pick up litter off a freeway for something I didn't do." So, at the age of sixty-four, he served four months in the L.A. County Jail, without a peep of complaint.

ONE DAY I went to his house—we were going out somewhere—and he was crying.

"Is there anything I can do, Jim?" I said.

"No, I'll be okay in a minute," he said. "I just heard that a friend of mine died."

"I'm sorry," I said. "Was it someone you played ball with?"

"Yeah, it was," he said. "He was white, and the finest man I've ever known."

Well, Jim Brown is the finest man *I've* ever known.

John Boorman
and Jon Voight

Early in 1971, John Boorman asked me to read for the part of Lewis Medlock in his next movie, *Deliverance*, based on James Dickey's bestselling novel. I'd admired Boorman's work, especially his last two pictures, *Point Blank* and *Hell in the Pacific*. After a few preliminaries, Boorman began describing the novel about four city boys from Atlanta on a weekend canoe trip that turns into a battle for survival against a raging river and two murderous mountain men.

"I read the book," I said. "And I've read Dickey's poetry."

Boorman seemed surprised, and he missed a beat. "Can you do a Southern accent?" he asked.

I didn't want to blow the part with a wisecrack, so I just said, "Yes." I didn't tell him that I'd spent twenty years trying to get rid of mine.

A week later I was in John's office at Warner Bros., listening to him talk about this very Southern novel in his very English accent. He obviously had a feeling for the story and empathy for the characters. His enthusiasm was contagious.

I wanted to know which of my movies had made him think of

me, so I began listing the pieces of crap I'd done. "Did you see me in *Navajo Joe? Sam Whiskey? 100 Rifles?*"

"Actually," he said, "I saw you hosting *The Tonight Show.*"

It was my turn to miss a beat.

Boorman said that he'd been impressed by how I took charge of the show and that he thought I was fearless, just like Lewis in the novel.

"I'm too stupid to be scared," I said.

Boorman said that he'd already cast Jon Voight in the part of Ed Gentry, and I was pleased. Jon was an accomplished actor, Oscar-nominated for his portrayal of Joe Buck in *Midnight Cowboy.* Boorman asked if I knew Jon, and as I started to say that we'd met only once or twice, he opened the door to the adjoining office and Jon came in. He'd been in the other room all the time.

Jon and I proceeded to do an hour of improvisation that seemed like ten minutes. We clicked, and the chemistry must have been obvious to Boorman, but he never told me, "You've got the part," so I broke down and said, "I feel good about the meeting, and I feel strange asking this . . . but am I in this movie or not?"

"You're in the movie!" he said with a big grin.

Jon seemed genuinely happy for me. There was a sweetness about it. We were instant pals, and our friendship grew during the making of the picture.

Boorman had originally considered Lee Marvin and Henry Fonda for the roles of Lewis and Ed. The studio wanted Jack Nicholson and Robert Redford. It was rumored that both Charlton Heston and Gene Hackman had wanted to play Lewis. But Boorman being Boorman, he wanted everyone to do their own stunts, and with big stars they would've used doubles, so he decided to go with the much younger Voight and some of his contemporaries. Jon was the linchpin for Boorman, and he was for me, too. I don't think I'd have been in the movie without his support.

I AGREED to $50,000 (with no back end) for three months' work, a lot less than I'd been making on *Dan August*. But I didn't care. It was a great script and a great opportunity. I knew I could get into Lewis's skin and I saw the role as a chance to finally gain some acting credibility.

Boorman found Ned Beatty and Ronny Cox doing *The Pueblo Incident* at the Arena Stage in Washington, D.C., and flew Jon and me there to see them. We agreed they'd be perfect for the parts of Bobby and Drew, and it was a thrill to be there when John told them he was casting them in what would be their first movie.

Voight is curious about everything. As an actor he wants to know as much as he can about the character because, more than anything, he wants to get it right . . . and for my money he always does. He taped hours of conversation with James Dickey and used it to get the Southern accent. He's also meticulous about clothing. Actors can say a lot with what they choose to wear. Lewis is proud of his biceps, so I went to an army/navy store in Atlanta, bought a wet suit, and cut the sleeves off. (They didn't sell them that way at the time.) Jon found just the right things for easygoing Ed, especially that little hat, although I thought the pipe was over the top.

Jon will do whatever's necessary to be faithful to the character, including risking his life: To protect his buddies after Lewis breaks his leg, Ed turns into a predator who stalks and kills a man with a bow and arrow. In one of the most gripping scenes in the picture, he scales the vertical face of a 200-foot cliff. Jon did most of the climbing himself, and we almost lost him.

JOHN BOORMAN is probably the best director I've ever worked with. He certainly knows how to handle actors. Before shooting began, he took me aside and said, "There's only one way this is going to work: Voight has to give the first half of the movie to you, and he will because he's unselfish. He *must* let you take it, and you *will* take it."

No director ever said anything like that to me before or since.

"But in the last half," Boorman said, "after Lewis gets hurt . . . from then on you're just a body in a boat. You're totally worthless. *You've* got to give it to *him*."

He was right, and I did.

He also gave me some good advice right when I needed it. "Don't act," he said. "Just behave. We'll wait for you, because we can't take our eyes off of you."

I didn't know he'd told the other guys the same thing.

John gave us the luxury of rehearsing every scene until it was right. The experience brought us together, and we got closer as the filming went on, talking endlessly about our characters and their relationships, not only with each other but with their unseen families, friends, and coworkers.

John started as a film critic, then made documentaries for the BBC before coming to the States in 1966 to make *Point Blank*. He knows his way around the camera and he's particular about the visual quality of his pictures. For *Deliverance*, he thought the actual scenery along the river was too lush for the grim content of the film, so he had them wash the color out in post-production to make the landscape look more menacing. He analyzes every line of dialogue, every camera angle, every piece of business, but unlike a lot of directors, he'll take suggestions from just about anyone.

Boorman came up with the best definition of the movie business I've ever heard: "Filmmaking is the process of turning money into light and then back into money again." As a writer-director, he isn't afraid to take risks in the pursuit of his vision. Though he's a master at turning money into light, he hasn't always turned it back into money, but all his films embody his devotion to craft.

John came over in 2012 for the fortieth anniversary *Deliverance* reunion. Jon, Ned, and Ronny were there, too. We had a wonderful time and everybody was laughing and telling lies. The four actors have stayed close over the years. We did everything ourselves in the picture, and each of us almost drowned more than once. We saved each other's lives, so we're like guys who've gone to war together. And they still think I'm Lewis. They said, "When can we go to dinner?" I still have to tell them everything.

But I felt something amiss with Boorman at the reunion. I think it dated back to 1973, when he'd wanted me to come to Ireland to play the lead in *Zardoz*, the movie he eventually did with Sean Connery. I wasn't crazy about the script, but that's not why I didn't go. I'd been sick and just wasn't up to it. I think he felt that I let him down, and I don't think he's ever forgiven me for it. If I could do it over, I'd go . . . in a hospital plane if necessary.

JAMES DICKEY was a great poet, and his bestselling novel *Deliverance* is a masterpiece that usually shows up on lists of the hundred best American novels. But he was a man who, after he'd had a few martinis, made you want to drop a grenade down his throat. I think he fancied himself a two-fisted poet, a kind of down-home Hemingway.

He was a big, wild-eyed bear of a man with a flair for the dramatic. He'd act out scenes from *Deliverance*, playing all the parts himself. He'd tell the same stories again and again—the same way every time. And when he read his poems to an audience, he'd deliver them with what seemed like deep emotion, but he'd always break down in tears at the same place.

Dickey liked to hang around the set, and one day during re-hearsals, after swearing me to secrecy and claiming he hadn't told another living soul, he confided that *Deliverance* was autobio-graphical, that everything in it had happened to him. He warned me not to tell the others because, he said, I was the only one who could handle it. I was shocked, but honored that he would take me into his confidence, and the more I thought about it, the more I admired him for turning painful experience into great literature.

Of course I mentioned it to Voight.

"Do you know what Dickey told me?" I said.

"I don't know what he told *you*," Jon said, "but he told *me* that everything in the novel happened to him."

We discovered that Dickey had also confided in Boorman, Ronny Cox, Ned Beatty, the cameraman, the archery coach, and proba-bly the key grip. We've since learned that he made up all kinds of things about his background, falsely claiming to have been a college football star, a combat pilot during World War II, and a working-class child of the Depression. In fact he played only one season of freshman ball; was a radar operator, not a pilot; and came from a well-to-do Atlanta family. Nor was he the whitewater expert he pretended to be. On a pre-production jaunt down the Chattooga, he managed to capsize his canoe in calm water.

Boorman saw each of the four main characters in *Deliverance* as a different facet of Dickey's personality: There was Ed, the cau-tious advertising man—Dickey had been a copywriter on the Coca-Cola account at McCann Erickson in the 1950s. Lewis, the macho survivalist, is the man Dickey wished he could be. The guitar-playing Drew is the poet. And as for obnoxious, overbearing Bobby . . . well.

I'm not sure I buy all that.

But I think Boorman did solve the mystery of Dickey's allergy to

Mom and Pop with Sammy Davis Jr. (circa 1980).

With Mom (circa 1989).

Big Burt on the ranch with Cathy, his favorite deer (circa 1995).

With Larry King and Pop on the set of *Larry King Live* (2000).

With my sister, Nancy Ann (2005).

With my niece, Nancy Lee Hess (2009).

Trespassing at Mar-A-Lago with "Headless Harry Smith" and Mo Mustaine (circa 1951).

With Ann Lawler, Mo Mustaine, and Marlene Zent at Palm Beach High's "Senior Skip Day" (1953).

Florida High School All-Star Game (1953). I'm first on the left, bottom row.

On the practice field at Florida State University (1954).

(© Florida State/Collegiate Images/ Getty Images)

On the sideline with Lee Corso (circa 2000).

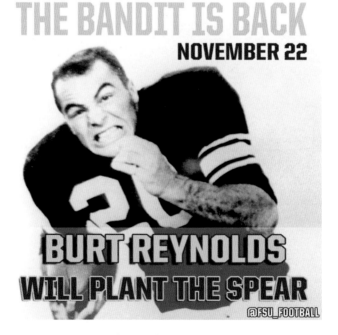

The Bandit is back . . .

. . . to plant the Seminole spear (Florida State versus Boston College, 2014).

(© Don Juan Moore/Getty Images)

ABOVE: In my home office, pretending to work (1967). *(© The Palm Beach Post/Zuma Wire)*

BELOW: In my living room, pretending to relax (1978). *(© The Palm Beach Post/Zuma Wire)*

Home on the ranch (1978).

Cruising in Palm Beach while shooting *B. L. Stryker* (1988).
(© The Palm Beach Post/Zuma Wire)

With my son,
Quinton, on the
Jupiter ranch
(circa 1992).

Inscription: "For 'Big Burt'—No more 'D' Day's for us—
with respect—Charley Durning."

With Charles Durning
as he receives the 44th
Screen Actors Guild Life
Achievement Award
(2008). *(© Kevin Winter/
Getty Images)*

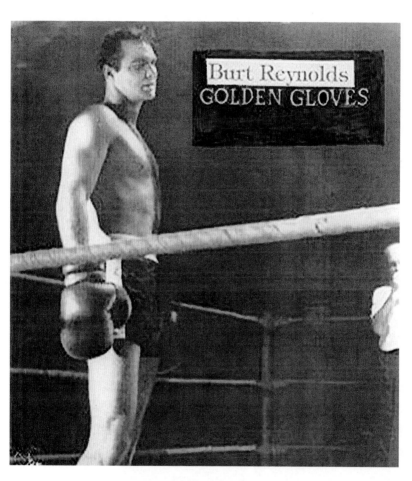

I retired undefeated after three bouts.

As "Hoke Adams" in *Angel Baby* (1961), my first major role in a feature film.

As "Rocky Rhodes," a Brando-like actor in a 1963 *Twilight Zone* episode.

On the set of *100 Rifles* with Jim Brown and Raquel Welch (1969).
(© 20th Century Fox Film Corp./Everett Collection)

Deliverance (1972). *(© Everett Collection)*

Deliverance (1972). *(© Everett Collection)*

Unwinding in the pool with Jon Voight after a hard day's work on *Deliverance* (1972).
(© Getty Images)

On the beach in Palm Beach (circa 1955).

the truth: "He used up all his honesty in his poems and had none left for his life."

DELIVERANCE IS ABOUT men facing down their fears and testing themselves against nature. A magnificent wild river is about to be turned into a placid lake by a dam built to supply power for air-conditioners in Atlanta. As Lewis says, it's the chance to see "the last untamed, unpolluted, un-fucked-up river in the South."

We filmed along the Chattooga, in the remote mountain country of Rabun County, Georgia, with its dense forests and whitewater rapids. At one time Rabun supplied most of the moonshine for Atlanta. Jim Dickey called it "the home of nine-fingered people" because nearly everybody there was missing a body part, either from inbreeding or poor medical treatment.

Our base camp was in Clayton, the Rabun county seat and a popular resort for Atlantans ("Where Spring Spends the Summer," according to the Chamber of Commerce). Clayton was already a popular movie location: *The Great Locomotive Chase* (1956), *The Long Riders* (1980), and *Whiskey Mountain* (1977) were all filmed there. After *Deliverance*, the area became a tourist trap where you could buy T-shirts that said, "Paddle faster, I hear banjos," and where ill-equipped novices tested themselves against the "Deliverance River." Dozens have drowned in the process.

Some people in Rabun County said the film unfairly portrays backcountry folks. That was never my intention, and I don't think it was anybody else's. Some of the reviews of the picture were condescending toward the locals, calling them "weasels" and hillbillies "inbred to the point of idiocy." I think we may have been painted with that brush.

Our accommodations were a pleasant contrast to the working

conditions. We stayed at Kingwood Country Club, with its condos, golf course, and clubhouse, which became our gathering place in the evenings.

One night I was sitting at the bar trying to ignore Dickey, who was across the room holding forth at a table with Jon and Ned.

"LEWIS!" he shouted. (Dickey called us all by our characters' names.) "I'm talkin' to ya, boy! Come ovah heah."

I didn't budge.

All of a sudden he was looming over me, all six-foot-seven of him, in full regalia: Stetson, fringed jacket, bowie knife. He locked his arms around my shoulders and bellowed, "LEWIS! How the fuck are ya, Lewis?"

I didn't answer.

Dickey bent down so his head was next to mine. "Lewis, I'm talkin' to ya, son. Why don'tcha answer me?"

"Because I'm not Lewis, I'm Burt. Tomorrow morning on the set I'll be Lewis. Until then, get the fuck out of my face!"

The room fell silent, and for an instant I thought he might cut me with the bowie knife.

Instead he laughed and said, "By God, that's just what Lewis woulda said!" Then he turned on his heels, went back to his table, and never came around me again.

But he did come around our rehearsals, usually with a drink in his hand and a bow on his shoulder. He wasn't shy about voicing his opinions, and every time he opened his mouth, he pissed somebody off. We'd be ready to do a scene and at the last minute he'd pull Jon aside and tell him how to play it. It drove Jon nuts, and you could tell it was getting to Boorman, who with typical understatement termed his relationship with Dickey "turbulent and bruising." Just like the Chattooga.

We called a meeting with Boorman and told him that we couldn't stand the son of a bitch, and John kicked him off the set, but only after promising him the part of the sheriff. Dickey insisted on speaking to us before he left. He came to a rehearsal and said, "Gentlemen, I understand that my presence will be more expeditious by my absence."

I asked Boorman, "Does that mean he's going or he's staying?"

Dickey came back two months later to play Sheriff Bullard, who has a few lines at the end of the picture. As an actor, James Dickey was a great poet, and Boorman had to work to extract a performance from him. After wrapping his last scene, Dickey wore the sheriff's outfit around town. He claimed he was so convincing in it that he'd collected graft from the local whorehouse, adding, "That wasn't all I got, either."

AT A DUSTY backwoods filling station on the way into the wilderness, Drew (Ronny Cox) is idly pickin' a few notes on his guitar when an inscrutable boy on a porch answers back with his banjo. The exchange turns into a call-and-response between the two instruments, and as it builds to a crescendo, the boy comes alive. But when the song ends, he goes back into his shell. When Ronny tries to communicate with him, he turns away.

The boy (Lonnie) was played by twelve-year-old Billy Redden. Boorman had wanted a certain look and found Billy in the Clayton Elementary School. He had him made up to match the description in the novel: "an albino boy with pink eyes like a white rabbit's."

Billy may have *looked* right for the part, but he couldn't play the banjo, so they cut a hole in his sleeve and a boy who could play stuck his arm through and did the fretting while Billy pretended to strum. Between takes, Billy would turn to the boy and say, "We sure can play this thing, can't we?"

It was all dubbed by a pair of bluegrass musicians from New York, Eric Weissberg and Steve Mandell. Warner Bros. released it as a single and it was a big hit. They paid royalties to Weissberg, and Boorman got a gold record that was later stolen from his house. It turned out that the melody was swiped, too, from "Feudin' Banjos," recorded in 1955. The rightful composer sued Warner's and got a big settlement.

Variations on the "Dueling Banjos" theme serve as the score of the film. Boorman did it to save money: the studio was constantly on his neck about the budget, so he fired the conductor and orchestra in favor of just the two string instruments.

Billy appears once more in the film, as a ghostly vision on a log bridge over the river. As we pass under him in our canoes (in a nifty 360-degree turning shot), Drew breaks into a big grin and tries to make eye contact, but Billy only turns away, ominously swinging his banjo like a pendulum.

THE RAPE of Bobby (Ned Beatty) by a mountain man is the other signature scene in *Deliverance*. It's a single shot that runs ten minutes on the screen. Boorman had five cameras rolling because he knew he could shoot it only once. He considered it the heart of the film and a metaphor for the rape of the river. (Lewis actually says it: "We're gonna rape this whole goddamn landscape. We gon' *rape* it.") For John, the rape is nature's revenge against the men who were violating the river. It figured to be one of the most powerful scenes ever filmed, but he couldn't find an actor with an authentic Southern accent and no front teeth to play the accomplice.

"I know a guy!" I said. Herbert "Cowboy" Coward. I'd met him at Ghost Town in the Sky, a Wild West tourist attraction in the Smoky Mountains of North Carolina where I'd worked as a stuntman, doing staged gunfights and high falls every hour on the hour for a hundred bucks a week.

Cowboy was in character from the moment he arrived on the set wearing clodhoppers and bib overalls. He stuttered a bit, but he said some funny things. When Boorman hired him, he asked, "Now, Cowboy, are you okay taking part in the rape of a man?" and Cowboy replied, "Hell, I've d-done worse things than th-that!"

When Cowboy was handed the script, it was obvious he couldn't read, so I ran the lines with him until he had them down. But with the camera rolling, they didn't always come out as written.

When he couldn't manage a word he ad-libbed around it, so that "Go over by the tree and pull down your pants," became "Get over by that sa-a-a-plain and take your p-panties down." The line "You ain't goin' nowhere" turned into "You ain't a'goin any damn wheres." But one of his lines was right from the script: "He got a real purty mouth, ain't he?"

Off the set Cowboy kept to himself. Every night back at the Heart of Rabun Motel, he'd put a case of beer on ice in the bathtub and work his way through it while sitting on the toilet seat.

Bill McKinney, the one who sodomizes Bobby, was a veteran character actor and a hell of an athlete—very fit and health-conscious. But he was one strange dude. Every time you looked at him, he was examining the veins in his forearm, and early mornings I'd see him running nude through the sprinklers on the golf course. After *Deliverance* he made some pictures with Clint Eastwood, always playing sickos.

But Bill was a pro: He had to play dead in the long sequence where we decide what to do with his body, and he went a full two minutes without blinking or breathing, despite a mosquito that landed on the white of his eye. Complete concentration. Told they needed substitute dialogue for the TV version, Bill ad-libbed a line that stayed in the movie: "Squeal like a pig!"

Forty years later, people on the street still yell that at Ned. The whole business had a powerful effect on him, and he couldn't stop talking about it.

"When am I going to get this out of my brain?" he kept saying.

One night he had a drink or two and confessed that he regretted ever doing the movie. "All they're gonna remember is that I was the guy that got boogered."

Ned's performance in that scene is devastating. He should have won the Oscar.

DELIVERANCE WAS a rough shoot, an adventure that mirrored the plot of the movie, with more than our share of accidents and injuries, including a couple of near drownings. It was so dangerous, we couldn't get insurance for the production.

The Chattooga is one of the most treacherous rivers in the United States, with more average drop per mile than the Colorado. Rated too difficult to navigate in an open canoe, it's recommended for kayaks only. We learned that you had to be very precise negotiating rapids with names like Corkscrew, Bull Sluice, and Screaming Left Turn. You had to enter each set at exactly the correct angle or you were in trouble.

It was the most fun I've ever had.

On the first day of filming, the whole company set off downriver in a fleet of rafts and canoes. Half of them capsized within the first mile. Nobody got hurt, but a camera and sound equipment went down with one of the rafts.

That's when I heard the prop man say, "We're gonna be here a long, long time."

For the whitewater scenes, Boorman would be in a little rubber boat with the cameraman and his assistant. (But no sound man: You couldn't hear what we were saying over the roaring river, so we dubbed the dialogue later.) We had a top-notch cinematographer in Vilmos Zsigmond, who, as a nineteen-year-old film student in 1956, had shot famous footage of Soviet tanks entering Budapest. Boorman figured that a man who'd been fired on by the Russians wouldn't be intimidated by a river.

There were other complications. Trees and rocks would get in the way and we'd have to retake the simplest shots again and again. The Chattooga formed the state line between Georgia and South Carolina, so if we filmed on one side of the river, we were under the jurisdiction of the New York union, but on the other side we had to use a Chicago crew. Union rules also forced Boorman to hire a separate cameraman, but because Vilmos was his own operator, the other guy spent most of his time at the motel.

Movies are almost always shot according to the logistics of the production and the scenes are later cut into the correct order. But *Deliverance* was shot in sequence.

When I asked John why, he said, "In case one of you drowns."

He had a notation right there in his script—"Lewis drowned today"—and I wasn't sure he was kidding. The drawback of shooting in sequence was that we all knew the rape scene was coming and we got more and more anxious as it approached.

Jon and I each lost ten pounds during the filming. We came in soft, but slowly built ourselves up, and by the end we were like rocks. We did a lot of training before the cameras rolled, learning how to climb rocks and shoot a bow and arrow.

I was having trouble finding the character and Boorman suggested I read *Zen in the Art of Archery*, which says that you don't shoot the arrow, the arrow shoots you. You don't consciously release it; rather, you pull it back and it goes where it's supposed to go by itself . . . when the time is right. I thought, Well, no harm in trying it.

If you see the movie, you hear dialogue over the titles that we actually shot at an archery range.

When it came time to shoot that scene, Boorman said, "Let's not rehearse, let's just fire the arrows," and he started rolling.

The target was fifty yards away, which meant that you had to kind of arc the arrow. The bow had a 65-pound pull. I was in great shape by then, but 65 pounds . . . it's hard not to quiver a bit. But I didn't quiver at all; I had it right there, steady as could be. I was saying my lines and all of sudden I noticed the arrow was gone. So I took another arrow out and talked some more and it was gone and I talked some more and another arrow was gone.

When Boorman called "Cut," all the arrows were in the bull's-eye.

Freddy Bear, who was our expert—Bear Bows are named after him—said, "I've never seen shooting like that in my life!"

"It's nothing," I said.

When we broke for lunch, I wanted to try it again and nearly shot myself in the foot. I could hardly pull the string all the way back and couldn't come close to the bull's-eye. I was only good between "Action" and "Cut," when I was Lewis. As Burt, I couldn't hit the side of a barn.

We also took canoeing lessons. Of the four of us, Ned, whose character Bobby was the worst canoer in the group, was the only one who'd ever paddled one before.

Boorman let us pick our own canoes. There were a few Indian-style wooden canoes and one made of aluminum. The wooden ones looked authentic, but the aluminum was kind of drab and industrial.

I told Jon to go first, hoping he'd take a pretty one, and he did! He told me later that he took it because it was "homey." Exactly what Ed would have done. It was an artistic choice that Jon came to regret, because it was too fragile for the rapids. Every time it hit a rock, he had the sickening feeling that it was breaking up under him.

By the end of the shoot we'd destroyed half a dozen wooden canoes but only dented the aluminum one. (Later I sent Jon a miniature wooden canoe with "Voight's Choice" painted on it.)

ONE MORNING I had a late call but couldn't understand why, because Lewis was scheduled to go over the waterfall that day. I got to the set at ten o'clock, just in time to see them filming a dummy (dubbed No Balls by the crew) going over the falls.

It looked like shit.

In those days I was fearless . . . to the point of insanity. I would take on anything, anybody, anywhere.

I went to Boorman and said, "John, I can go over the falls at least as good as that thing."

Boorman didn't doubt you. If you told him you could do something, he'd let you try.

There was a hydroelectric dam about four miles upriver and we had control of it. We could close the water down to a trickle to allow us to set up the stunt, then open the gates and release a torrent for the shot. In preparation, I had them pound a spike into a rock at the top of the falls and attach a rope to it. I swam out, grabbed the rope, signaled to let the water go, and lay out flat. Within a minute I heard a terrifying sound. I looked up and a mountain of water was on top of me. I ducked just as it hit, but it turned me head over heels under water and slammed me against the rock, cracking my tailbone. I surfaced long enough to gulp air, then plunged back under and did an involuntary triple axel, landing on my head. I'd been swallowed by a hydraulic, an underwater whirlpool that spins you around like a cement mixer.

Somehow I remembered one of the old-time stuntmen saying

years before that if you get caught in a hydro, don't try to swim out because you'll drown fighting it. Instead you swim to the bottom and the current will shoot you out from there. I swam down, and sure enough, it launched me like a torpedo. I finally surfaced a hundred yards downstream. The rocks had skinned me alive and the hydro had torn off my boots, socks, pants, everything.

Boorman said, "I saw a fit thirty-year-old actor go over the falls and a naked old man stumble out of the water."

Later that day, when he came to see me in the hospital, I asked him how it looked. "Like a dummy going over the falls," he said.

FOR THE SCENE where Lewis breaks his leg, I told Boorman that I didn't want the special effects guy or anybody else doing it. "Let me try something and if you don't like it we won't use it," I said.

I went to a local butcher, got the backbone of a lamb, and snapped it in half. I asked the butcher if he had any blood and he said, "Oh God yeah, I got me a lotta blood," and gave me three jars of it.

It looked real, not like Hollywood blood, and between takes I'd pour it over the "wound." It looked so bad, it almost made Ronny sick. Boorman loved it.

Ronny returned the favor. In the script they find Drew washed up on the rocks with his arm grotesquely bent around his neck. In the film it wasn't faked because Ronny was double-jointed and could throw his shoulder out at will. He didn't do it much because it hurt like hell, but he did it for the scene and it was gold. The sight of it shocked everyone but Boorman.

It isn't clear whether Drew is shot or commits suicide. Half the people I talk to think he was shot; the other half think he bailed because he couldn't accept the decision to cover up the killings.

Lewis believes Drew was shot, but Ed thinks he killed himself. Ronny later told me that he'd decided for his own purposes that Drew was neither shot nor a suicide, but the victim of some kind of accident.

DELIVERANCE DEALT WITH issues that Hollywood hadn't yet touched: the destruction of the natural world by humans, and something that was never discussed at the time: homosexual rape.

I saw a cut of the movie with Boorman from the back of the Cinerama Dome in Los Angeles. The place got so quiet between the action sequences, it was like being in church. When it got to the rape scene, he said, "I can't watch this. I didn't think it would be this powerful. I didn't think it would grab hold of you like that."

We went outside, and soon there were half a dozen men who couldn't watch either, and one of them was throwing up on the sidewalk. But the women in the audience were fine. Their reaction seemed to be "Okay, now you know what it's like!" (Before the release Barbra Streisand called Boorman and asked to see a rough cut because, she said, "I want to see a man raped for a change.")

IF I HAD to put only one of my movies in a time capsule, it would be *Deliverance*. I don't know if it's the best acting I've ever done, but it's the best movie I've ever been in. It proved I could act, not only to the public, but to me.

Just before *Deliverance* was released, I went to a screening at Warner Bros. with Lee Marvin, who took me aside and gave me some unsolicited advice: "Don't let 'em fuck you up, pardner! You're gonna be under a microscope and it's gonna change your life forever."

"I sure hope so," I said.

Lee grabbed me by the lapels. "No, listen to me! It's gonna change everything and you've got to be careful. *Don't let 'em fuck you up!*"

"I won't," I said.

"Goddamn it! You're not listening!"

And I wasn't.

I had no idea.

Helen Gurley Brown

I think *Deliverance* deserved more recognition from the Academy than it got. It was nominated for Best Picture of 1972, but *The Godfather* won the Oscar. John Boorman was nominated for Best Director, but Bob Fosse won for *Cabaret*. Tom Priestley was nominated for Best Film Editing, but David Bretherton got it *(Cabaret)*. Even though it was a tough year, I was surprised that Jon Voight and Ned Beatty weren't even nominated. Nor was Vilmos Zsigmond for cinematography. And I confess that I thought I had a shot, too.

Why were we snubbed?

It was my fault.

One night early in 1972, after *Deliverance* was in the can but before it was released, I was on *The Tonight Show* with Helen Gurley Brown, the longtime editor of *Cosmopolitan* and author of the bestselling book *Sex and the Single Girl*. During a commercial break she invited me to be the first male nude centerfold of the magazine.

Though no one had ever shown a naked man in a magazine before, Helen believed that women have the same "visual appetites" as men, who'd been looking at naked women in *Playboy* since

1953. She wanted the same prerogative for women. It would be a milestone in the sexual revolution and she said that I was the one man who could pull it off. I found out later that she'd asked Paul Newman first, but he turned her down.

Helen didn't have to talk me into it. I was flattered and intrigued. I wish I could say that I wanted to show my support for women's rights, but I just thought it would be fun. I said yes before we came back on the air. (I may or may not have had several cocktails in the greenroom before the show.)

Everybody I respected told me not to do it. Friends and relatives pleaded for self-restraint. My agent warned that it would cancel out whatever *Deliverance* might do to establish me as a serious actor.

Ned couldn't believe it: "You're gonna be nekkid?" he said. "They're gonna see your *tallywacker*? What the hell are you trying to prove?"

I did it anyway. I thought it was a big joke. I wanted to do it as a takeoff on the Playmate of the Month. I'd list my hobbies and favorite colors, there'd be a black-and-white shot of me pushing a supermarket cart, and a quote: "I love sunsets and hate mean people."

On the way to the photo shoot, I stopped for two quarts of vodka and finished one before we got to the studio, which was freezing cold (bad for a naked man's self-esteem).

The famed Francesco Scavullo photographed me on a bearskin rug. He took hundreds of shots: with a hat in front of my . . . tallywacker, with a dog in front of it, with my hand in front of it. (If I was trying to prove something, why would I cover it up with my hand? I have very small hands.) They promised to burn the outtakes and give me all the negatives.

The magazine hit the stands in April 1972, three months before *Deliverance* opened, and quickly sold all 1.5 million copies.

Suddenly my life was a carnival. I couldn't go anywhere without women asking me to sign their copies, each one a painful reminder of my stupidity. I did *The Rainmaker* in Chicago and the audiences were rowdy: instead of applause there were hoots and catcalls. While most of the mail was positive and polite, I also got some of the filthiest letters I've ever seen, many of which included Polaroids. I received regular shipments of pubic hair from a woman in Nova Scotia. (I worried about her in that cold climate.)

I was in Denmark promoting *Deliverance* and there I was on the cover of a Danish porno mag pretending to hump the bearskin rug. It was one of the outtakes that were supposed to have been destroyed.

The Catholic church condemned me.

And I got "Hey! I didn't recognize you with your clothes on" fifty times a day.

A cottage industry sprang up. I wasn't paid for the photos or for any sort of merchandising rights, but my centerfold appeared on panties, T-shirts, key chains, coasters, floor mats. The low point was when I checked into a hotel and found myself imprinted on the sheets. (The manager said he'd bought them at Macy's.)

It was a total fiasco. I thought people would be able to separate the fun-loving side of me from the serious actor, but I was wrong. I'm still embarrassed by it and I sorely regret doing it. It's been called one of the greatest publicity stunts of all time, but it was one of the biggest mistakes I've ever made, and I'm convinced it cost *Deliverance* the recognition it deserved.

Lee Marvin

L ee Marvin was a master storyteller. He had that wonderful deep voice, and he invented his own words, like *vicaries,* for vicarious thrills. He would also express himself without words, using a combination of gestures and whistles. He had an offbeat sense of humor and would say anything to get a reaction. Which is why journalists loved him: He gave great interview, with choice tidbits like "Reporters don't make actors sound stupid; they take care of that themselves." He once told me that he didn't care what was written about him, whether true or false, as long as it was interesting.

Lee was a shrewd judge of people and could sniff out bullshit a mile away. At the same time he had sympathy for anyone less fortunate than himself. But he did have an ornery streak, and it came out at an early age: He ran away from home when he was four and was later expelled from a series of exclusive boarding schools, including a Catholic academy in Florida "for pushing a kid out of a window," he said.

Lee joined the Marines at seventeen with his father's permission and saw action as a scout-sniper in the Pacific island-hopping campaign. On Eniwetok he killed half a dozen enemy soldiers with a grenade and bayoneted another in hand-to-hand combat. He got a Purple Heart for a near-fatal wound he received during the invasion of Saipan when a sniper's bullet hit him in the butt. "Not a very romantic place to be shot," he said. He thought it must have been a flat-nose round because it didn't leave a small entry hole, but a deep eight-inch gash across his backside just below the beltline that missed his spine by a fraction of an inch.

Lee believed that the wound saved his life. He'd been close to the breaking point and worried that he could no longer function in combat. The bullet put him out of action and, he said, kept him from embarrassing himself in the face of the enemy.

He was evacuated to a hospital ship anchored offshore. A nurse asked if he wanted anything—ice cream, ice water, whatever. "Moonlight Serenade" was playing over the PA. Lee could hear the gunfire from the battle still raging on the island, but he had ice cream, clean sheets, Glenn Miller, and nurses.

"My company, what was left of it, was still there," he said. "I was safe on a hospital ship. I was a deserter and a coward, and I cried." He could never shake the guilt from surviving while so many of his buddies died.

Lee obviously suffered from battle fatigue or PTSD or whatever you want to call it, but he thought it was cowardice and nobody could convince him otherwise. No matter how hard he tried to escape it, the war never left him. He had nightmares and once confessed that he relived the battle so vividly that he saw snipers in the trees.

After thirteen months in the hospital, Lee got a medical discharge and found a job as a plumber's assistant in Woodstock, New York. He was fixing a toilet at a community theater when an actor fell ill at the last minute. Lee was pressed into service and he was hooked. He went to New York and enrolled in the American Theatre Wing under the GI Bill. He made it to Broadway with a small part in the original production of *Billy Budd* (1951), then went to Hollywood and started working right away, mostly in Westerns and war movies.

For the first twenty years of his film career, he played so many sadistic heavies they called him "the merchant of menace." Some of those performances *are* chilling: He throws scalding coffee in Gloria Grahame's face in *The Big Heat* (1953) and enjoys it just a little too much. And for my money he blows Brando off the screen as a psycho motorcycle punk in *The Wild One* (1953).

Lee told me that he learned to act in the Marine Corps, trying to appear unafraid by concentrating on some task, like digging a foxhole or cleaning a weapon. He also credited the Marines for his actor's discipline: "The Corps teaches you that when it's time to toe the mark, you toe the mark," he said.

One of Lee's strengths as an actor was his power of observation. He noticed details that other actors ignored and it shows in his performances. He was especially knowledgeable about the technical details of firearms. He loved guns, and on the screen he handles them deliberately, almost lovingly. He was always original in whatever he did on the screen. He invented most of his own business and never repeated himself. As a supporting player and costar, he stole just about every scene he was in from some of the best actors in the business, including Spencer Tracy in *Bad Day at Black Rock* (1955) and Duke Wayne in *Donovan's Reef* (1963).

But Lee didn't begin to get the recognition he deserved until he appeared on television as Lieutenant Frank Ballinger in the police series *M Squad*, which he described as "*Dragnet* on speed."

It was the first TV show I ever did. On the first day I got a call sheet that read, "7:00 for 7:30." I assumed it was multiple choice. Hey, if that's the case, I'll take seven-thirty, I thought.

So I arrived at seven-thirty and the assistant director, a little wisp of a fella named Carter DeHaven, went berserk. He was chewing me out mercilessly in front of everybody, and I snapped.

"Listen, pal," I said, grabbing him by the throat, "If you don't shut the fuck up, I'm gonna hit you so hard both your parents will die."

At that instant Lee walked by and said, "What the hell's the matter?"

I told him the dumb thing I did with the seven o'clock call and he said, "Well, that makes sense to me," and we walked off together, leaving the poor AD muttering to himself.

We went to Lee's dressing room and I began to apologize. "I'm sorry, Mr. Marvin. I think it's because I'm scared."

"Me too!" he said. "Let me tell you what you should do, kid. Every morning before you shoot, go up to the camera and tell her you love her. Don't give a shit if anybody's watching you. Say, 'Good morning. I hope we have a good day today.' And if you want to give her a kiss, that's fine, too."

"Do you do that?" I asked.

"Yes!" he said. "It helps me get through the day. If the camera likes you, everybody likes you."

I've been doing it ever since.

LEE GOT BORED with *M Squad,* despite its success. He said it felt like a straitjacket creatively. He got out of the contract after three seasons and was happy to go back to feature films.

He got his first starring role in *Cat Ballou* (1965), a comedy Western in which he plays a drunken gunslinger who rides an equally drunken horse. In one of the great sight gags, a takeoff of the famous James Earle Fraser statue *The End of the Trail,* both Lee and the horse lean against a wall, both obviously soused. The

Academy doesn't usually give Best Actor Oscars for comedy performances, but Lee beat out Laurence Olivier (nominated for *Othello*), Richard Burton *(Who's Afraid of Virginia Woolf?)*, Rod Steiger *(The Pawnbroker)*, and Lee's *Ship of Fools* costar Oskar Werner.

It was a popular win. Lee took the podium to huge applause and said, "There are too many people to correctly thank for my career. I think, though, half of this belongs to a horse, someplace out in the Valley."

Cat Ballou finally tied Lee's name and face together for the public. His quote shot up to a million dollars a picture and he was suddenly a leading man. When Duke Wayne turned down the part of Major Reisman in *The Dirty Dozen* (1967), Lee took it. He hated the script, but couldn't resist the money. He wound up hating the picture, too. He thought it was way over the top. He believed that war should be shown in all its horror, not as an adventure. *The Dirty Dozen* was a huge hit—a "dummy money-maker," Lee called it, and it made him a superstar.

One of the things Lee and I had in common was our regard for John Boorman. They teamed up on *Point Blank* (1967), in which Lee plays a hard guy on a quest for revenge. By then Lee's star had risen so high, he was given control of the whole picture. He chose Boorman to direct and put him in charge of everything, including approval of the script, the cast, and the crew. Boorman made all the decisions and Lee backed him at every turn, even though it was Boorman's first Hollywood picture.

Lee made another picture with Boorman, *Hell in the Pacific* (1968), about an American pilot and a Japanese naval officer marooned on a Pacific island. Toshiro Mifune was the only other actor in the film and Lee said he loved working with him, even though they had no common language. The critics liked the film, but it flopped at the box office.

Lee was now making a million dollars a picture, but he was getting cynical about the business. He resented that Paul Newman made $200,000 more than he did on the Western comedy *Pocket Money* (1972). "You spend the first forty years of your life trying to get in this business, and the next forty years trying to get out," Lee said. He was also disgusted with being a movie star. "They put your name on a star in the sidewalk on Hollywood Boulevard and you walk down and find a pile of dog shit on it. That tells the whole story, baby."

Lee also began to have a problem with alcohol. "I quit drinking every morning and I start again every evening," he used to say. Like a lot of people, he got physical when he drank. He'd pick a fight with the toughest guy in the room and usually win. Sometimes he got so drunk he couldn't speak, just wave his arms. Or he'd do crazy things like go down to the Marine recruiting office in the middle of the night and try to reenlist.

One night Lee and I went for drinks and he got smashed and I said, "I promised your wife I'd get you back by one o'clock." I dragged him to the car and he got on the roof and wouldn't come down. I'd had a few drinks myself and I figured, what the hell, it's late, there's no traffic, I'll just go slow. So I drove at about ten miles an hour up the Pacific Coast Highway. I looked in the mirror and saw two cops in a cruiser behind us and thought, Oh, shit! But all they did was drive up beside us and go, "Hi, Lee," and drive off. I guess they were used to seeing Lee Marvin on the roof of a moving car.

I THINK MICHELLE TRIOLA started out as more or less a convenience for Lee, but she became a predicament. I don't think he loved her, but he might have been afraid of her or of what she was capable of doing. She threatened suicide more than once, and on the night of the Oscars, when Lee intended to take his ex-wife Betty, Michelle said that she'd kill herself if she couldn't go. Lee caved and took her instead of Betty.

Michelle was a wannabe actress and singer. She met Lee while working as a stand-in on *Ship of Fools* (1965). They became an item, and before long, Lee separated from his wife and Michelle moved into his Malibu house. She legally changed her name to Michelle Marvin. After living with Lee for six years she sued him for "palimony" in what became a landmark case.

Michelle demanded half of the millions Lee earned while they lived together, plus extra money for the loss of her "career." The judge denied her claim for Lee's income but awarded her $100,000 to help her learn a marketable skill. Lee appealed, and the judgment was thrown out on the same day that Michelle was arrested for shoplifting in Beverly Hills.

A short time later, Lee married his childhood sweetheart, Pamela Feeley, and settled down in Tucson. When he wasn't working, he was riding a motorcycle or big-game hunting or deep-sea fishing. ("Fishing gets rid of the bloodlust at sea, so I don't have to take it ashore with me.") But the booze and the four packs a day finally took their toll. He could never give up cigarettes despite violent coughing fits, and in his final days he would take off the oxygen mask to smoke.

Lee died of a heart attack in 1987 at age sixty-three. He's buried in Arlington National Cemetery. There's an old showbiz adage that you have to be lucky that somebody more famous doesn't die on the same day you do. The news of Lee's passing was overshadowed by the death of John Huston the day before, but I don't think Lee would give a damn.

Lee was a serious, intelligent actor who took pride in his craft, and a loyal friend who went out of his way to warn me of the perils of Hollywood success. Before Clint Eastwood, before Sam Peckinpah, Lee changed the way violence is portrayed on film. He hated senseless screen violence and made sure there was always a point to it in his performances. If the violence looks too easy, he believed, it becomes an invitation to try it. He wanted to make it so horrible that nobody would want any part of it, and I think he played all those "animal men," as he called them, not only because they were part of him, but also because he wanted to influence people not to be like them. But there's no doubt that the key to his personality was violence: the violence inside him, the violence he experienced in combat, and the violence he put on the screen. But, deep down— and he'd probably slug me for saying it—Lee was a gentle man.

Roy Rogers

Thomas "Snuff" Garrett (he got his nickname from Levi Garrett Chewing Tobacco) started as a disc jockey in Lubbock, Texas. Snuff didn't play an instrument, he didn't sing, but he had an uncanny ear for hits. He became a record producer and worked with everyone from Del Shannon to the Johnny Mann Singers. He wrote songs and owned his own record label. Back in the 1970s, he bought up all the old Republic Westerns and made a lot of money selling them on cassettes and DVDs. He retired to his ranch in Arizona and still lives there.

Snuff is one of the funniest people in the world. And legendary in Hollywood. You'd go to his house for dinner and you never knew who would be there, because he knew everybody.

Snuff produced the music for *Sharky's Machine* (1981) and *The Cannonball Run* (1981), which earned us music publishing royalties. When John Ford died, they auctioned off his paintings, and Snuff used our royalty money to buy two of them. One showed a scene from *The Searchers* (1956), the other from *Fort Apache* (1948). Snuff liked the one from *Fort Apache*, but he gave it to me because he thought it was a better painting, and he kept *The Searchers*.

Well, *The Searchers* is one of my favorite films, and I was disappointed, but I didn't say anything. A few weeks later I was having dinner with Snuff and his wife, Nettie, at their new house in Beverly Hills. We were sitting in the dining room with *The Searchers* hanging on the wall over us, and I couldn't take it anymore.

"How did *you* end up with the painting from my favorite movie, *The Searchers*?"

"You got the best goddamn painting, the one from *Fort Apache*," he said.

"I don't *want Fort Apache*."

"I'll tell you what," he said. "I never wanted the fuckin' *Searchers*."

The next morning we switched paintings.

SNUFF WAS A good friend of Roy Rogers. One day he said to Roy, "Would you record a song called 'Hoppy, Gene, and Me'?"

Roy said, "I don't know, I've never heard it."

And Snuff said, "I've never heard it either, Roy, because I just now got the fuckin' idea!"

Snuff came up with a song in about a week. Roy recorded it and it was a smash hit.

I'VE ALWAYS LOVED WESTERNS. As a boy I went to Saturday matinees to see Hoot Gibson, Charles Starrett, Rex Allen, Gene Autry, and my favorite, Roy Rogers, "The King of the Cowboys."

When I came to Hollywood, Snuff introduced me to Roy, and we hit it off right away. (I knew Gene Autry, too. Roy and Gene weren't the best of friends, but they pretended they were. They were always friendly in public, but they didn't much like each other.)

Roy and I talked a lot about the movies, and I loved running around with him, because wherever he went, people would go crazy. There was always a much bigger hubbub about him than about any other movie star I've ever been with, because they grew up with Roy and absolutely adored him. He was giving to his fans and kind to everyone who approached him for an autograph or just to chat. It was a great lesson for a young actor.

Roy's real name was Leonard Slye, and he was from Ohio. He didn't grow up on a ranch, but on a farm with cows and chickens. They did have one horse, and Roy taught himself to ride. He worked like hell with it, and by the time he became Roy Rogers, he knew what he was doing. Roy and his mother used to yodel to each other to communicate across distances on the farm, and yodeling became one of Roy's musical trademarks. He had a beautiful tenor voice, and long before he hit the silver screen he was the leader of the Sons of the Pioneers. The group performed what was then a new kind of popular music: not country, not bluegrass, but "Western" songs such as "Don't Fence Me In," "Tumbling Tumbleweeds," and "Cool Water."

One day Roy was in a hat shop in L.A. having his Stetson blocked when a guy ran in all out of breath and bought a cowboy hat. Roy overheard him tell the clerk that he needed the hat right away for an audition at Republic. Roy slipped out the back and snuck into the audition. He did a number on his guitar and they hired him and gave him a long-term contract on the spot beginning with a low-budget oater called *Under Western Stars* (1938).

Roy had these tiny little eyes, and of course Republic tried to change the thing that made him stand out. They made him use drops to widen them, but fans wrote in to protest, so they got rid of the drops and let Roy be Roy.

Audiences loved him. He went on to make nearly a hundred feature films, and they all made money. He shot each one in a couple of weeks for under $10,000, and on average they grossed $50,000. Between 1943 and 1954, Roy was the top Western star in Hollywood.

Even so, Republic wouldn't pay him more than $300 a week, so

Roy struck a deal for his own merchandising rights that turned into a bonanza. He was second only to Walt Disney in licensing sales, with Roy Rogers cap guns, pajamas, comic books, action figures, and of course about a billion lunch boxes. There's even a chain of Roy Rogers fast-food restaurants. He also had the Roy Rogers Museum in Apple Valley, California, where they had Roy's stuffed horse Trigger on display.

ROY WAS a straight shooter on the screen, but he didn't shoot to kill. When he plugged an hombre, he only winged him or shot the gun out of his hand. He was a marksman in real life, too, a champion shotgunner and big-game hunter with a den full of trophies. Not long after we met I went hunting with him and three or four other guys in Canada. It was one of the great thrills of my life. When everybody partnered up, I was honored that Roy asked to be with me.

The two of us took a small boat out to a remote island. We set up in a spot where Roy thought we'd have a good chance of finding game. We were talking about our favorite movies when we looked up and saw a moose walk out of the woods and begin to drink from a creek about fifty yards way. It was huge.

"Go ahead, take it!" Roy said.

"No, you go ahead," I said.

"No, it's yours."

"No, Mr. Rogers, please, *you* go ahead."

"Don't call me Mr. Rogers!"

The moose looked up from the stream and stared in our direction for a second, then went right back to drinking. Roy squeezed off a shot . . . and missed. He fired a second time and, believe it or not, missed again. The moose didn't seem to notice. It turned around and slowly disappeared into the trees.

It was an awkward moment until Roy said, "He's obviously never seen any of my movies."

Roy's was a sweet and gentle version of the Old West, and there was no attempt at realism. He liked to say that the reason they called it a Colt .45 was that they could shoot it forty-five times without reloading. The shows were little morality plays with simple plots: Roy was the good guy in the white hat and you knew he'd triumph over the black hats at the end of every film and TV show. He was a hero, not an antihero. He never drank or smoked, and "shucks" was the closest he ever got to cussing.

I'm glad he never got to see *Deadwood*.

Roy had a flair for showmanship. All decked out in those embroidered shirts, those fancy tooled boots, and that white Stetson, he looked like a stockbroker at a dude ranch. But he used to say, "If they're gonna call me the King of the Cowboys, then I've got to *be* the King of the Cowboys."

Roy's approach to acting was simple. "I never took any lessons on singing or acting or anything," he said. "So I'd read the script. If I had to play the bad guy, I'd frown. If I had to play the good guy, I'd smile."

Roy bought a palomino named Golden Cloud off the set of *The Adventures of Robin Hood* (1938), where it was ridden sidesaddle by Olivia de Havilland, and renamed him Trigger. He was a fabulous horse. Roy liked to say that Trigger could turn on a dime and give you nine cents change. The horse was a real trouper. He could do dozens of tricks and was billed as "The Smartest Horse in the Movies." He was popular with the public, who were unaware that there were actually two Triggers. The second was a body double used for chase scenes. When you run a horse hard, he's not going to be ready for his close-up.

Roy and his wife and costar, Dale Evans, moved to television in the early fifties with a half-hour series. In addition to Trigger, there was Roy's German shepherd, Bullet, the Wonder Dog, and Pat Brady as Roy's sidekick with his temperamental Jeep Nellybelle. (It was a "modern Western.") Roy and Dale sang "Happy Trails" at the end of each episode.

They were a great couple, though it was his third marriage and her fourth. They adopted five kids and had one of their own and were wonderful parents. Dale was the driving force there. She was smart, especially about business. Her problem was that she sized people up too quickly and didn't like half of them. I know she didn't like me. She thought I might be a bad influence on Roy . . . and she was right, because that's what I had in mind. But Roy didn't need much encouragement in that department. He only *sang* like a choirboy.

I liked Roy enormously. He was much more than a singing cowboy. Something a lot of people don't know about him is that he loved jazz. It was his quiet passion and he was knowledgeable about it, but he couldn't say anything because it didn't fit his image. It's strange how paranoid people in show business are about guarding their territory. Roy was afraid that his fans wouldn't like it if they knew.

When Trigger died in 1965, at the age of thirty-three, Roy couldn't bring himself to put him in the ground, so he had Trigger stuffed, in the rearing position, *anatomically correct*. He put him in the museum, where the sight of him startled the visitors. But Roy was thrilled. "Trigger was a stallion till the day he died," he liked to say.

Roy died of congestive heart failure in 1998 at the age of eighty-six. He's buried at Sunset Hills Memorial Park in Apple Valley, but if he had his way he'd have been stuffed and put up on Trigger.

Dinah Shore

In 1969 I went to the Philippines to do a movie called *Impasse*, a word that also described the state of my career. I stopped in Japan on the way because I'd heard about Kabuki theater and wanted to see it in person. It turned out to be everything I'd imagined and more. Young actors go there in their early teens and stay for ten or twelve years studying voice, dance, and acting. They live like monks and nuns while being immersed in the traditional Kabuki characters.

One evening I went to a theater in the suburbs of Tokyo, where I saw a young actress named Miko Mayama who absolutely bowled me over. She had black hair way down to there, a beautiful, shapely figure, and a throaty, almost sultry voice. I'd never seen anyone like her. She was in her early twenties and had been in Kabuki since the age of nine.

I went back after the performance and introduced myself. Miko didn't speak a word of English and I didn't speak a word of Japanese, but we had no trouble communicating. We saw each other every night for the next week. Before long, we'd decided that we wanted to be together and that she would come to America, but first we had to go to Miko's home in Osaka to get her parents' permission.

They were lovely people, but they didn't speak English either. Miko's brother did speak a few words and he interpreted for us. I told them that I wanted to bring Miko back to America with me. At first they wouldn't hear of it, but after a while they realized that she might have a career in American show business.

Miko loved Hollywood. She did a couple of movies and a bunch of television shows and played Yeoman Tamura in the original *Star Trek*. She learned to speak English by watching Bugs Bunny cartoons. The first thing she ever said to me in her adopted language was "What's up, doc?"

I knew my father had spent three years in Japan after the war, but I didn't dream that would cause a problem, so I brought Miko to Florida to meet him and my mom. The first thing he said was "What are you gonna do, open a restaurant?"

I let it go, even though I was furious. I grabbed Miko and left.

Miko and I lived together for four years, until I met the woman I thought I was going to spend the rest of my life with.

I KEPT HEARING that Dinah Shore wanted to have me on her daytime show, *Dinah's Place*. I didn't get it, but I thought, Well, okay, sure. I'd seen the show and thought it was terrific. The set was a replica of Dinah's house, so viewers felt like they were invited into her home. She'd often be cooking as she chatted with a guest. But it wasn't all fluff. Dinah always did her homework for interviews. After Walter Cronkite was a guest, he said he'd never been interviewed better by professional journalists. Like Johnny Carson, Dinah was always on the side of the guest, and whenever someone said anything embarrassing, she'd rush to their defense and try to help them cover.

There was a spot on the show where Dinah would open the closet door and be surprised by a guest. The staff didn't tell her who it would be. They arranged for me to be in the closet and somehow kept it a secret from Dinah. When she opened the door, I came out and grabbed her. I know it sounds crazy, but a shock went up my back. That had never happened before.

We sat down and just laughed and giggled. I forgot I was on a television show. It was just Dinah and me. We talked like two old friends, about the South and football and Bear Bryant, who had made a huge pass at her. He kept dropping by her house.

"He was so niiiice," she said.

"I'm sure he was," I said.

Finally I looked at her and blurted out, "Would you like to go to Palm Springs with me?"

She smiled and said yes without missing a beat.

"This weekend okay?"

"Perfect."

That's how it started, and it never stopped.

We did go to Palm Springs that weekend. Dinah was in a golf tournament and I was her caddie. We had a wonderful time, laughing and trading stories about our lives. We both knew we were already in love, but we didn't rush. We were savoring every moment. For the first time in my life I actually wanted a courtship to go slowly, respectfully. But in truth it wasn't my decision, because Dinah wasn't the kind of lady who jumped in the sack on the first date.

I followed her from city to city on a promotional tour for her show. At one point I had to leave her to do a play in Chicago. On opening night I looked out and she was in the audience. She invited me to her hotel after the show. We drank champagne and made love for the first time. It was a new experience for me. For the first time I was sharing intimacy with my heart full of genuine, unconditional love. I not only loved Dinah but admired her. I'd never felt that way about a woman before.

DINAH WAS ACCOMPLISHED in so many ways, yet she was humble and unaffected. The closest she ever got to boasting was when she said, "I know a lot of people because I have the best tennis court in Hollywood—and the best food!"

True on both counts. The court was always being resurfaced and repainted, and tennis pros used it free of charge to practice and for lessons. Whenever my jock friends would come over and we'd try to play tennis with her, she'd beat us all. She knew how to put the ball where you weren't. Getting beat by a woman wasn't thrilling for professional football players, but then she'd cook for everybody and all would be forgiven. She *loved* to cook, and no matter what time it was—three o'clock in the morning or whatever, she'd say, "Are you hungry?" and I'd say, "Well, um, I guess so," and she'd whip up a fabulous three-o'clock-in-the-morning dinner. She could cook anything and everything, including my favorite Southern dishes: hominy grits, black-eyed peas, turnip greens, hush puppies . . . and the desserts, of course: key lime pie, peach cobbler, pecan pie.

Her home in Beverly Hills was known as "Dinah's Bar and Grill." I can't count the number of times it wasn't meant to be a dinner or lunch but ended up that way. Whenever somebody came to the house, she'd find out where they were from and what their favorite dish was, and not only did she know how to make it, often as not they said she made it better than anybody else. Nobody who knew Dinah was surprised when she wrote a series of bestselling cookbooks.

Dinah's friends included some of the greats of show business: Mary and Jack Benny, George Burns and Gracie Allen, Mel Tormé, Ella Fitzgerald, and Groucho Marx. Groucho was hilarious, of course, and sarcastic as hell. I'd loved him since I was a boy. He was even funnier in person, when he was uncensored and uninhibited, than he was on his television show *You Bet Your Life*. His wife at the time—I'm not sure now which one—was studying with an acting teacher, and they put on a show of scenes. I went to see it with Groucho and his running commentary was hilarious, but so brutal it made me cringe.

I grew up listening to Jack Benny on the radio, so it was a thrill to not only meet him but get to know him. The first time I saw him in person, Dinah and I were at a screening. Jack came over, kissed me on the cheek, and said, "Forgive me, Dinah, but I have to go for the young ones." He was wonderful to me. Then again, he was such a mensch, he was nice to everybody. I could usually make him laugh, and I thought it was ironic that *he* thought *I* was funny.

Jack was in London when I was doing a TV show there and I asked him to come on and do a cameo. He looked right into the camera and said, "Burt Reynolds? Who *is* that?"

George Burns was terrific, too, but I don't think he liked me at first. Maybe he saw me as a young guy using Dinah to get ahead. He made a point of telling me that he'd never seen any of my movies. He eventually accepted me because of *The Tonight Show*. He mentioned one night that he'd seen me guest-host and thought I was funny, and from then on he was a lot friendlier.

Dinah and Ella Fitzgerald were good friends, and I knew Ella, too, because we were neighbors. She was a giant in the world of music, one of the great jazz singers of all time, yet she had no ego. I'd go to see her whenever she was playing at the Crescendo or other clubs around town. My sister, Nancy Ann, loved Ella, and once when she was in town visiting, we caught Ella's show and went backstage afterward. Ella couldn't have been nicer. She and Nancy Ann talked about all kinds of things. She was so warm, there was never a hint of "Well, time's up."

Ella and Dinah sang together often. Ella would come over and they'd have a piano player and sing all night. Most people don't know that Dinah could sing the blues. It goes back to her upbringing in Tennessee. But every so often I'd get her to sing a country song and we'd all be hysterical.

Mel Tormé was another "regular" at Dinah's. What a giant talent. He had that "Velvet Fog" voice and brilliant musicianship, but he was insecure. He'd sing and be phenomenal and then ask you fourteen times, "Was it all right?"

Mel and Ella were at Dinah's one night and he told me, "I'm not gonna sing tonight."

"Okay, Mel," I said.

"No, seriously, I'm not gonna sing."

A little later, as soon as Ella went to the piano and started singing, Mel came over and said, "Can I sing, too?"

"I thought you didn't want to!" I said.

"Where'd you get that idea?" he said.

DINAH WAS BORN Frances Rose Shore in Winchester, Tennessee. Her parents were Russian Jewish immigrants. Her father, Solomon, owned a small department store; her mother, Anna, was an aspiring opera singer. The Shores were the only Jewish family in town. One of Dinah's most vivid memories was of standing on their front porch watching a Ku Klux Klan parade. She was frightened by the sight of the figures in sheets and hoods, and as they marched by, her father named one man after another. Many of them were neighbors, and he recognized them by the shoes he'd sold them in the store.

I never played much tennis before I met Dinah, but I played a lot with her and it got old losing every time. She knew not to let me win, but she kept encouraging me: "You're getting better all the time," she'd say. I noticed that she'd start limping after a few games. I asked about it and she told me that she had polio as a child, but it was never "poor me." Self-pity wasn't Dinah's style.

She'd had a rough time of it when she was a girl. She was stricken at the age of eighteen months. Her right leg and foot were paralyzed. She was devastated by it, and her parents made her feel worse. They never mentioned polio out loud, but were always whispering about it, so Dinah was never allowed to forget that she was crippled. After a long course of painful treatments, she eventually recovered. But she was left with a limp that gave her an inferiority complex that I don't think she ever completely overcame.

Dinah was determined to get rid of the limp through exercise and physical therapy. She began swimming and playing tennis; she joined the fencing team, ran track, and took ballet lessons. By the time she was nine, her right leg was almost normal again and she could walk short distances without limping. The experience made her constantly strive to prove herself. She felt she had to compensate by running faster and jumping higher than everyone else.

Dinah began singing at an early age. She had an African-American nursemaid who was part of the family. Her name was Lillian Taylor, but everyone called her Paw-Paw. Dinah told me flat out that it was Paw-Paw who taught her to sing. She took Dinah to her church to hear the spirituals and sang Dinah the songs her mother sang to her when she was small. Paw-Paw called it "noodling."

Paw-Paw stayed with Dinah for the rest of Dinah's life. Nobody knew how old she was, but she was ageless. And fiercely protective of Dinah. She had an opinion about everyone in Dinah's life, and I was happy I came down on her good side.

By the time the Shores moved from Winchester to Nashville, Dinah had decided to become a professional singer. At first she had to study voice secretly, because her father disapproved. Later on, in addition to regular lessons, at the suggestion of her voice coach, Dinah sang in the choir at the First Presbyterian Church.

When Dinah was fourteen she talked the manager of a Nashville nightclub called the Pines into giving her a singing gig for ten dollars. She didn't dare tell her parents because she knew her father would forbid it. She borrowed her sister's prom dress and talked a boy into driving her to the club. She took a deep breath, walked up to the microphone, and launched into the one song she'd rehearsed, "Under a Blanket of Blue." Halfway through the number she looked out and saw her mother and father, who'd been tipped off. Her father told her she was too young to be a torch singer and that she'd have to finish high school and go to college.

While majoring in sociology at Vanderbilt University, she was a regular on a local radio show in Nashville. She sang the show's theme song, the old standard "Dinah," and people began calling her "the 'Dinah' girl." She'd always hated the name Frances, so when she landed an audition on WNEW Radio in New York, she renamed herself Dinah Shore. That's where she met a skinny young crooner from Hoboken named Frank Sinatra. They didn't get along at first—she thought he was arrogant, he didn't much care for her "magnolia accent"—but they eventually became friends.

In 1940 Dinah had her first hit records, "The Breeze and I" (with Xavier Cugat's orchestra) and "Yes, My Darling Daughter." Over the next fifteen years she had seventy more hits, including "Blues in the Night," "I'll Walk Alone," "The Anniversary Song," "Buttons and Bows," and "Dear Hearts and Gentle People."

During World War II she entertained the troops at USO shows and traveled to service hospitals to sing solo at the bedsides of wounded soldiers, and she was one of the first entertainers to visit GIs on the front lines.

When Dinah went to Hollywood in 1943 to make her first movie, the studio bobbed her nose, capped her teeth, and dyed her brown hair blond. She made seven pictures in all, including *Up in Arms* (1944) with Danny Kaye and *Till the Clouds Roll By* (1946), before she called it quits. She always said that she wasn't good on the big screen, that she'd failed as a movie star because she wasn't "photogenic," but I disagree. I thought she was a natural.

She went back to radio and signed a new record contract with Columbia, and by the end of the war she was an even bigger star. She was named Top Female Vocalist in all the polls and had a dozen more million-selling hits, including "Shoo Fly Pie and Apple Pan Dowdy," "Doin' What Comes Naturally," and "Baby, It's Cold Outside."

Dinah was always striving to improve as a singer. She rehearsed for hours, listening to playbacks, revising arrangements, analyzing and polishing her technique. Despite deadline pressure, she refused to release a record until it was perfect. She believed she had an obligation to give her best, and she studied fan mail and reviews to find out exactly what listeners wanted to hear.

Dinah was always open to fans, and it wasn't phony. She enjoyed meeting people. We'd miss planes because she'd be talking to strangers. Once we were going back to L.A. from New York and we both had to be on the set early the next morning. We were running late and missed our plane. Dinah worked the crowd while we waited for the next one. When it came time to board, she was having trouble breaking away. I said, "Dinah, we've already missed one flight, we can't miss the next one." I went to the man from the airline and said, "Please come over and tell her she has to get on the airplane!" The poor guy tried, but she wound him around her little finger. She asked him where he was from and told him about all the people she knew in his hometown . . . and we missed the second flight.

I couldn't be angry with Dinah, because I feel pretty much the same way. I think any actor who says, "My life is my life and I don't owe the public anything but a good performance," is an ingrate. I feel lucky to have people out there who've never deserted me, and they've given me more joy than any ten producers. I'm grateful to them and I'm thankful they still care.

Not long ago I dared to go to Costco. I was looking for a tiny paintbrush, and when I turned around, there were eight people staring at me. When I went to check out, people came up asking for autographs. If you sign one, you have to sign them all, and the people behind me were getting pissed off, so I got out of the line and kept signing.

The manager came over and said, "Can I help you get out of here?"

"Thanks, but I'll be fine," I said.

It took an hour to buy that brush, but I enjoyed every minute of it. When people come up to me in public, they want me to be a certain way, and I try not to disappoint. But I don't pretend to be something I'm not. They'll say nice things, and we might giggle about something in one of my movies. Some of them are surprised: "I always *said* you were a nice guy!"

"You mean there were people arguing?"

Sometimes they'll cross the line and get too personal . . . but I let them off the hook.

"Nah," I say, "we can't go there."

In the old days some people were disappointed if I didn't insult them or knock somebody down or burn rubber on the way out of the parking lot, but now everyone I meet is friendly and respectful, and I try to respond in kind. I don't do it for them, I do it for me. It makes me feel good. So if you see me in Costco, come over and say hello.

IN 1950, Dinah was up for the lead in the Hollywood version of *Showboat* but lost out to Ava Gardner (whose singing voice was dubbed in the movie). It was a big disappointment, but Dinah didn't mope. She launched a fifteen-minute television program that soon led to a Sunday-night variety show sponsored by Chevrolet that made Dinah the first woman with her own prime-time progam. At the close of each show she'd look into the camera and blow a kiss—"MMMMMM-WAH!"—and belt out her theme song, "See the USA, in your Chevrolet . . ."

The Dinah Shore Show ran for ten years and made her a household name. It was Dinah's personality as much as her singing that did it. She cared about people and it came through over the airwaves because she treated the camera—"old red-eye," she called it—like it was a single person.

Dinah never had a penny's worth of prejudice about anybody. In 1961, when she did a duet with Nat King Cole on her show, it was the first time a white woman had sung with a black man on American television, and it caused an uproar. Most of the affiliate stations in the South dropped the show. Dinah responded by having Sidney Poitier on the next week. That was her way of dealing with prejudice, and it worked. Eventually all the stations came back.

Dinah was amazing in terms of her friendships with blacks, on the one hand, and with people who couldn't put a governor on the way that they spoke, on the other. They'd make racist remarks, but she'd never tell them to shut up, which I know is what she wanted to say. She'd never confront people that way. Instead she'd quickly change the subject. Most of them got the message not to talk that way around her.

I had the same problem with people I knew, particularly some of the guys I played ball with. Like Dinah, I would try to change the subject, but if that didn't work I'd have to tell them: "I won't listen to that stuff. If you can't accept that, get the hell out."

IN 1973, I did a series of four television specials called *The Late Burt Reynolds Show*. For one show I took Merle Haggard, Jonathan Winters, and Dinah to Leavenworth Federal Penitentiary and we performed live for the prison population.

Merle had done time in San Quentin for robbery before he became a country music icon. I'd never met him and found him fascinating. I thought that if there ever was a born actor, it's this guy. He did play a couple of small film parts, but somebody should have given him a shot at something bigger, because he had something. He didn't try to act; he was just as real as he could be. He'd done hard time, but he wasn't bitter.

One day during rehearsals we were all standing around talking and I noticed that Dinah was gone, and nobody knew where she was.

"Goddamn it!" I said. "Wasn't anybody watching her?"

I was frantic. I started running all over the prison searching for her. I knew I'd find her in the worst place, with the baddest of the badasses, and I did. A group of inmates were having a cigarette break and Dinah was right in the middle of them, talking and laughing.

"Dinah," I said, "I think it's time for you to come sing your song."

"Really? Oh, okay."

She shook hands with every guy there, calling each one by name.

As we were walking away, one of them said, "You're a lucky son of a bitch."

Johnny Winters had spent time in a psychiatric hospital for bipolar disorder. He was frightened when we came to the front gate at Leavenworth, and when the big doors slammed shut behind us, he froze.

"Are you okay, Johnny?" I asked.

"I can't move," he said.

"It's that fuckin' sound, isn't it?"

"Yeah," he said. "I thought I'd never hear it again."

We talked for a few minutes until he said he was okay, and we walked in together.

Johnny was the funniest person I ever met. He lived to make people laugh and would perform for anyone on the street just because. When he lived in Manhattan, he couldn't get from his apartment to Rockefeller Center without stopping on every corner to do shtick for anyone who looked at him.

Johnny and I planned to do an improvisation in the Leavenworth show. I figured I'd just let him do his thing, with me as straight man. Before we went out, the warden told Johnny, "Look, I know the kind of stuff you do and it's fine, but I don't want you to mention the cook. You can talk about blacks, you can talk about gays, you can say anything you want, *but don't mention the cook.*"

Johnny and I came onstage and sat down on wooden stools.

I said to the audience, "Shout out anything and we'll do improv on it."

Three guys in different parts of the hall yelled, "THE COOK!"

"Anybody else, anybody . . ." I said.

"THE COOK!" they shouted.

Johnny whispered, "You be the cook."

And then he tore into me: "Same ol' shit! Same ol' shit ya gimme yesterday! It's shit!"

The inmates went wild, and Johnny went on to do the funniest twelve minutes I've ever seen.

But here's the kicker: A couple of days later they killed the cook. They knifed him and killed him dead. I called Johnny's manager and said, "I've got to talk to Johnny. I don't want to upset him, but they killed the cook at Leavenworth."

"We can't tell him that. He wouldn't handle it well," his manager said.

I didn't see Johnny again until a year later. I said to him, "It's been a long time, but I think you should know: they killed the cook at Leavenworth that night."

"Son of a bitch deserved it," he said.

MY DAD WAS over the moon about Dinah, and he didn't get over the moon too often. My mom thought she was wonderful, too. She just couldn't figure out what the hell Dinah saw in me.

Dinah and I attended the First Baptist Church in Palm Beach. It was just like Dinah, who'd been raised Jewish, to go with me to a Baptist church. *Southern* Baptist. Our pastor, the Reverend Dr. Jess Moody, came up with a clever way to get us in and out of the church without a fuss. It was like a military operation. We'd sneak in after the service started and stand in the back. Jess would have everyone bow their heads in prayer and we'd slip into our seats. When they raised their heads, there were two more people in the congregation.

Jess is retired now, but he was a great preacher. He brought humor to all of his sermons. It didn't matter which chapter in the Bible he was talking about, he'd find something funny in it. And he wasn't judgmental. I went to his church before I knew Dinah, for a while there with a different girl every Sunday. Jess would look out at me and smile.

Jess had a huge congregation, and the church was always packed on Sunday. It got so that he had speakers installed so the overflow crowd could sit outside by the lake and watch the boats go by while they listened to the service.

Jess recently lost his wife, Doris, after sixty-four years of marriage. Everyone who knew Doris will miss her. Jess's son Patrick is a lay preacher and an actor who has been in several of my films—not because he's Jess's son, but because he's a good actor and a delightful young man.

DINAH AND I were soul mates, but marriage wasn't in the cards. My career was on fire and my ego was out of control. I wanted to enjoy the fruits of my popularity and I didn't want to do it on the sly. And there was something else. I finally admitted to myself that the age difference did matter in one important respect: I wanted a child of my own. But I loved Dinah so much, I couldn't face life without her. I'd been at war with myself over it for a long time.

Dinah and I had the same doctor, a wonderful man. One day he told me, "You know, you can't go on like this. You'll end up breaking each other's heart, and I don't want that for either of you."

"That could never happen," I said.

"You're too smart to believe that," he said.

I hoped he said the same thing to her. I hoped it wasn't just me. But once he said it, I knew what I had to do.

Breaking up with Dinah was the hardest thing I'd ever done. She sat on the couch holding a hankie. She kept her composure, but I lost mine. I missed her the minute I walked out the door. I could barely function for weeks. I was in the kind of pain that she would have consoled me about.

In the spring of 1993, Dinah was diagnosed with ovarian cancer. I didn't know how sick she was until our doctor said, "You've got to expect the worst. If you want to spend more and more time with her, that's fine. I think that would be good. But at the same time, prepare yourself for the inevitable."

Dinah was not close with her children, and it was their fault. She wanted to have a good relationship, but for them it was all take and no give. And they weren't there for her at the end. They just didn't care, and I'll never forgive them for it.

When people wanted to know why I was with Dinah, I always said, "Why *not*? She's the most wonderful person I've ever known." We had so much in common. We were both from the South. We both loved sports, especially football, and she was knowledgeable about it. And in all the years I knew her, we never had a fight.

"But what about the age difference?" they'd say.

The answer is, Dinah was ageless. She had both wisdom and the eyes of a child. She was this extraordinary person whom I was lucky to be with. Despite all the negative publicity, I think our relationship appealed to women because it showed them that they could be interesting to a younger man. And men told me that it gave them the courage to be with an older woman.

Dinah was one of the rare people who are what they seem to be. I never met anybody who didn't like her. She hated gossip and never said a bad word about anyone. If you mentioned Hitler, she'd say, "Well, he was a good painter."

She kept everything negative to herself. She never wanted to burden others with her problems, and she never blew her stack. "I'm not a shouter, I'm a sulker," she always said.

It was against her nature to tell a lie.

She taught me about music, art, food, and wine; she taught me which fork to use; she taught me how to dress. And she was full of wisdom about show business. When I met Dinah I didn't have a clue about handling the press. They were horrible about our relationship, always questioning whether it was real, and I'd get angry.

But Dinah kept saying, "No, the worst thing you can do is get angry. Just smile and be happy."

Dinah always tried to encourage me: "You don't have to worry, honey," she said. "The camera is an X-ray machine. People look inside you and decide whether they like you. If they do, there's almost nothing you can do to change their minds."

OVER HER FIFTY YEARS in show business, Dinah was inducted into the Television Hall of Fame, had a dozen gold records, and won ten Emmys, a Golden Globe, and a Peabody (she was proudest of the Peabody). She was frequently among the Gallup Poll's Ten Most Admired Women in the World. But I think her greatest legacy is the love she gave so freely to everyone who crossed her path.

Frank Sinatra

I'd heard a lot of stories about Frank Sinatra, good and bad. I finally met him one night when I took Dinah to dinner at Nicky Blair's on Sunset Boulevard. When we walked in, he was seated at a corner table with the actor Harry Guardino, two bodyguards (Poochie East and Poochie West), and Jilly Rizzo, who owned Frank's favorite joint in New York.

Frank waved at us and we waved back. Then he motioned us over.

Dinah whispered, "I think he wants us to go join him."

I was feeling ornery and said, "Well, we're not going. I'm not a waiter here. We'll have dinner first and maybe go over later."

We sat down and ordered a drink.

Harry Guardino came over like a messenger. "Frank would like you to come say hello."

"Tell him we will when we finish eating," I said.

"Do you really want me to tell him that?"

"Yes, I do."

He went back to Frank's table and I could see him bend over and say something in Frank's ear.

And then I could read Frank's lips: *"What the fuck?"*

Dinah and I finished our meal and went over. "How do you do, Mr. Sinatra?" I said.

"Fine, pal. How'd you like to play a little poker?"

"Sure! When would that be?"

"Tonight. Right now, back in the kitchen."

I began to excuse myself because I had to take Dinah home, but she said, "Go ahead, I'll get a cab. It'll be an experience to play poker with Frank." So I put Dinah in a taxi, and when I came back, Frank, Jilly, Harry Guardino, Poochie East, and Poochie West were seated at a big round table in the middle of the kitchen, with all the waiters and busboys rushing back and forth.

I sat down and Frank called the game: five-card stud. But before he could deal the first card, there was a big crash. An unlucky bus-boy had dropped a tray of glassware.

Nicky Blair came running in, yelling at the poor busboy.

"Wait a minute, pal," Frank said. "How much do those glasses cost?"

"I don't know, Frank, a few bucks apiece," Nicky said.

Frank nodded to Poochie East, who hauled out a roll of hundreds the size of a calzone and counted out three thousand dollars. Frank took it and gave it to Nicky. Frank nodded again and Poochie East counted out another three thousand and Frank gave that to Nicky and said, "Now bring me three grand worth of glasses."

"I beg your pardon?" Nicky said.

"Bring me three grand worth of glasses," Frank repeated.

Nicky shrugged and went away.

A minute later, busboys were coming from all directions with glasses.

Frank said to the unlucky busboy, "What's your name, kid?"

"Hector."

"Hector . . . break 'em!" Frank said.

"*Qué?*"

"Break 'em!" Frank repeated.

Hector smashed them, one by one, until the floor was covered with broken glass.

I wondered what the customers thought was going on in the kitchen.

Frank told Nicky, "If I ever come in and don't see Hector, I'll never come back again. Understand?"

"I've always loved Hector," Nicky said.

Everybody turned back to the game.

As Poochie West shuffled the cards, I got up from the table and began crunching my way to the door.

"Where the hell are *you* going?" Frank said.

"Home," I said. "I got my Sinatra story."

AFTER THAT I saw Frank a lot, always with Dinah. They went way back, to the radio days in the early 1940s when they were both starting out. Frank had an amazing capacity for booze, but no matter how many bourbons he had, he never showed it. He was always a perfect gentleman around Dinah. He would tell me, in a kind of threatening tone, "I assume you know what a great woman you have there . . ."

I did a movie called *Shamus* (1973) that was produced by Bob Weitman, who had been the producer at the Paramount when Frank played there in 1942. Those were the "bobby-soxer" days: five thousand screaming girls, packed to the rafters for every show, and thousands more lined up in Times Square. The first time Frank walked onstage, the roar was so loud it stunned him, and he couldn't sing a note. All he could hear was the bandleader, Benny Goodman, saying, "What the fuck is *that*?"

Most of the kids would stay for all six shows. If they got up to go to the bathroom or buy popcorn they'd lose their seat, so they brought lunch and peed in their pants.

Weitman had a button he could push from way up in the booth to bring the curtain down. Frank would come onstage, wait for the pandemonium to die down a little, and then start to tell a joke. Weitman would push the button.

"I don't pay you to tell jokes, Frankie," he said. "Just shut up and sing."

That Paramount gig made Frank a superstar, and I'll bet that was the last time anybody spoke to him that way.

Frank was a caring and loyal friend—especially to those who'd stood by him when he was down—and he was a gracious host. He had so many houseguests people began calling him "the Innkeeper." When he gave a party, he was constantly refilling your drink or piling food on your plate. He gave expensive gifts for no reason and would ask friends, "What can I do for you?" And he meant it. He once told Shirley MacLaine, "I wish someone would hurt you, so I could kill them for you."

Frank could be so charming and thoughtful, it was scary. But he could also be unbelievably cruel. You never quite knew which way he would go. You could tell pretty quickly if it was a bad day, and you left him alone.

I think Frank could have been a terrific actor. He's wonderful as Maggio in *From Here to Eternity* (1953), the role that won him an Oscar and brought his career back from the dead. But after that, I think he got lazy. He didn't take acting seriously. He'd never want to do more than a couple of takes. Generally that was enough, and if you know what you're doing, it doesn't get better with more takes. But actors who worked with him said he was kind of slipshod. While they wanted to go deeper into a scene, he just wanted to get it over with.

But Frank was always serious about the music, and he was anything but slipshod when he made a record. I watched him cut "You'd Be So Nice to Come Home To." You needed a pass to get in, and there were a couple of his ape-shapes guarding the door.

In the studio there was a table, a glass of ice, a bottle of Jack Daniel's, a pack of Camels, and an ashtray. He came in, lit a cigarette, poured himself a drink, and nodded to the orchestra. They did a run-through and Frank said, "The oboe's off." He caught it. The oboe player made an adjustment and they did the song again. Frank would give the musicians notes between takes. They must have done the song a dozen times before he was satisfied. He was in total control and knew exactly what he wanted.

I KNEW THE GUYS who kidnapped Frank Sinatra Jr. I met them through Ryan O'Neal. We played softball together and they were also on the team. They were pretty good athletes and seemed like nice guys, but they were not the brightest bulbs in the building. Always looking for a scam. When I heard they'd kidnapped Frank Jr. I thought, Of all the people in the world, why would you take Frank Sinatra's kid? You'll have the police, the FBI, and the Mafia after you.

They grabbed Frank Jr. from his room at Harrah's Lake Tahoe, where he was appearing with the Tommy Dorsey band. They had a hideout ready in L.A., but they were so broke they had to get gas money from Frank Jr., who had just enough cash to get them there. When they asked him for his father's phone number, he said, "No way. Do whatever you want to me, but I'm not giving you his number."

One of the kidnappers heard that Frank was using a hotel in Reno as his headquarters, and they were able to get a call through to him. They'd planned to ask for exactly $240,000, but as soon as

Frank was convinced that they had his son, he offered them a million dollars.

"No!" these geniuses said. "We want $240,000 and not a penny more!"

They collected the ransom and actually got away, but they couldn't help bragging about it. They were caught a few days later after spending only a few thousand dollars on a living room set for the ex-wife of one of the kidnappers.

The FBI was ready to confiscate the furniture, but Frank said, "Nah, let the poor broad keep her couch."

Needless to say, Frank was pissed off.

I thought, Whatever the government does to these guys, it won't be half as bad as what will happen to them when they get *out* of prison. They were convicted and got long sentences, but they got out in a few years on a legal technicality. Frank never took revenge . . . as far as I know.

I didn't know Frank Jr. well. I was with him only a couple of times and thought he was the dullest man I'd ever met. The poor guy had no personality whatsoever. In all fairness, Frank Sr. was intimidating, to say the least, and having him for a father must have been impossible.

The daughters, Nancy and Tina, were not my favorites either. They were attractive enough, and Nancy was a good singer, but they weren't my kind of gals. Talk about a sense of entitlement. As Frank Sinatra's daughters, they considered it their birthright to be difficult.

For a while Tina was dating Doug McClure. Doug and I were both under contract at Universal and we became friends. Doug was scared to death of Frank, and I'd do silly things with him. One day I told him, "Frank called and said, 'What time did Doug bring Tina home last night?'"

Doug turned white and said, "What? What time did I bring her in? It wasn't late, it wasn't late." He called to apologize and Frank must have thought he was crazy.

Doug was always being ordered to do this or do that, go here or go there, and I said, "Doug, tell 'im to go to hell! Live your own life and he'll respect you more."

But Doug didn't think that was a good idea. He was a sweet-natured guy without an ounce of mean in him. People remember him best for his long run on *The Virginian* in the 1960s and '70s. He was also good at comedy, but he couldn't find the right projects. And he wasn't aggressive in the pursuit of any kind of success. He had no idea how to elbow his way into anything. Otherwise I think he could have had a big career.

The last time I saw Frank was on the set of *Cannonball Run II* (1984). It turned out to be the last movie he did. We were shooting in the desert near Las Vegas, and Frank flew in on his own jet, at his own expense. He was the first one on the set. Frank was in a good mood, joking with everybody. Sammy Davis Jr. and Dean Martin were there, making him laugh. Sammy was one of the most versatile and talented entertainers of the twentieth century. I first met him in New York, when he was playing clubs. We crossed paths many times after that and became friends. He'd come to my parties and always sing a song or two, but we never got to work together. Finally, when we were casting *Cannonball Run*, Sammy was the first one I wanted. I thought of him as the "anti-Dom"— skinny and black instead of portly and Italian, but just as gifted. During the shoot, Sammy did to Frank and Dean what I did to Dom: Push them over that edge and crack them up during a take. Like Dom, Sammy always cooked on the set. He took his pots and pans everywhere.

I loved Dean. He was so damn funny and likable, it was a party whenever he was around. I was once in Vegas standing with him backstage at one of his shows. He had a glass of bourbon in his hand when the stage manager came over, reached for the glass, and said, "You're on, Mr. Martin. I'll take your drink."

"Whoa, pally," Dean said, pulling the glass toward his chest. "I ain't goin' out there alone."

Our producer Al Ruddy told Frank he didn't know what to pay him and Frank said, "How about you donate a hundred thousand to my favorite charity?"

Done!

Al also gave Frank a model train set. If you'd told me a famous singer was a model train nut, Frank Sinatra is the last one I would have guessed.

Johnny Carson

Almost everything good that happened in my career started with Johnny Carson. More than anyone, he was the reason I got to do comedy in films. Before I met Johnny, I'd played a bunch of angry guys in a series of forgettable action movies, and people didn't know I had a sense of humor. My appearances on *The Tonight Show* changed that. My public image went from a constipated actor who never took a chance to a cocky, wisecracking character. And that's exactly what *The Tonight Show* Burt Reynolds was, a character . . . a swinging bachelor having a ball being rich and famous. The women, the booze, the limos, the private jets . . . this guy did everything but wink at the camera.

Actors plugging a movie on a talk show all say pretty much the same thing: "It was a privilege working with the director, and the leading lady was a joy—so lovely, so unselfish—and always *prepared*." Then the voice gets a little deeper: "And I *loved* everything about shooting in the Philippines, including dysentery and malaria. Everyone should go there."

But after a few vodka tonics in the greenroom, I'd come out and say, "It's a turkey. Don't waste your money."

If you were quoted in print saying that kind of thing, people thought you an ungrateful shit. But when you said it with a big grin on *The Tonight Show*, they loved it.

I didn't spare myself. If Johnny asked, "What are you doing after the show?" I'd say, "I'm gonna walk up and down Broadway trying to get recognized." If he brought up my string of flops, I'd say, "My movies are the kind they show in prisons and airplanes, because nobody can leave." It all showed that I didn't take myself too seriously, that off-camera I didn't just stand around wearing my Number 3 Virile Look.

I was a guest on *The Tonight Show* probably a hundred times, but one appearance stands out in my memory. It was in September 1974. There must have been a full moon that night, because before my spot there was a food fight with Dom DeLuise that ended with Johnny dropping an egg down Dom's pants and breaking it.

Just before I came out, I grabbed an egg and a can of whipped cream. As I walked on the set I sprayed whipped cream all over the front of Johnny's sports jacket and tossed the egg to Dom. I put the can down and Johnny grabbed it. He came out from behind the desk and we stood face-to-face. Without saying a word, he piped a bead of whipped cream up and down one of my legs and then put a gob of it on my crotch area. He gave me a "So there!" look and handed me the can. But before I could do anything, he rubbed the whipped cream in. With a circular motion.

I glanced over and Dom was on the floor. I scooped a dollop of cream from Johnny's tie and flicked it in his face.

He took the can and sprayed it down my shirtfront.

I grabbed the can, pulled out his waistband, aimed the nozzle down the front of his pants, and sprayed for about three seconds—Reddi-wip makes such a delicious sound—and calmly gave the can back to Johnny.

He took it, but this time, instead of retaliating, he sprayed it down the front of his own pants with a blissful smile on his face, ending the bit on a roaring laugh.

Everybody thought it was planned, but we hadn't even talked about it, let alone rehearsed it. Johnny had no idea what I would do. *I* had no idea what I would do. I just knew that he'd follow my lead, and that whatever he did would be funny.

We had that kind of rapport. We both loved Laurel and Hardy, especially their clockwork timing in the tit-for-tat routines where they traded blows or pies or attacks on each other's possessions in turn, each waiting calmly for the other to retaliate according to the unwritten laws of slapstick combat. Doing Laurel and Hardy with Johnny was the most fun I've ever had in front of a camera.

I MADE MY FIRST *Tonight Show* appearance in the mid-sixties, when it was still in New York. I'd been briefed not to touch Johnny or anything on his desk and not to speak to him during commercials, so at the first break I turned to Ed.

But Johnny leaned over and said, "Hey, want a drink?"

"Don't talk to me!" I said. "I'm sorry, but I don't talk to anyone during commercials."

Johnny got a kick out of that, and said, "How would you like to guest-host the show?"

I was stunned, but I was also too dumb to be scared, and without thinking I said, "Yeah!"

And that's how I became the first actor to guest-host *The Tonight Show*. Before that, only comedians had sat in for Johnny. For some reason I was cool about it. I shouldn't have been, but I was fearless in those days. I asked for Judy Carne as my first guest. It was a risky thing to do, but I thought it could be funny if it worked.

Judy and I were married in 1963 after dating for six months. We were divorced after three years, but the marriage was over long before that. It soon became obvious that we had very little in common. I couldn't get into her lifestyle—the nonstop partying, the hard drugs, the kinky sex—and she wasn't thrilled with my tendency toward fisticuffs. After one of my many brawls, she said, "God, you're boring." To this day I credit Judy, and to an even greater extent Dinah, with helping me discover that a guy doesn't need his fists to make a point.

In 1968, she was a sensation on *Rowan & Martin's Laugh-In.* She'd be dancing in a bikini and she'd say, "Sock it to me!" and be doused with water or hit with a pie. "Sock it to me!" became a national catchphrase, with everyone from Ringo Starr to Richard Nixon coming on the show to coin it.

When her career began to wane, Judy's substance abuse got worse, and she made a lot of money talking about me to the tabloids. She claimed I hit her, which was not true. It broke my heart.

When Judy came on *The Tonight Show,* we hadn't spoken in the six years since our divorce, and following Johnny's practice, I made sure not to see her before the show. I introduced her, and when she sat down, the first thing she said got the audience involved right away: "God, you look good."

"So do you, I'm sorry to say."

"Why did we ever get a divorce?" she said.

"I don't know," I said, "but whatever the problem was, it was my fault."

"No, Burt, it was my fault . . ."

We went back and forth like that, and the sparks kept flying until Judy made a crack about Dinah. "I hear you like older women," she said.

Well, you don't step on the flag. The crowd turned on her, and I had to slap her wrist.

"Not older, Judy, just classier."

They cheered.

Judy realized she'd made a terrible mistake, and I had to throw her a lifeline. "People don't know this, but you're a big fan of Dinah's, aren't you, Judy?"

"Yes, Burt, I love her."

"You have all her records, don't you?"

"Yes. Yes, I do."

"You're lying, but that's okay. The crowd still loves you too, don't you, folks?"

They applauded, and we went to a commercial.

I HAD NO IDEA how hard it is to host a talk show. Johnny made it look easy, but it's an unnatural act. The pressure is overwhelming. And exhausting. Dick Cavett likened it to going to two hundred cocktail parties in a row and being the life of them all. After the show you just want to go home and collapse. But not Johnny. He told me that the hour taping the show was the most alive he felt all day.

Johnny found his vocation at the age of twelve, while lying on the living room rug propped on his elbows, his face in his hands, listening to Jack Benny on the radio. He'd memorize the jokes and deliver them in the schoolyard the next day. But not just the jokes. He watched Benny's movies and absorbed his body language, his facial expressions, and above all, his pauses.

Benny was a master at milking the space between jokes, and he could wring more out of silence than most comedians could get from a punch line. Like Benny, Carson wasn't afraid of silence . . . as long as he'd created it. He could stretch a laugh forever without saying a word, then deliver the perfect capper. He was always cool on-camera. He could ad-lib a quip in any situation, and he could play off the unexpected and make a triumph out of a disaster, like the way he handled the Ed Ames incident.

The actor-singer who played a Native American on the NBC series *Daniel Boone* comes on the show to do a tomahawk-throwing demonstration. The target is a Western sheriff made of plywood. Ames throws the tomahawk, making a direct hit on the wooden sheriff's crotch, to the delight of the studio audience. When Ames moves to retrieve the weapon, Johnny stops him. Holding two tomahawks, Johnny pretends to sharpen them while he milks the moment, and when the laughter finally subsides, he says to Ames, "I didn't even know you were Jewish!"

Pandemonium.

When that dies down, Johnny says, "Welcome to frontier bris!"

More pandemonium.

Finally Ames asks Johnny, "Do you want to try it?"

"No," Johnny says, shaking his head. "I couldn't hurt him any more than you did."

FOR AS LONG AS we were friends, Johnny complained about his mother. He grew up in Norfolk, Nebraska. His father, Homer, was an executive at the local power company, his mother, Ruth, a homemaker who said she didn't like boys because they were "dirty." Throughout her life she never expressed pride in his accomplishments: A reporter once got the idea to watch *The Tonight Show* with Ruth to get the proud mother's reaction. After silently frowning all through the monologue she said, "That wasn't funny," and left the room.

When Johnny got an award from the Television Academy, he called Ruth.

"Mom, they're giving me the Governor's Award. It's for lifetime achievement in the television industry," he said.

"Well," she said, "I suppose they know what they're doing."

No wonder Johnny called her Lady Macbeth and "the toughest son of a bitch of them all." He even blamed her for his failed marriages: "There is no goddamn way to please that woman," he told me.

And when she died, he refused to go to the funeral. "The wicked witch is dead!" he told everyone.

Yet they found a big box in her house full of clippings from her son's career. Johnny took that box and kept it in his bedroom closet for the rest of his life.

This was something Johnny and I had in common. I had the same thing with my father. I tried everything I could think of to earn his approval but got nothing. Not a single "attaboy" or pat on the head.

As a young boy on construction jobs with him, I'd work extra hard. I'd load the wheelbarrow with dirt, push it as fast and as far as I could, unload it, and rush back.

One time he said, "You keep that up and you'll be built like Joe Louis."

That was the closest my dad ever came to giving me a compliment.

When I shined on the football field—he did come to all the games with my mom—I thought, Well, when I get home tonight he'll say, "You played a good game, son." But . . . nothing. When the papers the next day would have glowing write-ups . . . still nothing. And when I made First Team All State, he didn't say a word. I kept hoping that someday he'd tell me what a good football player I was, but he never did. He just didn't know how to say it.

Men of his generation did not show affection easily. They didn't hug or say, "I love you." I would have settled for a hug. I would have *killed* for a hug. My dad lived to be ninety-five, and in the last few years of his life we talked a lot. When he finally said he was proud of me, it made me cry. It still does. I'm grateful that he lived long enough to say it.

JOHNNY'S RUN as host of *The Tonight Show* began on October 1, 1962, with Groucho Marx introducing him. The other guests that night were Tony Bennett, Mel Brooks, Joan Crawford, and Rudy Vallee. Skitch Henderson was the bandleader (later replaced by Doc Severinsen), and Ed McMahon was the announcer delivering his first "Heeeere's Johnny!"

Johnny was an instant hit. Though he'd inherited the show from Jack Paar, he quickly made it his own. It was live on tape so they almost never stopped rolling or edited. In fact *The Tonight Show* was the closest you could get to live television. "I never want the show to feel too planned," Johnny told me. "We create it while it's on the air."

The nightly monologue was written by a staff of four or five writers and blue-penciled by Johnny. But he wasn't just an editor of other people's material. He knew when a joke worked and when it didn't and usually added some of his own. People stayed up to watch the monologue because they knew that everybody would be talking about it at the water cooler the next day. That's why I insisted on doing a monologue when I guest-hosted. They looked at me like I was crazy, but I did it, including some of Johnny's shtick, like doing a slow burn or tapping the mic when a joke bombed.

Johnny was at his best when the monologue wasn't going well. The rule among comedians is, never acknowledge a bad joke. Just keep talking like nothing is wrong. But Johnny got laughs based on the fact that he wasn't getting laughs. As Ed McMahon put it, "Nobody died better than Johnny."

Once, when the audience actually booed, Johnny raised an eyebrow and said, "You didn't boo me when I smothered a grenade at Guadalcanal." It got so you *wanted* a joke to bomb so you could hear the saver, and some people said that he purposely put bad jokes in the monologue. But Johnny was too much of a pro for that. Once in a great while when even the saver failed, there was never a hint of flop sweat. Doc and the band would strike up "Tea for Two" and Johnny would break into a soft-shoe.

A lot of comedians don't laugh. Johnny laughed. Fully, with genuine appreciation. I was always thrilled when I could make him laugh. If you were a comic and you did your routine and Johnny said, "Funny stuff!" or gave you the okay sign, you'd be flooded with bookings the next morning. If you looked over and he was wiping his eyes, your price doubled. If he was on the floor, it tripled. And if Johnny called you over to the couch, you were a certified professional comedian with a big career ahead of you.

Johnny understood that television is an intimate medium and made sure there was a slave camera aimed at him at all times. The director could go to it for close-up reaction shots—"looks," Johnny called them. He drew you in by playing to that camera as if it were another person in the room. Like millions of other Americans, you'd lie in bed watching Johnny through your toes. He'd do a look right into the lens and suddenly you were accomplices.

I asked him about it once and he told me that he'd never forgotten seeing Oliver Hardy sigh directly into the camera in a silent film. Johnny decided to use the camera the same way. If a guest was boring or said something stupid, Johnny would stare into the lens with an expression that said, *Do you believe this?*

Well, just as Johnny had learned from Oliver Hardy, I used Johnny's looks in my films, and he would always call me on it.

"You did my look!" he'd say, pretending to be annoyed.

"Yeah, I did. And I'm glad."

JOHNNY DOMINATED his late-night time slot, beating all the talk-show hosts who challenged him, including Joey Bishop, Merv Griffin, Jerry Lewis, David Brenner, Arsenio Hall, Alan Thicke, and Joan Rivers. Joan had been a frequent guest on the show and was both the first woman to guest-host and the only permanent guest host. Having boosted her career, Johnny considered her a friend. He never forgave her after she jumped to Fox to host a competing show without telling him first. He felt betrayed and never spoke to her again. Joan's show lasted a year.

My experience with Joan wasn't fun, either. She had a vendetta against me because I'd said something critical about her. I privately told someone close to Joan that I didn't think she was a nice person and that it isn't funny to say nasty things about people who can't respond. Of course it got back to Joan and she said vile things about me in a magazine interview, then hired a guy who looked like me to sit in the audience at her Vegas act. She'd introduce him as Burt Reynolds, berate him, and then kick him out. People kept asking me to respond, but I tried to take the high road. I managed to keep my mouth shut until one reporter too many asked for a comment and I blurted out: "I never answer female impersonators."

JOHNNY WASN'T PERFECT. He had a temper, but thank God he never unleashed it on me. And he could really hold a grudge. There was a board in the office with names written in Magic Marker. One day I'm with Freddie De Cordova and I look up and see the list and I say, "Oh, a wall of fame," and Freddie says, "No, these are people who will never be on the show again because they came on drunk or coked up or they went over the line with Johnny."

There were some big names on that wall who were banished for-ever on Johnny's orders.

Johnny's timing was perfect. In fact, there was a pillow in his office embroidered with the motto *It's All in the Timing*. He was also a master straight man. He'd let you talk when you were on a roll or jump in when you needed help. He wanted you to succeed because he understood that if the guest scores, the show wins. It doesn't matter who gets the laughs. He'd learned that from Jack Benny, one of the few radio comedians who allowed others to de-liver punch lines. But it was still Johnny's show and he never lost control. The official title was *The Tonight Show Starring Johnny Carson*, just so nobody forgot.

At the same time, I loved to watch how he handled a difficult guest. If someone was drunk or over-the-top, he ended it with a well-aimed zinger. He once stopped Zsa Zsa Gabor's rambling with "The Stage Deli just called. They want to nail up your tongue in the window."

But he was gentle with ordinary folks, like the hundred-year-old woman with a black belt in karate or the birdcall guy or the man who made jewelry out of bird droppings. As far as I know, the clos-est Johnny ever came to being mean to a civilian was with the lady who brought out her precious collection of potato chips that re-sembled animals. While Ed distracted her, Johnny crunched loudly into a chip. The poor woman whirled around with a look of horror on her face, until Johnny revealed that he had his own bowl of chips hidden behind the desk.

Though Johnny didn't invent the late-night TV talk show, he per-fected it. His monologue/guests/musical act structure set the pat-tern for every talk show that followed, just as Johnny set the mark for all other talk-show hosts.

For a long time he was the most familiar face on American television, but he never got overexposed. In fact he was an enigma. People were curious about him because they sensed there was more there than met the fisheye. The joke around town was that Johnny existed only on television, and at least once a week someone would ask me, "What's Johnny Carson really like?" It became a national catchphrase.

What was Johnny really like?

He was a good man. Yes, he could be cold. But if he was your friend, he would lie down in front of something for you and he'd show you that he cared through countless acts of kindness. But wordlessly, and from a distance.

And he was loyal. Not long after we first met, Johnny invited me to his apartment for a drink. Ed McMahon was there and we all had a few too many. For no reason Ed started busting my chops. I don't know where it came from—whether it was some kind of jealousy about my friendship with Johnny or what—but Ed was really on my case. Sober, he was Mister Congeniality, but he was also an ex-Marine and he was drunk. The insults kept coming, and they were hurting my feelings.

Just as I was about to take a poke at him, Johnny stepped in.

"That's enough, Ed," Johnny said.

Ed ignored him and kept on me.

"Ed, I want you to leave."

"What?"

"You heard me. I want you to leave."

Ed looked at Johnny like, "You're taking his side over mine?"

Johnny looked back as if to say, "Yes, I am."

Ed left.

I'll never forget that Johnny did that for me.

Johnny didn't handle alcohol well either. I won't say he was a nasty drunk . . . more like dangerous. He was also a cheap drunk. Two whiskey sours and he'd be ready to take on the world, and he often tried. He'd pick fights with total strangers, and I heard that a contract was put out on him after he made a drunken pass at a mobster's girlfriend.

In the New York days, he and Ed would do the rounds at P. J. Clarke's, Sardi's, Danny's Hideaway, and Jilly's, where one night at about two a.m. Johnny was sitting at the bar when Sinatra walked in.

Without looking up, Johnny said, "I told you twelve-thirty, Frank!"

When it finally dawned on Johnny that he had a problem, he cut way back and pretty much quit the hard stuff. After that, I never saw him drink more than a glass or two of wine.

JOHNNY WAS AT HOME in front of an audience but uncomfortable in a small group. "I'm good with ten million people, lousy with ten," he often said. At parties you'd find him in a corner doing magic tricks for a few people. He explained it simply: "On the show I'm in control. Socially I'm not."

He wasn't on all the time like a lot of performers. Compliments embarrassed him. He knew who he was and didn't need his ego stroked. People thought he was cold and aloof. But he wasn't cold and he wasn't aloof. He was shy, yet I think he was very secure. I don't believe he envied or felt inferior to anyone. He hated publicity and seldom granted interviews. On the few occasions when he did one, it was an ordeal for both journalist and subject.

Johnny was a loner, but I don't think he was lonely. He enjoyed his own company, spending his free time at solitary pursuits like astronomy. He had telescopes all over the house. He'd call you over and say, "Look at this!" Whenever someone asked him how he became a star, he'd say, "I started in a gaseous state and then I cooled." He was also into photography, flying, scuba diving, playing the drums—he was a damn good amateur—and above all, reading. Johnny was curious about everything. He was one of the best-read people I've ever known, and there was hardly a subject he couldn't discuss knowledgeably.

SOMEBODY ONCE SAID that Johnny did for divorce what Lucille Ball had done for pregnancy on *I Love Lucy*. First there was Jody Wolcott, his college sweetheart and the mother of his three sons. Then there was Joanne Copeland and then Joanna Holland. Johnny met Alexis Maas when she strolled by his Malibu beach house in a bikini. He was in his sixties, she in her thirties, but they were happy together because she thought he was funny. It helps a lot when your wife thinks you're funny.

Though Johnny played the divorces for laughs on the show ("I heard from my cat's lawyer. My cat wants twelve thousand a week for Tender Vittles"), he once admitted to me that his failed marriages were among his deepest regrets.

The first marriage produced Johnny's only children, his sons Chris, Ricky, and Cory. He was a distant father to say the least, as aloof and uncommunicative as his own parents. Johnny's brother Dick once tried to describe the Carson reserve. "Put it this way— we're not Italian. Nobody in our family ever says what they really think or feel to anyone else."

I think Johnny loved his sons, but like his mother—and my dad—he couldn't express it. He knew that show business wouldn't let him down, but he was never sure about people, even his own children, so he focused on his career at the expense of his family.

It took thirty-nine-year-old Ricky's death in a freak accident to bring it out. Ricky was a professional photographer on assignment when his SUV rolled down an embankment. Johnny had never talked about his sons in public before, but on his return to the show after a period of mourning, he eulogized Rick and displayed his photographs. At one point he welled up and said, "He tried so darn hard to please." He closed the show with Rick's photo of a sunset. Johnny never talked about it with me, but there was obviously a lot of pain and regret there, and I don't think he ever got over it.

FOR AS LONG AS I knew him, Johnny carried a gun. I assumed he had a permit, but we never talked about it. It was a snub-nose .38 that he packed in a holster or in his man-purse. He refused to have bodyguards despite a climate of danger for celebrities and constant death threats against him personally: Before killing John Lennon, Mark David Chapman had targeted Johnny.

Over the years, I've had death threats, too. I never went to the police about them. I just recognized that there were lots of crazies out there and kept a pistol in my car. My dad was a police chief and he put me on the range when I was fifteen, so I knew how to handle a gun. I figured it wouldn't hurt to talk about that on *The Tonight Show*, so one night I said, "I have a gun!" and the audience laughed, but I'll bet there was at least one wacko out there in TV-land who thought, Not screwin' with *him*!

There was an incident when Johnny found a hand grenade in his driveway along with a note threatening his family and demanding a $250,000 ransom. Despite strong discouragement from the FBI, Johnny insisted on making the drop himself. It was a point of honor with him. The G-men followed from a distance as he dropped the "cash"—actually cut-up newspapers—in a Burbank Laundromat. When the blackmailer picked it up, they arrested him. The grenade turned out to be a dummy, just like the guy who put it there, who went to prison for five years.

Johnny didn't kowtow to corporate brass or suck up to sponsors.

Once, after a McDonald's commercial claiming "over twenty million burgers sold," Johnny said, "Gee, that's what, fifty pounds of meat?" One Christmas he announced that General Electric, then the parent company of NBC, had sent him a card announcing that "in lieu of a gift, a GE employee has been laid off in your name."

The Tonight Show was a money machine, one of the most profitable shows ever, and it produced a big chunk of NBC's profits every year. When Fred Silverman became president of the network in 1979, he publicly scolded Johnny for taking too much time off. Johnny's response was to announce his retirement, causing the price of NBC's stock to drop like a stone. The network did a quick one-eighty and gave Johnny more than he'd ever dreamed of: a three-year contract at $5 million a year—then the biggest salary in television and double his previous pay—plus sole ownership of *The Tonight Show.*

When Johnny began hosting *The Tonight Show* in 1962, it ran an hour and forty-five minutes and he worked forty-seven weeks a year. The show was reduced to ninety minutes in 1967 and to sixty minutes in 1980, with Johnny working four nights a week. Eventually he worked only three nights a week for twenty-five weeks a year. When he started, his salary was $100,000 a year. When he retired in 1992, it was $1 million a week.

Anyone who was alive and conscious at the time remembers his last two shows, though people are confused about which was which. It was on the next-to-last show—not the finale—that Bette Midler serenaded Johnny with "You Made Me Love You" and "One for My Baby." Then Bette and Johnny fell into a duet of his favorite song, "Here's That Rainy Day." Robin Williams, the only other guest that night, later said that it gave him goose bumps. It was certainly one of the tenderest moments I've ever seen on television.

The final show, on the following night, May 22, 1992, drew fifty million viewers. Johnny showed highlights from past shows. His sons were in the audience and he addressed them before signing off: "I realize that being an offspring of someone who is constantly in the public eye is not easy, so, guys, I want you to know that I love you. I hope that your old man has not caused you too much discomfort."

Johnny quit at the top of his game and left 'em wanting more. He told me that he preferred people asking him "Why did you quit?" over "Why didn't you quit?" When he walked away, he walked away for good and stuck to his decision despite countless offers to appear on talk shows and sitcoms and awards shows, saying that he'd "rather sit in Malibu and watch the hummingbirds mate."

Johnny was an entrepreneur and an investor who amassed a huge estate. He had his own apparel company and a large real estate portfolio, and at one time owned several TV stations. His company, Carson Productions, owned not only *The Tonight Show* but also *The Late Show with David Letterman*.

He left most of his money to charity. A lot of people were surprised by that, but I wasn't. All his adult life he had committed quiet acts of philanthropy. He'd see an item in the newspaper about someone in need and would anonymously send a check. And he never forgot where he came from: He made a series of gifts to his hometown of Norfolk, including a library, a museum, a football field, a gymnasium, a theater, a senior center, and a zoo. And he gave millions to the University of Nebraska.

Before Johnny died, he created a $200 million charitable foundation that makes large contributions to a variety of causes. And, in case you're wondering, he left multimillion-dollar trusts to his widow and two surviving sons.

JOHNNY ALWAYS HAD a lit cigarette within reach, even during the show. He puffed openly until the 1964 surgeon general's report on the harmful effects of smoking; then he started hiding it. He had the habit of nervously drumming his cigarette, but replaced it with a pencil with erasers on both ends. He moved the ashtray to a shelf under the desk and had an exhaust fan installed. He'd wait to inhale until the camera was on the guest, but sometimes, coming back from a commercial, he'd get caught sneaking one last drag. He didn't seem to worry about the hazards of smoking. Whenever the subject came up, he'd say, "Maybe I should check in to one of those places where they shock you or show you reruns of *Gilligan's Island* to make you quit smoking." I guess he was in denial. Maybe he thought that his genes would protect him—both his parents had lived well into their nineties. And he rationalized: "I know a man who gave up smoking, drinking, sex, and rich food," Johnny said. "He was healthy right up to the day he killed himself."

Johnny died from emphysema at seventy-nine. According to his wishes, there was no memorial service. Years before, when someone asked what he wanted for his epitaph, he said, "I'd prefer not to have one at all, but okay, something like, 'I'll be right back.'"

Since his death, things have been written portraying Johnny as a monster. That's not the man I knew. I think he was a national treasure, and his contribution wasn't fully appreciated until after he was gone. Only then did we begin to realize that he was a bigger part of our lives than we'd thought. Off-camera he may have been difficult at times, but I didn't see that side of him. I saw only a generous, loyal friend.

Destaphanado

Clint Eastwood and I both went to Italy to make spaghetti Westerns during the 1960s. He got Sergio Leone and a trilogy of pictures that made him an international star. I got Sergio Corbucci and *Navajo Joe* (1966).

Dino De Laurentiis was the producer. He was an old-school movie mogul with eyes like a cobra. Crystal green. The most dangerous eyes I ever saw. He was very smart and very persuasive. He could charm you into doing anything, and if that didn't work he'd break your legs. But we got along fine. I think he liked me because I didn't act like I was afraid of him.

I'd never heard of the director, Sergio Corbucci. He gave a cocktail party at his house the night before we started shooting and all the top actors in Italy were there. He held court and was very funny. I decided I liked him.

I spent years playing the third Indian from the left. I never got a funny line. I just took my shirt off as I got shot. I've played every Native American but Pocahontas, and I hated Navajo Joe because he was such a stereotype. Corbucci's idea of the way he would talk was, "You come. Follow."

My dad had Native American blood. By the time it got down

to me there wasn't much left, but I was proud of what there was. I had the writers change the dialogue in *Sam Whiskey* because I found it insulting. I've had to do that in several Westerns over the years, and Native Americans have thanked me for playing them with dignity.

The first day on the set the costume guy chopped up a ratty old wig and glued it on my head. It was the worst wig I've ever had, and that's saying something. It made me look like Natalie Wood. My grandmother was Cherokee and my mother was Italian, which is probably why half of me wants to grow hair and the other half doesn't.

When I was working at Universal, I went into makeup one day and there was Ray Milland having a hairpiece fitted. He was walking around in the hallway being funny and charming . . . with no hair. I thought, My God, that's brave. I'd been a big fan ever since *The Lost Weekend* (1945), and watching him joke about his baldness gave me a whole new respect for him and a sense of how to handle myself in a similar situation.

I started wearing a hairpiece in the middle of *Hawk*, and it was just awful. I was asked to do a test for a movie and the assistant director who was interviewing me said, "Why do you wear that awful rug?"

"Because I had a good one and nobody asked me any stupid questions," I said.

One night I went on the Carson show and Johnny said, "Oh, you're going gray," and I grabbed it and said, "You want it?"

I've always been frank about my hair because if you deny it, you're fooling yourself. Everybody else will do jokes about it. It's better if *you* do the jokes first. When somebody asks me if I wear a hairpiece I say, "Of course! Do you think I'm crazy? But I take it off at night to let my head breathe."

Women have been great about it, and if they compliment me

on it, I say, "Sure, you're just trying to get me to take the damn thing off."

But the reaction from men hasn't always been positive. One night in a bar in New York some idiot came over and made a crack about a "pelt" on my head and I said, "If you can get it off before I beat the shit out of you, you can have it."

The mustache is a different story. I had to grow it for *100 Rifles* in 1968. That was fine, because I was tired of hearing that I looked like Brando. It got lots of compliments, so I decided to keep it.

I shaved it off one night on *The Tonight Show* when Steve Martin was the guest host. Steve is multitalented, of course. And of course he's funny and of course he's bright. Since his start doing magic tricks at Disneyland when he was in high school, he's been a juggler, a comedy writer, a stand-up comic, a film and stage actor, a screenwriter, a producer, a novelist, a playwright, a musician, an art collector, and a tweeter (whatever that is).

But before I went on that night, I wasn't sure about Steve. I knew Johnny would always hit the ball back over the net, but I'd never met Steve, so I thought about being a little more outrageous with him.

"I've been thinking about shaving off the mustache," I said.

"You don't have the guts!" he said.

I called for a razor and they brought out an electric. Shaving off a mustache with an electric razor is like pulling the hairs out with tweezers. (Not that I know what that feels like.) I shaved half of it off and put the mirror in the middle and asked the audience to vote. They liked the mustache better. Of course I had to shave the other half off in that moment, and then couldn't wait for it to grow back. I've kept it ever since, and it's so much a part of me now, if I shave it off, I feel like I've lost my nose.

Steve and I got to be pretty good friends after that. When I won a Photoplay Award in 1978, I asked him to present it, and he was so funny and charming, it couldn't have been better.

ON THE FIRST DAY shooting *Navajo Joe*, I had to choose a mount from a corral full of horses. The wrangler was a Spanish Gypsy named Mahan. He rode up on an old, swaybacked thing that looked like Don Quixote's horse. His ears were bent down and he didn't have a mane or a tail. But he had a kind of pride about him.

"Which horse do you like?" Mahan said.

"I'll take the one you're on," I said.

"Ah, but he is *my* horse."

"I know, but he's the one I want."

"As you wish," he said. "His name is Destaphanado."

My dad put me on a horse when I was eight and I'd been riding ever since. In those days I could scissor a horse—just step up and *pfffft*, I was on his back. So I jumped on Destaphanado, whipped him around, and rode off. He didn't need a saddle or reins, I steered him with my knees. You always know right away when you get on a horse. He felt like Powerglide.

I thought an Indian should have a pinto, so I told the makeup man to get some water-based paint and put spots on Destaphanado, and give him a thick mane and a tail down to the ground. When I came to work the next morning, he looked like Ricardo Montalbán.

I think he somehow knew that I was responsible for his makeover, because he walked a little taller and he let me do anything with him. There was a stunt where I had to ride next to a moving train and step onto it. Most horses will not run against a train, but old Destaphanado took me right up to it and the transfer was smooth as silk. I could see him looking backward to see what happened to me.

Sergio Corbucci was all about body count. He thought that making a great Western involved killing a lot of people. He figured that if I killed more people than Clint Eastwood, *Navajo Joe* would make more money than *A Fistful of Dollars*. By the end of the first week I'd done so many stunts and killed so many people, I asked Corbucci to put in a love scene just so I could have a rest. He laughed and said, "We make American Western-a better. We take out love scenes and-a talk."

Before I left for Italy I'd done the pilot for *Hawk*. The producer, Renée Valente, called and said, "I've got good news and bad news. The good news is the pilot sold. The bad news is, you've got to be back here in a week." I had three weeks left on *Navajo Joe*, but they had to release me under the contract.

Sergio was a good sport. "Okay," he said, "We kill-a people faster."

I shot everybody in sight. I shot fourteen people in one scene. We got down to twelve guys and I had one day left on the picture. We were stumped on how to kill them in a different way until Sergio's eyes lit up and he said, "Dy-no-mite-a!"

The next day, as I was leaving to go back to the States, I asked the driver to stop the car. I rolled down the window and whistled, and Destaphanado trotted over. With tears in my eyes, I got out of the car and kissed him on the forehead.

Clint Eastwood

C lint Eastwood is one of the great filmmakers of all time. In the last fifty years, as an actor-producer-director, Clint has created a staggering body of work, in both quantity and quality. The Dirty Harry pictures of the 1970s and '80s made him a top box-office draw. He single-handedly revived the Western with *Hang 'Em High* (1968), *The Outlaw Josey Wales* (1976), *Pale Rider* (1985), and *Unforgiven* (1992), one of the greatest Westerns ever made. And just to show he could handle any genre, he threw in a psychological thriller, *Play Misty for Me* (1971); action comedies like *Every Which Way but Loose* (1978) and *Any Which Way You Can* (1980); a prison film, *Escape from Alcatraz* (1979); a suspense thriller, *Tightrope* (1984); an action thriller, *In the Line of Fire* (1993); a romantic drama, *The Bridges of Madison County* (1995); the sports drama *Million Dollar Baby* (2004); and war films like *Letters from Iwo Jima* (2006) and *American Sniper* (2014).

And he makes it look easy. He's so relaxed on the set that people think he's about to doze off, but that's just a game he plays. What he really does is go into his bus and do his homework. He knows what he wants and how to get it. He also saves the studio more money than any ten directors because he's good with actors.

Clint and I have been friends since the 1950s, when we were both under contract at Universal. One day an executive called us in and released us both. The guy said Clint's Adam's apple stuck out too far.

"What about me?" I said.

"*You* can't act," he said.

We were walking through the studio gate when I told Clint, "You're in a lot of trouble."

"Why?" he said.

"Because," I said, "*I* can learn to act."

CLINT LIVES QUIETLY, and he's very private. It was a long time before he even invited me to his house for dinner. There was another guest there who asked me how long I knew Clint.

"You first," I said.

"I went to high school with him," he said.

"I've known him for fifteen years," I said.

"Fifteen years?" he said. "Nobody's ever been invited after only fifteen years."

One Christmas I gave Clint a basset hound because I thought it would be a perfect dog for him. He fell in love with it and named it Grunk. I have no idea what that means. They were perfect together. When Clint went to work, he'd throw Grunk in the car and take him along. Nobody ever worried about him screwing up the take by barking or whatever. He'd just flop down and watch Clint with adoring eyes.

I won't say Clint was shy, but in those days he only said about nine words a year. And he did have a bit of a temper. When it came out, you had to give him a wide berth. Like the time we were sitting at a bar and a woman came over and said something to him that he didn't like. I don't know what it was because I was talking to somebody else and Clint and I were back to back. I turned around just in time to see her pour a beer over his head.

He didn't say anything. He just stood up, picked up a beer, and poured it over *her* head. And then he picked up another one, and another, and another. He poured four or five beers all over her. Then he said, "I'll see you later," and walked out.

Nobody in the place said a word.

By this time the woman was crying and she said, "Doesn't anybody here have any balls?"

"Apparently not," I said.

WHEN I WAS a teenager in Riviera Beach, we used to go to Palm Beach in the summer, when all the rich Yankees were gone. Their winter homes were boarded up, and we'd sneak into them. We didn't steal or destroy anything, we just brought our Pepsi and portable radios and danced. We were intimate with the homes of Doris Duke, Porfirio Rubirosa, and with Mar-A-Lago, the palace on Palm Beach Island owned by Marjorie Merriweather Post. Years later, Mrs. Post asked me to a party there, and when I arrived she said, "Let me show you around," and I said, "No, let me show *you* around."

One thing I noticed about wealthy people's homes was that they had lots of paintings on the walls. Paintings came to represent success to me. There was a Western artist named Olaf Wieghorst, who's mentioned along with Frederic Remington and Charles Russell as one of the great painters of the American West. He was a wonderful colorist and had a great eye for composition. Wieghorst was both a man of action and an artist. At age nine he'd been a circus rider in his native Denmark, and when he came to America he joined the U.S. Cavalry and rode against Pancho Villa. After a stint as a mounted policeman in New York, he settled in Southern California to paint full-time.

I've always loved Western art, and when I first came to Hollywood, I went to his studio and said, "Mr. Wieghorst, I'd love to have one of your paintings, but I'm just starting out and I don't think I can afford one. I was wondering if you could paint something for me. Maybe a tiny little Indian? And don't charge me for the clouds?"

He laughed and said, "Well, son, how much do you think that would be worth?"

And I said the most money I could think of. "A thousand dollars?"

"Done!" he said.

I scraped up the thousand bucks and he sent me a small painting of a tiny Indian standing under fluffy white clouds floating in a pale blue sky, with a plaque on the bottom that read: *Olaf Wieghorst. No Charge for the Clouds.*

About five years later, after I'd made a bunch of movies and my career was going strong, I learned that Clint owned a Russell and I was jealous. I decided I'd get a Remington, who was famous for his dynamic horses and vivid colors. I was doing pretty well in the picture business and had a few bucks, so I went into a gallery and asked if they had a Remington.

"Yes, sir," the man said. "We have one Remington."

It was magnificent.

"How much is it?" I asked.

"A million two," he said.

"I don't like it!" I said.

He called around and located a Remington for sale for $80,000 and I bought it sight unseen while I was away on location. After the picture wrapped, I flew back to L.A. and raced home from the airport to see my new painting. I dropped my bags in the hallway and ran into the living room. The picture was so dark I could barely see it on the wall. It was the only picture Remington ever did in black and white. No cowboys, no horses, just a couple of mangy goats and a skinny little Indian in the background who looked like Gandhi.

The next time Clint came to the house, he squinted at it and said, "Who the hell did *that?*"

TWENTY YEARS LATER and thirty years after we met, Clint and I still hadn't worked together, and I was looking forward to making *City Heat* (1984). It was Clint's project all the way. Blake Edwards was set to direct, but for some reason Clint didn't feel he was right. I thought Blake would have been good, but Clint was adamant. Dick Benjamin took over, but I don't think Clint spoke to him the whole time. I thought Dick was a good guy, and he'd just directed a wonderful picture called *My Favorite Year.* But he wasn't somebody who was going to direct Clint Eastwood because he was scared to death of him.

The first night of shooting was magical. The timing was perfect, the jokes were working, and everyone was having fun. The last shot of the night was a fight scene. I was supposed to get hit in the head with a breakaway chair, but the guy grabbed a metal chair by mistake and caught me flush on the jaw. I went down, but my first impulse was to shake it off, so I got up and finished the scene.

The next morning it hurt like hell. I had a blinding headache and ringing in my ears. I could barely open my mouth, and every time I tried to speak my face clicked. My bite was so lopsided I couldn't chew. I could only drink liquids, and I began losing weight.

But I willed myself to keep working. A few nights later I took a break to lie down in my bus (we had buses instead of trailers) and Clint came in.

"How ya doin'?" he said.

"I'm okay."

"No, you're not."

"No, I'm not. But I'll make it."

"Well, I'm not feeling too hot myself. I'm going home."

It was typical of Clint to pretend he was tired just to give me the chance to rest without having to admit I was hurt. He didn't want to make a big deal out of it. I tried to thank him, but he just walked away. He didn't want credit.

A day off didn't help. I should have gone to the hospital, but that would have shut the production down, and I didn't want to disappoint Clint. So I popped pain pills and finished the job. The public wanted *Boom Town*. They got *Dirty Harry vs. The Wimp*. I ruined the movie. Clint never complained about it, of course, and didn't allow it to affect our friendship.

I didn't work again for two years.

THE 1980S BROUGHT a deadly new disease: acquired immune deficiency syndrome (AIDS). Though doctors assured the public that it could not be spread by casual contact, the nation was gripped by hysteria. There wasn't much knowledge about AIDS, just a lot of misinformation and fearmongering. Anyone suspected of having it became untouchable.

A nine-year-old hemophiliac named Ryan White who had contracted AIDS from a blood transfusion was barred from school because parents were keeping their children home. The Social Security Administration banned AIDS patients from their offices.

Catholic churches stopped using communion cups. Hollywood actors started private blood banks and actresses refused to do love scenes with gay costars. When an actor who was thought to have AIDS did a cameo in a feature film, the makeup artist burned all the brushes.

A rumor started that I had AIDS. I told everyone it was a broken jaw, but nobody believed me. They wanted to think that I was dying of AIDS. It wasn't just the usual assholes; it was people I thought were my good friends.

My makeup man and my dentist refused to touch me. I lost forty pounds, which only added fuel to the fire. I wasn't well enough to work, but nobody wanted me anyway, and I couldn't blame them. Why would you hire someone who was terminally ill?

"Let's give him $5 million and see if he makes it till Friday."

One night I began hyperventilating, and my heart was pounding so fast, I thought my chest would explode. I called for an ambulance and gave them my address. I was on all the movie star maps, so every tourist in the world found my house . . . but not the ambulance driver. I watched from the window as he passed by three times. I dragged myself onto the lawn and began waving as he went by the fourth time. He still didn't see me. I had to crawl into the street to get him to stop.

When I got to the hospital, they did a bunch of tests and put me in a room with three old Jewish guys. I was finally dropping off to sleep when one of them came over and said, "You play pinochle?"

"I'm dying," I said.

"We're all dying," he said.

So we sat there in our wheelchairs playing cards.

In the hospital I met a girl with the same symptoms. She was in terrible pain and we commiserated with one another. I could tell she was on the edge. I kept trying to encourage her, but a week later, I heard that she'd killed herself.

I wasn't suicidal—never have been in my life—but if I had died at that time, it would have been okay with me. It was the lowest point in my life. I was so depressed I just wanted to curl up in the fetal position. I couldn't go out in public to deny the rumors because I was exactly what they said, a bag of bones. But not because I had AIDS.

I had temporomandibular disorder (TMD or TMJ), which affects the joint that connects the lower jaw with the skull. It messes with your balance and your sensory perception. It's like being seasick all the time. I couldn't lie down, I couldn't stand bright light, and if the phone rang, I'd fall on the floor with a pillow over my ears. It felt as if I had an army of people in my head and they were trying to get out through my eyes, nose, mouth, and ears. I kept losing weight and I looked like a cadaver.

I saw a dozen dentists who had no idea how to treat it. One of them sawed all of my bottom teeth off. It didn't help my condition, but I could stick my tongue through the gap with my mouth closed. Another one prescribed a new drug called Halcion. It was the only thing that would relax my jaw. Of *course* you didn't feel pain, you didn't feel anything. It put you *out*. I was a zombie but didn't care. I would have done anything for relief. I kept taking Halcion and my tolerance went up. It got to where I was taking fifty a day and I was sleeping longer and longer.

I finally found a retired dentist in San Diego named Gus Schwab. He was a cranky old coot, but he knew what he was doing. I drove down from Los Angeles every other day and he realigned every tooth in my mouth. It cost a fortune, but I would have sold my house at that point if it meant that I would feel better.

And wouldn't you know it? Very slowly, I began to get better.

So many friends had deserted me, I joked that I was saving lots of money on Christmas cards. I'll never forget the people who stood by me: Dom DeLuise, Ann-Margret, Charles Nelson Reilly,

Charley Durning, Angie Dickinson, Jon Voight, Hal Needham, Clint Eastwood, Johnny Carson, Elizabeth Taylor, and about five hundred stuntmen.

Elizabeth had gone through the same thing with her jaw and she told anyone who'd listen: "He can't eat! That's what it is. At one time or another, all of us fat broads wish we had TMJ."

Johnny kept calling and telling me to "get up and get out." He made it clear that I was welcome on the show to dispel the rumors whenever I was ready. But I was still concerned about my appearance. I'd lost so much weight, I didn't want a camera in my face. But I knew it was time to fight back, so I finally accepted Johnny's invitation.

When I walked on *The Tonight Show*, I had a prop with me, a little black address book. I held it up and said it contained the names of all the people who had deserted me through the illness, the AIDS rumors, the tabloid headlines. I said, "It's always nice to know who your friends are." Then I opened the book and began tearing pages out. That's when Johnny said, "You know, I've done that, too. It makes a hell of a fire." The audience erupted, and for the first time in months, I felt hope for the future.

Pretty soon I got hired for a show where I had to kiss a girl good night. Her name was Gigi, and I'll never forget her. She really planted one on me—if I'd been a slot machine the eyes would have been spinning. Later I told her how touched I was by the fact that she wasn't afraid and she said, "Oh, people are full of shit. Besides, I've been waiting a long time to kiss you."

That was just what I needed.

Looking back, I feel as though it all made me stronger in the end. But I still can't forgive the people who deserted me.

The AIDS hysteria eventually died down. I think it began to change when Rock Hudson came out as the first celebrity with the disease. He went on television and he looked horrible. Doris Day stood next to him when he made the announcement and she seemed to be holding him up. A few weeks before Rock died, Elizabeth asked me to appear at a fund-raiser for AIDS Project Los Angeles, and I was proud to be one of the hosts for the evening. When I got up to read a letter of support from President Ronald Reagan, the audience booed because they felt he hadn't done enough to fight the disease.

Afterward I got calls from reporters asking me why I would appear at an AIDS fund-raiser. I'd done benefits for lots of causes and nobody had ever asked that before.

"If it had been a benefit for cancer victims," I said, "nobody would be asking such a stupid question."

Unfortunately, it took me longer to get off Halcion than it did to cure my TMJ. My doctor wanted me to check myself into the Betty Ford Clinic, but at that time it was important to me not to be seen as a drug addict, so I went cold turkey. I fell into a coma, and at one point the doctors thought I might die, but after about eight or nine hours I regained consciousness. I never took another Halcion. Years later I became dependent on prescription painkillers following back surgery. I was in denial for a long time, but finally realized I couldn't beat the problem on my own and checked myself into rehab. It's a good thing I did, because I wouldn't be here otherwise.

Hal Needham

H al was a pioneer and an innovator who made stunt work into an art form. He worked as a stuntman or stunt coordinator on three hundred feature films and three thousand television episodes, and beginning with *Smokey and the Bandit,* he directed nine feature films.

Hal doubled for me on *Riverboat* and *Gunsmoke* on TV, and in a bunch of features: *Lucky Lady, The Man Who Loved Cat Dancing, W.W. and the Dixie Dancekings, White Lightning, Gator.* He did everything with style. In a fight you could always recognize him because he had a unique way of throwing a punch and then coming back across his chest with the same hand. Stuntmen call it a Needham.

I've always had great affection for stuntmen, and many of them are among my best friends in the business. Most of the stuntmen I've known were jocks, and a few were rodeo performers. I'd go out to Hal's house in Thousand Oaks on weekends and there would always be four or five stunt guys there, with Hal coaching them. They'd rehearse fights and work up new gags.

The first time I went there, Hal said, "Let's go out back and do some high falls." I had no idea what he was talking about, but I said, "Sure!"

Behind the house there was a tree that must have been sixty feet high, with a rope on it and a net below. Hal said, "Go on out, swing back and forth, and let go of the rope. Just before you hit the net, do a flip and land on your back."

Sounded easy enough, and I did it, and it *was* easy. I graduated to tree fights: Another guy would get up in the high branches and we'd swing at each other forty feet in the air and try to knock each other into the net. It was crazy. But I have to admit that it was fun.

We'd also work on fights. Hal taught me how to give and take a punch on-camera. A lot of actors don't do that well.

We all had motorcycles—mostly Harleys—and we did crazy stuff with them. They were junk bikes—pieces of this and pieces of that. You could tell they'd been in crashes. A guy would go over a hill and disappear, and when you followed him over, he'd be upside down. Everybody crashed and burned sooner or later. It was a miracle that nobody got seriously hurt. And everybody had a dirt bike. We raced them out in the desert. We'd map out a track through the cactus and rattlesnake nests. We chipped in to buy a trophy. I thought it was a big deal to win a stuntman's trophy. When we weren't practicing gags or racing bikes, we'd play touch football. I had a team made up mostly of stuntmen and we beat everybody.

Those guys were the best in the business. It's a tight-knit community and they trusted me, which is the greatest compliment anyone can get from them. I never saw a real fight between stuntmen, I think because they respect each other so much.

When a real fistfight breaks out on a movie set, it's usually the actor's fault, not the stuntman's. The actor makes a stupid remark about the right way to do a fall, or he complains that a stuntman hit him on purpose. Whenever I saw that, I'd take the actor aside and say, "Don't you understand? If he hit you on purpose you'd be asleep now. Just keep your mouth shut."

Some actors feel insecure around stuntmen, who can do all the things the actor is supposed to be doing himself. (There are actors who use a stunt double to open a car door for them.) It's worse when the actor's wife or girlfriend is on the set. Some actors can't handle it and they get belligerent.

HAL WAS ONE of only two stuntmen to ever receive an Academy Award. The other was Yakima Canutt. They both took stunt work to new levels. Yakima was a rodeo rider who went into acting. He did leading roles in silent Westerns, but he had a high voice, so when talkies came in, he was reduced to playing quiet villains. He began to do stunt work, and by the mid-1930s he was the lead stuntman at Republic, where he doubled for Gene Autry, the Lone Ranger, and Zorro. Since Zorro wears a mask, Yakima did almost all the nonspeaking scenes himself.

Yakima was the first to plan and prepare stunts carefully, which made stunt work less dangerous and the stunts more thrilling. He also invented a bunch of riding tricks, like the Crupper Mount, a leapfrog into the saddle from the rear. Over his long career he stunted for Tyrone Power, Errol Flynn, Henry Fonda, Randolph Scott, Tex Ritter, and Roy Rogers. He taught Duke Wayne how to fall off a horse, and Duke once admitted that he'd studied Yakima to see how a real cowboy walked and talked. Having known them both, I can attest that Duke's famous rolling stride is pure Yakima.

Yakima doubled for Clark Gable in *Gone with the Wind* (1939). He staged the chariot race in *Ben-Hur* (1959) and trained not only the horses but also Stephen Boyd and Charlton Heston. (He told Chuck, "Just stay in the damn chariot and I guarantee you'll win the race.") As stunt coordinator on *Cat Ballou* (1965), Yakima was the one who got Lee Marvin's horse to play drunk. He also did great work in *Spartacus* (1960), *El Cid* (1961), *Where*

Eagles Dare (1968), *A Man Called Horse* (1970), and *Breakheart Pass* (1975). His most famous stunt is in John Ford's *Stagecoach* (1939), where, as an attacking Indian, he jumps from his horse at full gallop onto a six-horse team pulling a stagecoach. He drops down between horses and allows himself to be dragged along the ground, then lets go as the horses and coach speed over him.

Yakima was in a wheelchair by the time he came to visit me on the set of a picture I directed called *The End* (1978). We were shooting out at a big ranch with a bridge over a shallow creek. I could tell it was killing him to watch everybody doing stunts, so I said, "Yak, you wanna do something?"

"YEAH!" he said.

"Okay," I said. "How 'bout if I come by and knock you off the bridge?"

"GREAT!" he said.

We blocked it out, and we did it in one take!

When I yelled, "Cut!" we all ran in. Yakima was sitting in the creek with a big grin on his face. Everybody else was standing around with their mouths open.

Hal picked up where Yakima left off. He invented technology and stunts that were pure Needham. He was respected by everyone—producers, directors, actors, and above all, fellow stuntmen. He was the best there ever was in terms of versatility. I guess Dar Robinson was better at high falls, but Hal was the best at horse falls, the best at stair falls, the best at fights, the best at underwater stuff . . . He was just incredible.

HAL USED TO SAY, "I'll never win an Academy Award, but I'll be a rich son of a bitch." Well, he did both. He made a bunch of money. He had profit participation on *Smokey*, which was unusual for a first-time director. And he received not one but two Oscars: a scientific and engineering award for technical innovation, and a Governor's Award for life achievement on both sides of the camera. All that success didn't change him one bit.

Nobody has more respect for stuntmen than I do. I appreciate their athleticism, physical courage, and creativity. A good stuntman is a world-class athlete. Make that stunt *person*: women have come into their own since I started in the business, when small men would double for females.

Everyone on a movie set works hard. Stunt people work hard *and* risk their necks. They crash vehicles, jump from buildings, set themselves on fire. Everybody in the business recognizes their importance. Except the Academy of Motion Picture Arts and Sciences, which refuses to give them their own Oscar.

There are Oscars for costume design, makeup, set decoration, sound mixing . . . but not for stunt work. Is it because the studios don't want to bring attention to the fact that actors don't do their own stunts? That's not exactly a secret. Everybody knows it's not the actor. They understand that insurance companies won't let actors do dangerous stunts, because if the lead actor gets hurt, the production closes down, which costs money and puts people out of work. Stunts *are* the action in action films, which year after year are the biggest draw at the box office.

Hal wasn't a fan of computer-generated imagery (CGI), and neither am I. CGI creates scenes that aren't physically possible. Yes, it's convenient and cost-effective to be able to climb Mount Everest without leaving the studio, but I think audiences would rather have real stunts.

That's why the pendulum is swinging away from CGI and back to physical stunts. Because people can tell the difference between what's real and what's fake, and they know what stunt performers do and they appreciate it.

The Academy Awards show is already too long, so let's give the stunt performers their Oscar in a separate ceremony along with the technical awards. It's the Academy of Motion Picture Arts and Sciences, right? Well, stunt coordinating is both an art and a science. It's time we recognize these people.

HAL WAS BORN in Memphis during the Great Depression. His sharecropper stepfather moved the family to Arkansas when Hal was four. They lived so deep in the Ozarks that they "had to pump in the sunshine," Hal said. No roads, just rutted dirt tracks. They couldn't get a car within three miles of the place—not that they had one. Their transportation was their two feet. They were a family of seven in a two-room shack with a dirt floor and no electricity or indoor plumbing, just a two-holer out back. They had to carry all their water from a mountain spring five hundred yards down the hill, and they did all their cooking on a woodstove. Their only artificial light was from kerosene lamps, and the only heat was from a fireplace. Hal gathered berries, cut firewood, and hunted rabbit and squirrel to put meat on the table. He got his clothes from the Salvation Army and never saw a movie until he was ten.

Hal left school after the eighth grade and worked as a bowling pin setter and later as a tree topper, whose job it was to use iron hooks to climb tall pines, chopping off branches on the way up. One day he cut too low and fell seventy feet. Luckily he landed on a pile of leaves and branches and walked away with just a few cuts and bruises. (His first stunt!)

Hal joined the 82nd Airborne in 1951. He tested parachutes and earned extra money on weekends doing jumps at air shows. During one performance his chute failed to open and he fell thousands of feet before he could work his reserve chute free, only a few seconds before hitting the ground. (His second stunt!)

After the army Hal knew he wasn't qualified for any high-paying profession, but he was ambitious and figured he'd have to do something dangerous to make good money. He went to California and got into the stunt business through a TV show called *You Asked for It*, hosted by Art Baker.

People would write in and say, "I'd like to see somebody eat a pigeon," and they'd arrange to have it done on the air. Hal wrote his own letter that said, "I want to see somebody jump from an airplane and bulldog a man off a galloping horse." He went down to the studio a few days later and said, "Hi. I jump off airplanes and bulldog people off horses. Any call for that?"

"That's odd," they said. "Why, just the other day . . ."

Hal went to Chuck Roberson, who was Duke Wayne's stuntman, and said, "Chuck, I've got a job for us. I'm gonna bulldog you off a horse."

"How much money?" Chuck said.

"A thousand dollars," Hal said.

"I'll do it," Chuck said. "What'll you be riding?"

"Cessna 150."

"*Cessna 150?*"

"Cessna 150."

"Well, how fast will you be going?"

"I don't know. It's never been done before."

It's an amazing piece of film. The plane had to be going at least fifty miles an hour to avoid a stall. Hal jumps from the wheel of the plane and brushes Chuck off the horse. Chuck slams into the ground, and then Hal hits even harder.

It was a tough way to earn a thousand bucks, but it got Hal work in Western movies, doing fights and saddle falls, stirrup drags and wagon wrecks. When Westerns dried up, Hal switched to car stunts and high falls. He did parachute and wing-walking gags in *The Spirit of St. Louis* (1957) and then landed on TV as an extra on Richard Boone's *Have Gun—Will Travel*.

In one episode a stunt guy was supposed to climb a tall tree, get shot, and fall into the water, but he wasn't going high enough and it looked lousy. Hal said, "Fuck it, let me do it." He went up the tree like a monkey (or a tree topper), got as high as he could, did a half flip, and hit the water. He walked out and said, "How was that, Mr. Boone?"

"You're my man!" Boone said.

From then on, Boone wouldn't make a move without Hal, who choreographed all the stunts and fight scenes on the show. Boone saw that Hal had the charisma to be an actor, so he started giving him small parts. By the end of the show's five-year run, Hal had acted in dozens of episodes.

EVERYBODY WHO MADE action films loved Hal, including Duke Wayne. Hal worked on probably a dozen movies with Duke and loved to tell the story of how he taught him to throw a punch. On the set of *The Undefeated* (1969), with the camera behind him, Duke was having trouble delivering a punch that looked real. He was throwing a straight jab that was missing the side of the guy's face by a mile. Hal had the guts to step forward and correct Duke in front of everyone, suggesting he throw a roundhouse instead. Hal said there were a few anxious moments when he wondered if he'd ever work again, but Duke finally thanked him and demanded him on all his pictures from then on.

Hal graduated to second unit director and stunt coordinator. Second unit directors shoot the action sequences, inserts, and other scenes that don't involve the principals. Stunt coordinators look at the script and figure out how to make the action scenes more exciting. They hire and supervise stuntmen and decide which stunts an actor can do and which ones require a professional stunt person. They design and choreograph stunts and rehearse them for days and sometimes weeks to make sure they're executed safely. Stunt people know that lack of preparation is not only dangerous but also sloppy. They have an expression: "Bullshit doesn't photograph."

Despite what I jokingly said many times, Hal wasn't crazy. He planned and rehearsed every move he made to eliminate as much risk as possible, and he never did a stunt until he thought he was ready. But you can't have a great stunt without danger, and Hal told me that he was scared sometimes, but the confidence he got from calculating the stunt overcame the fear.

And he was reliable. He was known in the business as a guy who got the job done, and he was proud of the fact that he never turned down a stunt in his life. Though he charged more than other stunt people, he was cheaper in the long run because he almost always did it on the first try.

Glenn Wilder is another one of the greatest stuntmen of all time and one of my favorite people in the world. He's more fun than anybody, and one of the best-liked guys in the business. I was staying with him on his ranch near L.A. during the 1971 Sylmar quake, a 6.7 on the Richter scale. Hurricanes don't bother me, but earthquakes scare me to death. You just don't know what to do. Glenn had about seven horses and they all went crazy and ran not *over* the fences but *through* them. People were running around screaming, but Glenn laughed the whole thing off. He thought it was all wonderful.

Ronnie Rondell is another world-class stuntman and a terrific guy. There was nothing he couldn't do. And he's so good-looking I always wondered why he wasn't an actor.

Hal, Glenn, and Ronnie didn't like that the old-timers in the

Cracking up with Johnny Carson and Dom DeLuise on *The Tonight Show* (1982).
(© Bettmann/Corbis/AP Images)

With Dom DeLuise in *The Cannonball Run* (1981). *(© Everett Collection)*

With Elizabeth Taylor at the Starlight Foundation award benefit gala in New York (1985). *(© Getty Images)*

Backstage with Frank Sinatra and Sammy Davis Jr. (circa 1987).

With Quinton and Hal Needham at the First Annual Taurus Foundation World Stunt Awards (2001).
(© Gregg DeGuire/Getty Images)

Doing my James Stewart impression for James Stewart (circa 1989).
(© The LIFE Picture Collection/ Getty Images)

With Chris Evert (1996).
(© Globe Photos/Zuma Wire)

Aboard Destaphanado, my beloved costar in *Navajo Joe* (1966).

(© Everett Collection)

With Dinah on her show
Dinah's Place (1973).
(© NBC Universal)

With Dinah at the
1973 Academy Awards.
(© Globe Photos/Zuma Wire)

Dinah and Mom (circa 1975).

With Jackie Gleason in a scene from *Smokey and the Bandit* (1977). *(© Everett Collection)*

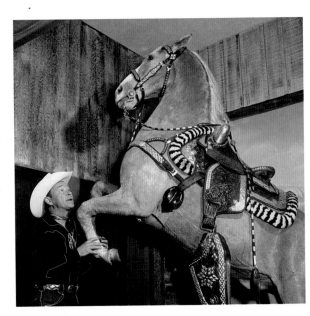

Roy Rogers with the (anatomically correct) stuffed Trigger (1965).
(© AP Images/Corbis/Bettmann)

With Hal Needham, Jerry Reed, and the real star of *Smokey and the Bandit*, "Fred" the basset hound (1977). *(© Universal Studios/Getty Images)*

With Sally on the set of *Smokey and the Bandit* (1977).
(© Mary Evans/Ronald Grant/Everett Collection)

The iconic hammock shot in *Smokey and the Bandit* (1977).
(© 1977 Universal City Studios, Inc.)

In the famous Trans Am, *Smokey and the Bandit II* (1980). *(© Everett Collection)*

Out to dinner with Sally in L.A. (1978).

(© Ron Galella/Wire Image)

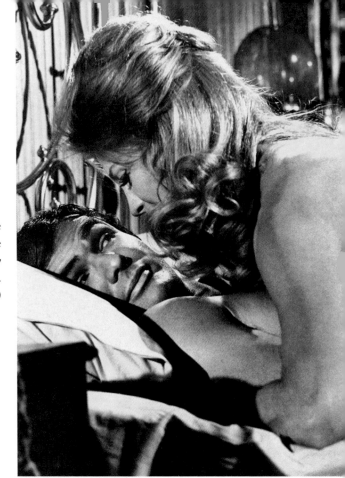

With Angie
Dickinson on the
set of *Sam Whiskey*
(1969).
(© Everett Collection)

With Carol Burnett (1972).
(© Everett Collection)

With Clint Walker and Ossie Davis on the *Sam Whiskey* set (1969).

A scene from *Hustle* (1975) with Catherine Deneuve.
(© Everett Collection)

With Clint Eastwood
in *City Heat* (1984).
*(© Warner Bros./Everett
Collection)*

Nancy Ann, Dolly Parton, Mom, and Pop on the set of
The Best Little Whorehouse in Texas (1982).

With Raquel Welch on the set of *Evening Shade* (circa 1992).

(© *CBS/Everett Collection*)

With Loni at the Burt Reynolds Dinner Theatre (1989).

(© The Palm Beach Post/Zuma Wire)

With Loni (1993). *(© John Krondes/Globe Photos/Zuma Wire)*

With Mark Wahlberg in a scene from *Boogie Nights* (1997).

(© New Line Cinema/Everett Collection)

Backstage after a concert with Cooper Getschal and Willie Nelson (2010).

With Dudley Remus and Patrick Moody in the Town of Lake Park Mirror Ballroom, where my acting career began (2013).
(© C. Todd Vittum)

Stuntmen's Association wouldn't admit women or minorities, so they broke away and formed Stunts Unlimited. The two groups didn't like each other and it got to be stupid. I paid no attention to it and hired guys from both because I had friends in both. Hal would get pissed off at me, but I told him, "Look, I can't dislike someone because you dislike them." It was the only time we ever argued, but it didn't hurt our friendship.

Hal was the real deal. If you went into a badass bar with him, you felt safe. One time on location in Arkansas we were having a beer in some dive when a guy came over and started giving him shit.

"Look," Hal said, "I don't want to get into a fight. I have a date and I don't want to get all sweaty."

"What makes you think you're gonna get sweaty?" the guy asked. "It may not last that long."

That's when Hal nailed him. The guy was out before he hit the floor. Hal turned to me and said, "He was right. I didn't get sweaty."

Hal *loved* to fight. It was one of the highlights of his evening. "What a great night we had!" he'd say. He was totally fearless of pain or injury. If anybody came over and said something stupid like "You're supposed to be the toughest guy in the world," you knew it was coming. But Hal would just smile. He thought it was wonderful. And it was never personal. They wanted to be able to brag that they'd been in a fight with the great stuntman Hal Needham, and Hal was happy to oblige.

HAL AND I made a movie called *White Lightning* (1973) in Little Rock, Arkansas. One of the gags was a car-jump onto a barge.

"I can do this, Hal," I said.

"Yeah," he said, "but let's have the barge pulling away."

"That's nuts," I said. "They won't even know it's moving. And what if it moves too far? I'll wind up in the drink."

"Then let *me* do it."

Hal told the barge captain exactly how fast to go. He got in the car and sped down the ramp doing about eighty. He didn't know that for some reason the captain firewalled the throttle, so the barge was farther out than planned. The car slammed into the barge nose first and the back wheels landed in the water. If the front wheels slid off the barge, Hal would have been swept away by the current and would have probably drowned. Fortunately the car stayed put. We all thought he'd wrecked not only the car but himself, too. He opened the door, stumbled out, and passed out.

We sent Hal to the hospital and went on with the day's work. I had somebody lined up and ready to go for the next stunt, but guess who came back?

"What the hell are you doing here?" I said when Hal walked in. "You're supposed to be in the hospital."

"Nah, I'm fine," he said.

"Are you hurt?"

"Well, I've got a little headache, but they gave me some Percodeens."

Hal did the stunt on the first take.

He always had "Percodeens." In fact Percodans were in every stuntman's bag. In those days we took a pill without a second thought and got back in the game. We weren't taking them to get high, we were taking them so we could work. We didn't know about any long-term effects. When I had to do a fight scene or a rough stunt, I'd pop a couple of Percodans first. I never missed a beat, never hit anybody, never did anything that people supposedly do when they're hooked on painkillers. And I never saw Hal visibly impaired in any way, either.

Hal was so good on vehicle stunts they called him "the master of suspension." He was one of the first to use rockets, and in a demo for General Motors, he sailed a rocket-powered pickup truck across a 112-foot-wide canal. He made it with room to spare, but with only a seat belt and harness and no roll cage, he broke his back on the landing.

Hal was one of the first humans to crash-test automobile airbags. Wearing just a lap-style seat belt, he ran head-on into a brick wall at 20 miles per hour and testified before Congress about it.

Hal decided he wanted to be the first to cross the sound barrier in a land vehicle and made a deal with Budweiser and CBS to build a rocket car. When he got in that thing, I knew he'd either get the record or blow it up. He got the record: 733.666 miles per hour. Today the car is in the Smithsonian.

Then he decided to get into stock car racing. He put a NASCAR deal together and asked if I'd be interested in being his partner. "It's a lot of money," I said. "Let's do it!" Hal built the team from the ground up and revolutionized the sport. We named the car the Skoal Bandit for *Smokey and the Bandit*. No race car had ever had its own name before. Hal was the first to use telemetry and the first to take charge of the pit crew and improve their performance. He drilled those guys as if they were rehearsing stunts. He was the first to dress them in fire suits covered with logos just like the drivers. He had a great commercial mind about things like that. He came up with stuff that made you think, *That was obvious*, but it wasn't obvious until he did it.

HAL WAS A GREAT INNOVATOR. He invented things that made stunt work safer and more spectacular, like a giant airbag for high falls, a car-flipping cannon, and the Shotmaker, a crane that allows the camera to swoop around a moving car and shoot from any angle. All of them are still in use.

Before Hal, stunt people used wooden sawhorses with mattresses and cardboard boxes on top of one-by-twelves for falls. The boards would bend before they snapped, absorbing some of the force, but they could handle a fall from only forty or fifty feet. Hal got the idea from the giant air-filled bag used by pole-vaulters. He filled a much bigger bag with helium, which allowed much higher and safer falls.

He also revolutionized explosions. In the old days they'd put a charge into a hole in the ground and detonate it just as the stuntman tried to fling himself as far away as he could. Hal invented a hydraulic launch pad that throws the stuntman much farther without his having to come near the explosion. It looks like he's really getting blown up. And Hal came up with a trunk-mounted cannon that can flip a speeding car without a ramp. In the first test, it snapped the car in half and sent Hal to the hospital with a broken back (again).

Over the years he had all sorts of injuries. He broke dozens of bones, had a shoulder replaced, punctured a lung, and lost a bunch of teeth. He always said that broken bones don't count, and that you're not hurt unless you have to go to the hospital. That's typical of not just Hal, but of all the great stuntmen. When Glenn Wilder's son, Scott, a top stunt guy himself, broke his pelvis doing a stair fall, somebody made the mistake of calling it a "serious injury."

"That's not serious," Scott said. "Serious is when you're dead."

I've never known anybody with Hal's pain threshold. When he broke his back the second time, I went to the hospital with him.

Hal walked in and said, "My back is broken."

I'll never forget the doctor . . . he didn't even shave yet. He said, "If your back was broken, you wouldn't be able to walk in here."

"Do I have to whip ya to convince you my back is broken?" Hal said.

The technician x-rayed him, and sure enough, he had two crushed vertebrae and fluid in one lung. Meanwhile, Hal was busy flirting with the nurse.

The doctor brought out the longest needle I've ever seen and said, "Mr. Needham, I have to drain that lung and it's going to hurt like hell, so I suggest you stand up and put your hands on the wall to brace yourself."

By this time they had him in one of those hospital gowns with the open back, and the doctor told the nurse, "You'd better support him because he'll probably faint."

She knelt down and grabbed hold of his legs.

"That's very kind of you, honey," Hal said, still pitching.

The doctor clearly didn't like Hal. Maybe he was dating the nurse. He came up behind Hal with that needle and WHAM, he plunged it into Hal's back and slowly began to withdraw the fluid from his lung.

I watched Hal for a reaction. Nothing. Not a blink, not even a bead of sweat.

But his bowels emptied all over himself and the nurse.

Without missing a beat, Hal looked down and said, "Does this mean I won't be getting your number, honey?"

Smokey

W hen Hal got his divorce, he said, "Do you think I could stay
with you a couple of nights?"

"Sure," I said. "You can stay in the pool house."

Twelve years later he was still there. But we didn't see each other
much because I never went down to the pool house. I was afraid I'd
find a bunch of waitresses. And at least one of us was always away
on location. But one day when we were both in town, Hal came up
to the house and said, "Roomie, I've written a movie."

The "script" was handwritten on yellow pads.

I read it and said, "Hal, if you can get somebody to give you the
money, I'll star in it and you can direct it."

My agent advised me to do more films like *Deliverance*, not a
screwball comedy written and directed by a stuntman who'd never
done either before. My friends got down on their knees with tears
in their eyes and begged me not do it.

A year later those same people said, "I'm sure glad I convinced
you to make that picture."

IN THE 1970S, you couldn't buy Coors beer east of the Mississippi. It didn't have preservatives, so it had to be kept cold all the
way from the brewery to the customer. It cost too much to ship it

refrigerated across the continent, so the company sold it only in the West, and people were smuggling it in their suitcases, which was technically bootlegging.

When Hal and I were getting ready to shoot *Gator* (1976) in Georgia, the traffic captain put a bunch of Coors on the truck in L.A. and took it down there. He gave Hal a couple of cases for his condo. Hal put a few bottles in the refrigerator, but the next time he looked, they were gone. He put a few more in and they disappeared, too. He figured it was an inside job and he was right. It was the maid. He caught her red-handed with two bottles in her cart. He asked her why she was stealing Coors beer and she said, "You can't get it around here and my husband loves it."

In Hal's mind, smuggling Coors became the MacGuffin for a movie, the thread that would tie the action together. He loved that it wasn't about killing or hurting people, but that it was still illegal. The story he came up with is simple: a truck driver, Snowman, tries to bootleg a load of Coors from Texarkana, Texas, to Atlanta, Georgia. His buddy, Bo "Bandit" Darville, acts as a decoy to allow Snowman to slip past his nemesis, Sheriff Buford T. Justice, aka Smokey.

Hal and I took the script to Universal. They wanted to make a movie with us, but not *Smokey*. They wanted us to do *Convoy* instead. We stood our ground and said *Smokey* or nothing, and they finally gave in. (*Convoy* was eventually made with Kris Kristofferson and Ali MacGraw, directed by Sam Peckinpah.)

The studio wanted Richard Boone to play the sheriff. He was a wonderful actor and might have been good, but I wanted someone a little crazier, a little more dangerous, and a lot funnier. "How about Jackie Gleason?" I said.

Orson Welles dubbed Jackie "the Great One," and it stuck. (When Orson dubbed you anything, it stuck.) Jackie was a huge TV star in the 1950s, first with a variety show and then on *The*

Honeymooners (1955–1956). He did interesting work in the movies in the 1960s: *The Hustler, Requiem for a Heavyweight, Soldier in the Rain,* but by the time we were casting *Smokey,* he hadn't made a movie in seven years and all the Universal execs were wary except the boss, Lew Wasserman, who loved the idea. His marketing brain kicked in right away. "I see eight million Jackie Gleason sheriff dolls!" he said.

I went to see Jackie and told him about the part. I think he was intrigued by the chance to build a character from the ground up. I told Jackie that my father was a police chief, and Jackie wanted to know all about him.

"My dad is so cop, he bleeds cop," I said. "All my life he'd say 'sumbitch!' instead of 'son of a bitch.'"

"Sumbitch?" Jackie said. I could see his eyes light up.

So Jackie said "sumbitch" in the picture and it became part of the Southern lexicon. For a long time, whenever *Smokey* aired on television, the censors overdubbed "sumbitch" with "scum bum," which became so popular with kids that Hot Wheels put it on the tail of its Trans Am.

Jackie was a master. He said, "I can't be in the car alone. Put someone in there with me to play off of." So we got a Rams linebacker named Mike Henry to play Jackie's doofus son and they were terrific together. I've always prided myself on being able to make chicken salad out of chicken shit, but Jackie could make it into cordon bleu. He never did anything the same way twice on-camera, and he put everyone on the floor. We had to bite our lips to keep from ruining takes. I watched him ad-lib his way through the whole movie. He never said a single word in the script. (Every once in a while, Hal would say, "Okay, I guess that's a cut.")

I loved every minute of it, and it was a great lesson: When you're with somebody that good, just fly with them. Hal was smart in that regard. He didn't let his ego get in the way. I don't think many other directors would have given Jackie such free rein. The result is an amazing performance, and I think Sheriff Buford T. Justice is right up there with Jackie's other great characters: Ralph Kramden, Joe the Bartender, the Poor Soul, and Reginald Van Gleason III.

Jackie started drinking at eight in the morning and drank all day, but he never got drunk, he just got funnier. He had a guy named Mal working for him. When he wanted a drink, he'd say, "Mal, hamburger!" That meant "Bring me a huge glass of vodka."

I asked him, "Why do you call it 'hamburger'?"

"I don't want the crew to know I'm drinking," he said.

One day Jackie and I were sitting outside in director's chairs. He was telling a story like he always did, with a "hamburger" in his hand. He was leaning back in the chair, and all of a sudden he tipped over backward and disappeared into the tall grass.

"Jackie, Jackie, are you all right?" I said.

A hand shot straight up holding the glass skyward and a triumphant voice shouted, "Didn't spill a drop!"

JERRY REED was a guitar player and singer-songwriter who'd signed his first record contract when he was seventeen. He had a string of hits in the 1970s and '80s, including "Amos Moses," "When You're Hot, You're Hot," and "The Bird." He was a natural comedian who could also play heavies because he had the smarts to do it in a charming way.

Nobody could talk faster than Jerry—he was like a sewing machine. He was fun to work with and gave you everything he had in a scene. At night he'd go out and get wasted, but he'd be right there the next morning ready to go, and he always knew his lines. We wound up doing half a dozen pictures together.

Jerry had promised to write a song for the movie, but by the end of filming, he still hadn't come up with it.

"What are you gonna do about the music?" Hal asked.

"I'll give you something in the morning," Jerry said.

He was out all night as usual, but the next morning he sang "Eastbound and Down" for Hal, who was so blown away he couldn't speak.

"If you don't like it, I can change it," Jerry said.

"If you change one goddamn note, I'll fuckin' kill you!" Hal said.

As Hal liked to say, "Eastbound and Down" was real "gettin'-down-the-road-truckin' music," and it was perfect for the movie. It became a monster hit and was Jerry's theme song from then on.

Pat McCormick played Big Enos and Paul Williams played his son, Little Enos. The two of them were like a polished comedy team, though they'd never met before. On the *Smokey* set they'd go away for ten minutes and come back with a scene. If you didn't like it, they'd go away for ten minutes more and come back with a better one.

I knew Pat from *The Tonight Show*—he was one of Johnny's top writers. I always thought he was hilariously warped. I'd met Paul at parties and liked him enormously. Besides being a popular singer-songwriter, Paul had a wicked sense of humor. Pat was six-seven, 280; Paul was all of five-two. The first time I saw them together, I broke up.

In my first shot of the picture, I'm in a hammock with my cowboy hat down over my face. The two of them come over, and I lift the hat up to see them standing there dressed in matching suits, and I burst out laughing. It's the most visceral, most natural, most satisfying laugh I've ever had, on or off the screen.

TWO DAYS BEFORE the cameras rolled, the studio cut the budget from five million to four million. Hal spent the next forty-eight hours revising the script. He had a professional movie dog all lined up but fired it to save money, so when we got to Georgia to begin shooting, we needed a replacement. Hal put an ad in the paper that I'd be judging a contest to pick a dog for "a major motion picture," and the next day there were two thousand dogs in the park. I put my hand over each of the "finalists," and a basset hound won. That's how Fred became a movie star. Jackie was the only one who could steal a scene from him.

We filmed mostly in Lithonia, McDonough, and Jonesboro, Georgia, but a few key scenes were shot in and around Ojai, California. Hal broke every day at five o'clock, and the cast and crew would be in the local bar by five-fifteen. Jackie would hold court and Jerry would sing country songs into the wee smalls, but at six the next morning everybody would be on the set ready to go.

Hal saw a picture in a magazine of a 1976 Pontiac Trans Am, the model with the T-top and the gold Thunder Chicken decal on the hood. He thought I'd look cool in one, and that it might make a good product placement, so we went to Pontiac and they gave us four Trans Ams for me and two LeManses for Jackie's cruiser. We wrecked 'em all. When a car couldn't run anymore, we kept it handy to scavenge parts. For the last scene we filmed, the one Trans Am we had left wouldn't start and we had to push it into the shot.

After *Smokey* came out, Trans Am sales went up 700 percent, and the president of Pontiac promised me a new one every year for life. A few years later a car didn't come. I didn't want to complain, but I thought something might have happened in delivery, so I called Pontiac and spoke to a very businesslike lady.

"Excuse me," I said, "this is Burt Reynolds. I guess there's been a mix-up. The Trans Am didn't arrive. Maybe it went to the wrong place."

"No," she said, "we didn't send one."

"Well," I said, "I don't mean to be pushy, but the president of the company said I'd get one every year."

"We have a new president now," she said. "It was our former president who made the promise, the one who *likes* your movies."

THE *SMOKEY* CAST and crew were watching rushes one night and a couple of the outtakes were hysterical.

"Hal," I said, "what if we run these at the end of the movie?"

"Ya think?" he said.

"Yeah," I said. "The great thing about it is that everybody's in character, so you're not hurting the movie. The audience finds out that these people laugh at each other."

So that's what Hal did. Instead of putting *The End* after the last scene, he let the screen go black and rolled outtakes next to the credits. For a long time afterward, everybody was doing it.

We did something else that wasn't done. We broke the fourth wall between the actor and the audience. I got behind the wheel of the Trans Am and eased into frame. I stopped in front of the camera, looked into the lens, and winked. I was saying to the people, "I hope you're having as much fun as we are."

And I meant it. It was the best time I ever had making a movie.

UNIVERSAL DECIDED to open *Smokey and the Bandit* at Radio City Music Hall in New York. We told them they were crazy, but they went ahead and it didn't make enough money to pay the Rockettes. They went to plan B and opened it wide in the South, and it found its audience.

I was in Florida when *Smokey* opened there. I wondered if anybody would go to see it, so one night I slipped into a mall theater that had five screens. *Smokey* was playing on all five, and there was a line around the block. With word of mouth behind it, *Smokey* was a smash hit. Universal was amazed at the business it did everywhere, including in Boston, Philadelphia, and even New York.

I've always been blue-collar, not white-collar. I can count on one hand the times I've played a college graduate. But I've played a lot of Southerners, from Lewis Medlock to Bo Darville, and I hated the labels the critics gave my films, like "hick flicks" and "redneck movies." They thought the IQ of everyone who saw them dropped ten points. This made me angry. They weren't "hick flicks," they were movies about the South.

Lots of movies ridiculed Southerners, and I resented them. I wanted to play a Southern hero, a guy who was proud of being from the South. *Smokey* gave me the chance to do that. And to make a movie for people in "flyover country"—the Midwest, the Northwest, and especially the South. Most of those folks are middle-of-the-road, not left or right. They believe in God, they work hard, and they love their country. They're the people I grew up with, and I like them.

Most of the critics panned *Smokey*. The best reviews came from the audience, and the only movie that grossed more that year was *Star Wars*. So if you want to know about a film, don't read the reviews, listen to the word of mouth from people who've seen it.

Alfred Hitchcock was quoted as saying—and his daughter later confirmed it—that *Smokey and the Bandit* was his favorite movie. But Billy Bob Thornton had the last word. "You know," he said, "down South, we consider *Smokey and the Bandit* a documentary."

Sally Field

When I told Universal that I wanted Sally Field for *Smokey and the Bandit*, they said, "Why would you want the goddamn Flying Nun?"

"Because she has talent," I said.

"She isn't ready to star in a feature film, and she isn't sexy."

"You don't understand," I said. "Talent is sexy."

The execs still weren't convinced, so I went to Lew Wasserman again, and he made it happen.

When I called Sally to ask her to be in the picture, she wasn't exactly thrilled. "I know your movies are commercial, but it's not the kind of thing I want to do," she said. "Then again, my agents tell me I need a commercial movie . . ."

I wasn't exactly overjoyed at her reaction, but I decided to take it as a left-handed compliment.

We didn't meet until the first rehearsal, and I was taken with her immediately. She was strong and funny and spectacular in the cold reading.

One of the things people say about *Smokey* is that you watch two people fall in love on the screen, and it's true. If ever the old cliché "chemistry" applied . . . I mean, the sexual tension was bouncing off the walls! But there was friction, too. Throughout the filming, Sally would get pissed off because we weren't doing the work. She hated that we were giggling and laughing and never saying the dialogue in the script. I tried to make her laugh in a scene whenever I could, and I succeeded now and then. It was a big deal for her to break character like that, because she was such a pro. She'd get mad at herself and mad at me because, I think, she was afraid of it.

"There's no script here!" she'd say.

"We'll wing it," I'd say.

"I'm not from the improv school!" she'd say.

"Trust me," I'd say.

And she did, a little. She loosened up to the point that in one scene, out of nowhere, she broke into a marvelous improvisation. We were in the car, and she put her feet on the windshield and started dancing and talking about how she'd always wanted to be in a play. She went on and on with funny, open-book kind of stuff that was brave and real. That's when I realized I was falling in love.

SALLY GREW UP in Hollywood. Her mother was an actress and her dad was an army officer. They divorced when Sally was four, and her mom married the actor-stuntman Jock Mahoney. Jock had doubled for Errol Flynn, and I remembered one incredible stunt he did in *Adventures of Don Juan* (1948). He's at the top of a staircase sword fighting, and a bunch of guys run up the stairs to get him. He dives off, flies through the air, lands on three guys, gets up, and fights his way out. The first time I saw it on the screen, I knew it was a lot tougher to do and a lot more dangerous than it looked.

It was hard for me to hate Jock because I had such respect for him as a professional. But I was angry at the way he'd treated Sally.

There were two girls, Sally and Jock's natural daughter, Princess. Jock treated her . . . well . . . like a princess. When he wasn't being mean to Sally, he was ignoring her. Until she started winning awards. That pissed me off. And I can't prove it, but he may have been physically abusive. Sally never said so, but I could read between the lines.

While we were together, I tried to guide Sally's career, and one day she asked me to read a script. "What do you think?" she said.

"Nomination!" I said. "This is your chance to stick it in their ear and show what you can do. Don't pass it up."

The script was *Norma Rae* (1979), and it would be her breakout film.

Then again, I also advised her to do *Beyond the Poseidon Adventure* (1979). I thought she needed to do another commercial film to balance it all out. It was one of those "disaster" pictures that was guaranteed to make money. She did it reluctantly, and she was not happy with me or with her performance.

Sally has spent most of her professional life working for respect. She started in television, first as *Gidget* (1965–66) and then as *The Flying Nun* (1967–70), and spent the next ten years trying to live those roles down. That explains why, when she won her second Oscar, for *Places in the Heart* (1984), she said, "I haven't had an orthodox career, and I've wanted more than anything to have your respect. The first time I didn't feel it, but this time I feel it—and I can't deny the fact that you like me, right now, you like me!" She was making a reference to a line in *Norma Rae,* but nobody got the joke, and Sally got slammed for it. To make it worse, people misquoted her as saying, "You like me, you *really* like me!" That line has been dogging her ever since.

Since then, I think her acting has been interesting and full of truth. I just wish she'd work more often. It may have something to do with the lack of roles for older women, but Sally's not *like* a lot

John Bassett
and Donald Trump

In 1982, John Bassett had a vision for a new professional football league at a time when the NFL had a monopoly and a reputation as a stodgy, "no-fun" league. John wanted to make pro football fun again. He cofounded the United States Football League and formed a team in Tampa Bay, Florida. I became a partner and we took the name Bandits, after *Smokey and the Bandit*.

John had been one of the founders of both World TeamTennis and the World Football League, where he made a landmark deal to bring Miami Dolphins superstars Jim Kiick, Paul Warfield, and Larry Csonka to the league. The WFL lasted only two seasons, and John's franchise went belly-up. He could have declared bankruptcy, but he insisted on paying off all the team's debts.

The USFL began play in 1983. John's idea was to play in the spring, the NFL's off-season, both to satisfy hard-core football fans suffering from withdrawal and to avoid competing directly with the established league.

The Bandits got off to a fast start. John had learned a lot from his WFL experience and was determined to do things the right way in the USFL. He hired the famous Florida Gators quarterback Steve Spurrier to his first head-coaching job in professional football. Steve assembled a team of guys who dreamed of being pro football players but couldn't make the cut in the NFL. Some of them were real bandits—when they weren't playing football, they were doing time—which gave the team a certain swagger. Not the most talented bunch, but they had plenty of guts. It was a lot like *The Longest Yard*.

John was a showman. He wanted the Bandits to be fun to watch, and he made what came to be called Bandit Ball colorful and unpredictable. It was a wide-open, freewheeling style of football played in fan-friendly Tampa Stadium, affectionately known as "The Big Sombrero."

They weren't just football games, they were happenings. There was always some kind of promotion: We had a Dolly Parton lookalike contest, a mortgage-burning night, and whenever the team scored, our masked mascot, Bandit, galloped across the field on his trusty steed Smokey. I went to all the games and did publicity for the team whenever and wherever I could. Jerry Reed wrote and recorded the fight song, and Loni Anderson appeared on billboards wearing a Bandits jersey with the team motto: *All the fun the law allows*.

Bandit Ball was a hit. The team drew forty thousand fans a game, got good TV ratings, and had a winning record. We were more popular than Tampa Bay's NFL franchise, the Buccaneers. Some of the other USFL teams weren't so successful, but the exciting championship game the first year between the Michigan Panthers and Philadelphia Stars was a welcome change from the boring NFL Super Bowls, and it lifted the whole league.

Unfortunately, some of the USFL franchises were underfunded and some of the owners weren't exactly sportsmen. There are always guys who come out of the woodwork and take everything they can get. Donald Trump was one such offender. He swooped in and bought the New Jersey Generals. He wanted us to go head-to-head with the NFL and play our games in the fall. But we weren't near the quality level of the NFL and couldn't compete with them for fans or advertisers. John and I both told that to Donald: "You can't go against the NFL. It's too big of an apple." We tried to convince him that the USFL should stand alone and continue to play in the spring, when the NFL was inactive.

John and Donald were both rich kids, but that's where the similarity ended. Donald was born on third and thought he hit a triple. John was the son of a Canadian media mogul, but it didn't turn him into a jerk. He worked hard to build his own fortune without help from his father. Unlike Donald, he'd been a jock himself, having played college football and high-level tennis as a member of the Canadian Davis Cup team. He had a permanent limp from multiple knee operations. (John's daughter Carling was quite an athlete, too. At the age of sixteen she came out of nowhere to make the finals in the WTA Championships and then won a tournament in France. And she was a real character. She reminded me of a lot of jocks I knew who didn't always abide by the rules but gave everything they had in competition.)

John wanted to keep improving the quality of play and grow the USFL into something that would someday rival the NFL. Donald didn't have John's vision or passion for the game. He admitted that he came into the league intending to move the games to the fall to compete directly with the NFL. I had the feeling that instead of trying to develop the brand, Donald was angling for a merger with the NFL so he could wind up with an NFL franchise for a song.

In my opinion, it was Donald's fault that the USFL didn't survive. Now don't get me wrong. I like Donald. I hold on to my wallet when we shake hands, but I like him. I just think his personal ambition sank the USFL. He was interested in only two things: money and publicity. John summed it up when he said that Donald's "ego transcended his business sense." (In the years since, every time Donald runs for president, I pray he never gets the chance to do to the USA what he did to the USFL.)

When John got sick with cancer, the way he broke it to me was typical of his dark humor. I called to say that I was coming to Canada to do a film and that I hoped we could spend time together.

"I may not be around, pal," he said.

"Oh? Where are you going?"

"I'll be dead. I've got a couple of inoperable tumors."

Within a month he died of brain cancer. He was forty-seven.

I think John might have held the league together, but after he died, Donald was like a shark in a tank full of guppies. The other owners were in awe of him because he'd made a lot of money in real estate. But he knew nothing about football. Donald won the battle, but we all lost the war. The NFL didn't want him or anyone else from the USFL, and our league folded after the third season.

Almost two hundred USFL players went to the NFL, including marquee names like Steve Young, Mike Rozier, Reggie White, Brian Sipe, Doug Flutie, and the great Jim Kelly, who was the toughest guy we had. Forget that he was a quarterback, he thought he was a tackle. He went to the Buffalo Bills and became the first former USFL player to make it into the Hall of Fame. The USFL pioneered the instant replay challenge, the two-point conversion, and the overhead suspended camera, all of which were later adopted by the NFL. Above all, I think the NFL took the lesson that they needed to make their "product" more exciting.

John Bassett was gallant and brave. He wasn't afraid to gamble everything on what he believed in. If he lost, he went out and made more money and started again. I'll always remember him as a true sportsman with an old-fashioned sense of honor and a deep respect for athletes. Because of him, a lot of people still remember the USFL fondly.

Charles Nelson Reilly

When I told my dad I wanted to be an actor, he said, "If you ever bring any of those sissy boys around here, I'll shoot 'em and make a rug out of 'em for your mother." At the end of his life, whenever he saw Charles, he kissed him on the cheek. Dad always called him Chuck, because Charles had this other personality. He'd affect a deep voice and introduce himself to some of the real butch guys I knew, including my dad, as Chuck Reilly. Dad must have known that Charles was gay, but he never talked about it. He just looked at him kind of sideways. And then one day he said, "You know, I like Chuck. He's a good guy." That was high praise coming from Big Burt.

Our 150-acre spread in Jupiter was a working ranch complete with livestock. We had a few head of cattle and we were loaded with horses. The first time I brought Charles around, Dad said, "Do you ride?"

"Like the wind!" Charles said.

So they went down to the corral. A young man walked by who could have been played by Brad Pitt. (Charles had the habit of saying who would play the people in his stories. You knew how he felt about them by who he would "cast.") "Brad Pitt" was leading a beautiful stallion.

"That's some stud, isn't it, Chuck?" my father said.

"The horse isn't bad, either," Charles said.

I met Charles in 1957, when I was in a Broadway revival of *Mister Roberts* (directed by John Forsythe and starring Charlton Heston as Roberts, Orson Bean as Pulver, and Fred Clark as Doc) and he came backstage after the show.

Charles was a great raconteur. Everything reminded him of a story. He acted out all the parts and could go for half an hour without ever touching on his topic. But he was never boring. He was one of the best guests on *The Tonight Show*. If he was on the panel, all the guests could relax. You'd do three spots with him before you realized that you'd bumped two other guests. He lived near the NBC studios in Burbank and they'd call him at the last minute to replace no-shows.

Charles was a marvelous performer. His autobiographical one-man show, *Save It for the Stage: The Life of Reilly*, cowritten and directed by Paul Linke, was brilliant. In it he talked a lot about his childhood in Hartford, Connecticut.

Though Charles was a man of the theater, he never sat in an audience. It went back to a horrible childhood experience: One hot July afternoon in 1944, when Charles was thirteen, he went to the circus in Hartford. Eight thousand people were crowded under a 500-foot-long big top to watch a matinee performance of the Ringling Bros. and Barnum & Bailey Circus.

Twenty minutes into the show, with the Great Wallendas on the high wire, flames began crawling up the sidewall of the tent toward the roof, which had been waterproofed with paraffin and gasoline. When the roof ignited, there was an explosion that turned the big top into an inferno. In the chaos, people were trampled to death and others fell from the bleachers. It took only ten minutes for the tent to burn to the ground. In what is still one of the worst fire disasters in U.S. history, almost two hundred people were killed and hundreds more—mostly women and children—were badly burned or seriously injured.

Charles got out unharmed, but he could never sit in any kind of auditorium for the rest of his life. He joked that he should join Audiences Anonymous, but he was deeply scarred.

Charles had another demon: his Swedish mother. She was hell on wheels and scared everybody to death. When he was growing up, she had an arsenal of racial and ethnic insults that she would rain down on passersby from her apartment window. She was so unpopular in the neighborhood that she had to take a baseball bat whenever she went out.

"I spent my adolescence in an Ingmar Bergman movie," Charles said.

I met her once, backstage at one of Charles's shows. She was General MacArthur in a dress.

I think Charles was underrated as an actor. Maybe it was because he was on so many game shows. But long before he ever did *The Match Game* or *The Hollywood Squares*, he'd created unforgettable roles on Broadway in *Bye Bye Birdie* and *Hello, Dolly!* and won a Tony for the role of Bud Frump in *How to Succeed in Business Without Really Trying*.

Charles studied acting with Uta Hagen and became a wonderful teacher himself at the Herbert Berghof Studio in New York. He also trained to be an opera singer, but the voice wasn't there. Whenever we talked about it, I'd say, "I don't understand opera," and he'd say, "I didn't either." But that wasn't true. He wrote and directed operas and was a commentator on Metropolitan Opera radio broadcasts.

Charles directed Julie Harris in *The Belle of Amherst* and won a Tony nomination for directing her again in a revival of *The Gin Game*. He also directed a bunch of TV shows, including quite a few *Evening Shade* episodes.

And, of all things, Charles was a yachtsman! He always had a big boat. People would laugh and say, "No way will I go out on the water with *him*," but he was a good captain. He even made a series of powerboat training films for the U.S. Coast Guard.

Charles never tried to conceal his gayness, but he never found it necessary to proclaim it, either. Early in his career a network executive dismissed him with the words, "They don't let queers on television." Maybe Charles did all those game shows to prove the guy wrong a thousand times over.

One night I took Charles to the fights. We visited the dressing room first and a guy came in wearing boxing headgear and Charles said, "That's *my* part." We sat in the front row. The chances of it happening are one in a million, but in the first round of the first fight, a boxer got knocked out of the ring and landed in our laps.

"Are we winning?" Charles said.

CHARLES DIRECTED, I think, seventeen shows at the Burt Reynolds Dinner Theatre. It surprised a lot of people who didn't know how talented he was.

When Charles first came to Jupiter to direct, I made a grand gesture. I had two houses on the beach, and I was in a generous mood when I said to him, "If you want this house, you can have it." I drove Charles to the house and said, "This is your home from now on." And then I couldn't get out of the car. It was the house I'd lived in with Sally and I couldn't go inside. Too many memories. Here I was trying to give him this wonderful present but couldn't show it to him.

"Can we do take two?" he said.

I tried, but I still couldn't go in. I felt terrible, but I couldn't help it. We sat there without speaking for a long time and I could see that he was getting impatient.

"Give me the keys," he said. "*I hardly knew her!*"

Loni and Quinton

About a year ago Loni Anderson decided that I should sell personal items to satisfy an old debt. She got a judge to order me to auction off the memorabilia I'd collected over the years, including my high school football trophies, my Emmy, my Golden Globe for *Boogie Nights*, my People's Choice Award, my autographed photos, my Western art. Those things meant a lot to me, and I didn't think it was fair that I had to part with them. But my lawyers told me I had no choice. I had to give it all up, so I held a yard sale in Las Vegas. I wouldn't have done it voluntarily, but now I'm glad I did. I'm a pack rat, and I had so much stuff it became a burden. Most of it didn't mean anything anymore. I was sick of so many pictures of myself in my own home, and who needs two dozen pairs of cowboy boots?

The auction turned out to be a liberating experience. Going in, I thought, If the stuff sells for half the estimates, I won't have to work for the rest of my life. As it turned out, many of the items went for three or four times the amount. That's nice, and not just for the money. It showed that people all over the world still think kindly of me.

I MET LONI on *The Merv Griffin Show.* I'd seen her on *WKRP in Cincinnati.* She's damn good at comedy, and the part of an intelligent blond was perfect for her. I'd never seen anyone quite so striking . . . but I was with Sally then, so that was the extent of it. I didn't see Loni again until a few years later, at an awards gala, after Sally and I had broken up. She asked me to dance and whispered in my ear, "I want to have your baby."

"Right here?" I said.

"You know what I mean," she said.

"Yeah, I know what you mean and I'm flattered, but don't you think we should find out if we like each other first?"

The truth is, I never did like her. We'd be together and she'd be gorgeous, though I always thought she wore too much makeup. It would be nice and all that, but I'd be thinking, This is not the person for me. What the hell am I doing with her? I don't remember actually asking her to marry me. There was just this pressure in that direction . . . coming from her direction. I kept telling her that we'd get married as soon as I finished building the chapel on my ranch. It took four years because I kept adding on. When it was finally done, I had no excuse.

So why did I marry her? Besides the physical attraction, it was the force of her personality. Her determination. It was something she wanted and she would not be denied. She was that way about everything. Anything she went after, she got. Did I have a choice? Of course I did. What was I thinking? Obviously, I wasn't thinking at all.

We had to make all the wedding arrangements in secret to fool the tabloids. The county clerk brought the marriage license to the house to save us a trip to the courthouse. We placed orders for the reception, like for the two tons of ice, in the name of one of my students. And we waited until the last minute to invite the guests.

On the way to the ceremony my best man, Vic Prinzi, said, "Do you really want to do this?"

"No, I don't," I said.

"Then let's get the hell out of here," he said. "We'll go to Miami."

"But my mom and dad are sitting there waiting for me. My mom loves Loni. It'll kill her."

"I hate to break this to you," Vic said, "but your mother can't stand Loni."

I paused in the doorway of the chapel. As I stood there looking at the assembled guests, Mom caught my eye. She was shaking her head NO.

But I didn't have the guts to pull the plug.

The Reverend Jess Moody performed the ceremony. Jim Nabors sang "The Lord's Prayer" and "Our Love Is Here to Stay." Bert Convy sang "Just the Way You Are." Some of my dearest friends were there, including Ann-Margret and her husband, Roger Smith.

After the reception, with press helicopters swarming like killer bees, Ann-Margret and Roger boarded a decoy chopper and flew to Miami, with the killer bees right behind them. Ann-Margret is fragile-looking, like a porcelain doll, but she's tough as nails. When they landed in Miami, they were met by a bunch of pissed-off paparazzi.

We'd jumped on our own helicopter and flew to Key West, where we boarded a 120-foot yacht loaned by a friend. We'd planned a cruise to the Bahamas, but Loni was seasick.

"Don't you think we should cast off first?" I said.

Instead of sailing to the Bahamas on the Atlantic, we turned around and motored up the Intracoastal Waterway back to Jupiter. Not a good omen.

It didn't help that we lived out our marriage in a fishbowl. To keep my sanity in the face of all the idiotic things that have been written about me, I've had to adopt a don't-give-a-damn attitude. And Dinah taught me that you can't treat the press like an enemy, even when they attack you.

But it can really sting. Rags like the *National Enquirer* don't care about the truth. They make things up out of whole cloth and dare you to sue them, because they know how hard it is for a public figure to win. Carol Burnett was one of the few to sue them successfully. The *Enquirer* reported that she was falling-down drunk in a Washington, D.C., restaurant and that she had a shouting match with Henry Kissinger. The truth was that she had a glass of wine and was introduced to Kissinger on her way out of the restaurant. She spent a lot of time and money to win a retraction and $150,000, which didn't cover her legal fees.

As Carol said, it's a shame we don't have a system where the losing team has to pay the winning team's lawyers. But she did accomplish one thing: The paper left her alone after that.

The *Enquirer* was headquartered in Lantana, about twenty-five miles from Jupiter. They bragged about how they had the tallest Christmas tree in the United States, and tourists came from everywhere to see it. On Christmas Eve my pilot and I loaded a bucket of horseshit under my helicopter, flew over the *Enquirer* building, and dropped it on the tree. I thought it was fitting, given the crap they were writing about us.

THE FIRST TIME I called Loni "The Countess," she beamed, and from then on it was in her contract.

She bought everything in triplicate, from everyday dresses to jewelry to china and linens. She bought designer gowns for ten thousand dollars a pop and wore them only once. "I never wear a dress after it's been photographed," she said. "I have to dress like a star."

I gave her a platinum American Express card with a $45,000 credit limit. She maxed it out in half an hour. Her spending was plunging me into debt, but my attitude was, whatever makes her happy is okay. But eventually the well ran dry.

We called it quits after five years of marriage. When we announced the separation, the press went into high gear. Princess Diana sent me a thank-you note for keeping her off the cover of *People* magazine. For a long time after the divorce, the tabloids were still calling Loni and me "cheesecake and beefcake."

The worst part of the divorce was losing custody of Quinton. He was only six at the time, and the judge decided he'd be better off with his mother. We got Quinton when he was three days old. We named him for Quint Asper, my character in *Gunsmoke*, and for the great Quentin Reynolds, the radio journalist I idolized when I was a boy.

I fell in love the second I laid eyes on Quinton. I took him everywhere with me, carrying him around like a football. I didn't want to let go of him. When it came to showing affection, I was determined to be the opposite of my dad. I was always demonstrative with Quinton and made sure he knew how much I loved him. It would embarrass him sometimes when I'd hug and kiss him, but he got used to it and I think he even came to like it.

Quinton knew he was adopted from an early age because somebody close to us decided to tell him so. He never asked me about it. If he had, I would have said, "I was lucky. I got to pick you." He was a bright child with a precocious sense of humor. One Sunday when he was four or five, I got up late, and when I walked into the kitchen he said, "Daddy! What are you doing up? It's still daylight."

When Quinton was in preschool he learned to say the blessing for lunch: "God is great, God is good." One day I was driving him and a friend home from school and gave them a snack of peanut butter and jelly sandwiches. The other boy said, "Wait! We gotta say, 'God is great, God is good,' and Quinton said, "It's only a sandwich."

When he was twelve he said, "When you go to an actor's house, there's a picture of the actor and other actors. If you go to a producer's house, there are Picassos. I think I'll be a producer."

I tried to keep him out of the spotlight when he was growing up, and the last thing I wanted was for him to have his heart broken in show business. But he wound up in the business after all, as a film editor, and he's doing great. He edited his first picture in 2011, and the film editor Nick McLean, who I've worked with a lot over the years, made Quinton an assistant editor. He's done several films with Nicky in the last couple of years.

It's been hard because he lives in California, across the street from his mother. I don't think he's heard the greatest things in the world from her about me. We talk on the phone, but it's not a great relationship. I love him so much and I think he loves me. It's just hard. When I'm in L.A., we have dinner, but we don't get to spend as much time as I'd like to.

Quinton never had the chance to know my dad. He met him when he was little, he sat on his grandfather's lap and all that stuff, and Big Burt thought Quinton was terrific, but they didn't bond the way I would have liked.

Big Burt never told me I was a man, but Quinton did.

One of the hardest things I ever had to do was tell Quinton that Loni and I were separating. We went for a walk on the beach, but I couldn't say it. Finally, Quinton looked up at me and said, "Daddy, is the dance over?"

"That's right," I said. "Mommy and I started the dance together, but the dance is over and now she's going to her side and I'm going to mine."

"It'll be all right, Daddy," he said. "You're a man."

Ossie Davis

Hattie McDaniel was the first African-American to win an Academy Award. It was a Supporting Actress Oscar for playing a slave in *Gone with the Wind* (1939), and she had to sit in the back of the auditorium at the awards ceremony. It was more than twenty years before Sidney Poitier became the first black to star in a Hollywood film and the first since Hattie McDaniel to win an Oscar (for *Lilies of the Field* in 1963).

When I was studying acting in New York in the 1950s, there were blacks in my acting class, and coming from the South, I was surprised they were working in the theater and stunned to see them playing "white" parts. Growing up watching movies, I was used to seeing African-Americans only playing slaves or domestics.

There was a young black actor named Ossie Davis in the class, and I was so impressed by his talent and his manner, I tried to do as many scenes with him as I could. We became friends, and Ossie told me that he always felt he had to conduct himself with dignity because he knew that whenever he was seen, he would be judged.

Like everybody else, I had a crush on Ossie's wife, Ruby Dee, and I tried to do every scene I could with her, too. (I don't think Ossie was crazy about that.) Ruby was a talented actor and a wonderful person, and she and Ossie were devoted to each other. Their marriage lasted almost sixty years, until Ossie's death in 2005.

I once told Ossie that at Florida State I was the fastest guy on the team in the 100, 220, and 440.

"How many blacks did you have?" he said.

"None," I said.

"Well," he said, "that might have had something to do with it."

When I was growing up in Florida, football, along with just about everything else, was segregated. There were white schools and black schools, and they didn't play against each other. At Palm Beach High we played our games on Friday night. The black high school, Roosevelt, played on Saturday night, and I went to their games. I'd be the only white in the stands. The black students returned the favor by coming to my games, though they had to sit in the end zone. If I scored a touchdown, I'd go over and throw them the ball. The place would go crazy, because you weren't supposed to do that. People kept telling me to stop making waves.

I didn't play against a black player until college, and even then almost all the teams were completely white, and there were no black coaches. Jake Gaither was legendary in our part of the country. As head coach of the all-black Florida A&M University from 1945 to 1969, he invented the split-T formation and was a great motivator of players. "I like my boys to be agile, mobile, and hostile," he liked to say.

Gaither won six black college national championships and achieved an incredible .844 winning percentage, to this day one of the all-time best records of any college football coach. But he could never get a job at a white university.

OSSIE USED TO tell me, "You know, you're the only actor in the world liked by both African-Americans and the Ku Klux Klan." I didn't like to think that the Klan part was true, and I wanted to remove any doubt about where I stood.

Early in 1965, I asked Ossie if I could join the planned march from Selma, Alabama, to the state capital of Montgomery to protest the state's denial of voting rights to African-Americans.

"Of course you can," he said. "But are you sure you want to get involved? You might lose friends."

"The hell with 'em!" I said.

As the date approached, it turned out that I had to go to Thailand first, to shoot *Operation C.I.A.* When the production wrapped, instead of going home I flew straight to Alabama, but when I landed in Birmingham I collapsed and wound up in the hospital.

At first the doctors thought it was Hodgkin's disease, but they eventually diagnosed schistosomiasis—snail-parasite eggs in the bloodstream! I'd almost certainly contracted it shooting a fight scene in a polluted Thai river. The problem was, the eggs were beginning to hatch. They brought in a microscope and showed me the little buggers wriggling around in my blood. It might not have been so severe, they said, if I'd had a spleen to purify my blood. Luckily, a cure for schistosomiasis had been discovered a few years before. They gave me a series of shots and I gradually recovered, but not in time for the historic march.

IF THERE'S ANY CONFUSION about my birthplace, it's my fault. I was born in Lansing, Michigan. We moved to Florida when I was five. I grew up a Southern boy who didn't want to be a Yankee, so for a long time I told people that I was born in Waycross, Georgia.

Why Waycross, Georgia? I liked the sound of it.

I still live in Florida. That's where I feel at home. Though I thrived on the excitement of New York when I was starting out as an actor, I was never comfortable living there. And I wasn't crazy about L.A. I prefer the South. I feel about it the same way I feel about America: I love it, but there are things about it I'd like to change.

I NEVER GOT into golf and never wanted to. I don't understand why people are so passionate about it. But I occasionally used to sneak on a local course and play nine holes, more for the walking than the game itself. The members would see me and they didn't seem to care; some of them were downright friendly.

One day I took football greats Bernie Casey and Rosey Grier with me as my "guests" and we played the back nine. A couple of days later two club members came by and said, "You're welcome to play if you join and pay dues, but we don't want any of your friends."

"What do you mean by that?" I asked, knowing full well what they meant. I just wanted to make them say it.

"We think you know what we mean."

"No, I don't," I said. "Tell me. Does it have anything to do with the color of their skin?"

They didn't answer. They just politely excused themselves and left.

I never went back. I was damned if I'd sneak into a place like that.

EVENING SHADE (1990–1994) was the most satisfying thing I've done on television. Ossie hadn't done a sitcom, and when I called to ask him to be on the show, his response was poetic. "I'm afraid I'm too heavy," he said. "My feet are too big and my head is too solid. I can't float on the surface that the sitcom tends to generate."

Fortunately, Ossie overcame his reluctance, and he became the backbone of the show. Whenever my character had a problem, he'd go to Ossie's Ponder Blue character for advice and he'd have the answer. Ossie was like that in real life, too.

The budget was high because of the quality of the cast. Marilu Henner played my wife and Hal Holbrook played her newspaper-publisher father. Charley Durning was the cranky town doctor, with Ann Wedgeworth as his wife. Ossie played the owner of the barbecue joint where we all hung out, and he was also the narrator of the show. When he summed up every episode at the end, it was like hearing the voice of God. We were also lucky to have Elizabeth Ashley, Michael Jeter, and a young Hilary Swank.

Hillary Clinton, then the first lady of Arkansas, was a friend of the producers, Harry Thomason and Linda Bloodworth-Thomason. Hillary suggested we name the show *Evening Shade*, after an actual town in the state, but it was really based on the small town in Missouri where Linda Thomason grew up.

Linda was a brilliant writer. She wrote the pilot and about every third or fourth show herself, and you could always recognize her episodes because they were funny and had lots of heart. And she knew how to write for an actor's rhythms.

As the creative force behind the show, Linda supervised all the scripts, and she was open to suggestions. She even let us improvise a little. At one point early in the series I ad-libbed a line and the script girl told Linda about it and she said, "That's all right, he writes 'em better than I do anyway." I'd never, ever heard her give me a compliment like that. It was so generous. I was floored . . . and grateful.

We'd have a meeting and she'd say, "We need a joke here." And I'd make a suggestion and she'd say, "That's great!" and we'd do it. I'd meet with the writers every Monday and we would talk about what I thought might be a good story for each character. Like Jim Arness on *Gunsmoke*, I wanted everyone to have a show.

With the exception of *The Tonight Show*, *Evening Shade* was the first time I worked in front of a live audience and I loved it. Everything seemed to click. We'd do a run-through with an audience as a kind of dress rehearsal, and it was usually so good we didn't do a second one.

I stayed friends with everybody in the cast. I talk to Marilu all the time. Fabulous girl. She's got that twinkle in her eye and she knows how to twist men around her finger. I always had fun with her and have always thought she's one of the sexiest women in the world. We used to say to each other that we just missed. When she was going with somebody I was loose, and when I was going with somebody she was loose, so we never got together. When she started having kids she told me, "I waited as long as I could, but you didn't ask me."

The character I played in *Evening Shade*, Wood Newton, is me. Making him a coach was my idea. If I hadn't been an actor, I'd have been a football coach. I love football, and I love young people and think I can communicate with them. But I didn't want Wood to be a successful coach. He'd been All Pro himself, but you can't coach without decent players, and he never won a game the whole time we were on the air. I also wanted him to be an ex–Pittsburgh Steeler because they were tough guys and I had friends on the team. Terry Bradshaw and some of his teammates even came on the show, and it was great fun. We also got Bobby Bowden to come on.

Bobby was one of the greatest college football coaches of all time. In his thirty-three seasons at Florida State, he won two national titles and twelve Atlantic Coast Conference championships. His career record of 377-129-4 is second only to Joe Paterno's of Penn State. One of the keys to his success is that he was a father figure to a lot of his players who didn't have dads in their lives. He had outlaws on his teams, but they behaved themselves because he was a straight arrow with them.

Just as we were about to shoot Bobby's episode, the director told me, "He doesn't know his lines!" I got the cast together and said, "If he messes up his words, just go with it." And they did, and he was wonderful.

Afterward Bobby said, "I ought to do more of these shows!"

THE THOMASONS had a big hit with *Designing Women* (1986–93) and wanted to do something that showed that not all Southerners are rednecks. They wanted the warm relationships of Andy Griffith's Mayberry, but with a layer of sophistication. The way we treated Ossie and the way he treated us was different from anything I'd ever seen on television. Nobody seemed to notice he was black, and that's the way it should be.

Jack Horner

Boogie Nights revived my career, but I did my best not to do it. In 1997, a twenty-seven-year-old director named Paul Thomas Anderson called to say he was making a film about the porn industry and that he wanted me to play Jack Horner, a director of adult films. I thought that glamorizing pornography was a terrible idea, and I told him so. But he kept calling. And I kept turning him down.

Finally, just to get rid of him, I agreed to a meeting. He came to my hotel room and I said, "Look, you don't get it. The answer is NO!" He made a smart-ass remark, and I blew up. At the end of my tirade he said, "If you can do that in the movie, you'll get nominated for an Academy Award."

His composure impressed me as much as what he said.

At first I didn't like Jack Horner, and not just because of how he makes his living. I don't respect a man who doesn't respect women. And I still didn't like the subject matter of the film. But I liked the challenge. I thought about it and finally decided that a real actor should be able to play any role, so I went after it with everything that I had.

But it *was* a challenge. It took a long time and a lot of work to "get" the character. I searched for something positive in him: a sense of humor, a desire to do good work even though deep down he knew it wasn't appreciated. I began to think of *Boogie Nights* as a family saga, with Jack as the father figure. I think he enjoyed that role. He also thought of himself as an artist. I suppose he was also a voyeur, but I didn't want to admit it. I didn't realize it when I finally had him. I never talked to anyone about it, but one day I noticed that people were looking at me differently.

Paul was mild-mannered and kept a loose rein on the set, without letting anyone forget that he was in charge. We had disagreements, but none of them were his fault, they were mine. I just couldn't say the lines he wanted me to say. I couldn't say, "Okay, fuck her in the ass." I asked for a meeting with Paul and our producer, John Lyons.

"I don't think I can deliver that line," I said.

"Well, we'll be here until you can," Paul said.

"Can't we do it another way?"

"No, I like it the way it is."

I thought, Where did *this* hard-ass come from? But I tried to reason with him. "I can *say* the line, but I don't think I can say it very well, because I'm not comfortable with it, and I thought that since you wrote it, you might have another way of doing it."

"No, I don't. You'll have to find a way to say it as written. It's what you were hired for."

That's when John Lyons grabbed my arm before I could punch Paul in the face. I'm glad he stepped in and thanked him for it later. I took a day off and came to the conclusion that I wasn't going to win the argument, so I went back and said the line.

I have to admit that it wasn't easy working with such a young director. After hundreds of TV shows and dozens of feature films, I wasn't crazy about being told to turn left at the couch by a guy who's younger than some sandwiches I've had. On the other hand, it was refreshing to find a young filmmaker with a sense of the history of our business. Paul knows every camera angle in every picture John Ford ever made. The first shot in *Boogie Nights* is one of the longest in movie history . . . on purpose.

"Have you timed this?" I asked him. "It's longer than *Citizen Kane!*"

"As a matter of fact," he said, "it's three seconds longer."

Paul's knowledge of old Hollywood came out all the time, and he could be just a little pompous with it. I learned not to get into arguments with him about classic films, even though I fancy myself a movie buff. I don't want to say he was opinionated, but if Bogdanovich had a son, it would be him. By the same token, we weren't likely to discuss yesterday's football game, because as far as I could tell, he wasn't interested in sports.

I think Paul treated me differently from the rest of the cast, I guess because of the age difference, and as we went along I was less and less thrilled about going to work every day. But he pulled me through the picture. I wouldn't have wanted him to know that, but I guess he will now. In some ways he's very talented. Most of his pictures are good. He just isn't my kind of director.

Some people have said that the characters in *Boogie Nights* are pathetic. Not on moral grounds, but because they're just clueless, and I think that's true. As actors, we were floating around trying to figure out what we were doing there because, I think, the characters themselves are lost souls. Which makes the performances of my fellow cast members all the more remarkable. I'd never met a lot of them and never *heard* of a few, but I was astonished by their talent. I felt comfortable with them from the first reading, when Mark Wahlberg sat down next to me and said, "How are ya, Dad?"

I like Mark. At one point he was having a tough time, which made him do strange things. He got very Methody and was walking around the set with a fake erection all the time. I stopped him and said, "What the hell are you doing? You're a good actor. Just act." I think he was wounded because we had that father-son relationship. I didn't mean to hurt him, but at the same time I didn't want to see him go that route because I like him so much. Mark is a talented guy who doesn't need gimmicks. I'm glad he's proven what he can do in a bunch of films since *Boogie Nights*.

Julianne Moore is wonderful in everything she does. Off-camera she's exactly like she seems: Bambi's mother. Sweet. Dear. Just lovely. People ask me about the relationship between Jack and Julianne's character, Amber Waves. I think he's in love with her, as much as he can love anybody. But he's selfish. He fakes it a lot.

I think one of the key scenes in the movie is when Philip Baker Hall (Floyd Gondolli) and Jack have a showdown in Jack's office about whether to switch from film to video. Floyd wants to go to video because it's more profitable. Jack wants to stick with film because, in a funny way, he's a purist. I got away from the script but Paul kept it, I think because I was basically quoting something I'd heard him say. I went for it as strongly as I could and Philip stayed right there with me. He's a fine actor and I enjoyed working with him.

Philip Seymour Hoffman is shattering in the role of a young gay man who's struggling to come to terms with himself. Philip was a magnificent actor and his early death was a tragic loss.

And, just like in the film, Heather Graham, as Rollergirl, wore the roller skates the whole time: at lunch, in her trailer . . . all the time. But no bra. I was more enthralled with the skates. She'd come to the set with half her clothes off. I don't think I'm a prude, but I didn't find it sexy.

Ricky Jay, who plays Jack's cameraman, remembered something

that happened in the scene where Dirk Diggler and Jack Horner almost come to blows. Dirk has hit bottom with his cocaine addiction, and Jack gets angry and refuses to film him in his strung-out condition.

Jack: "You're high and you need to sleep it off. You've been up for two days."

Dirk: "You're not the boss of me!"

Jack: "Nevertheless . . ."

When we shot the scene, Ricky had to fight back a smile every time I said, "Nevertheless." We must have done ten takes before he could manage to keep a straight face. He later explained that when he was a boy he went to a football game and the announcer introduced "The Star-Spangled Banner": "Ladies and gentlemen, to sing our national anthem, Miss Helen Forrest."

At that moment some goon in the stands yelled, "Helen Forrest sucks cock!"

Without missing a beat the announcer said, "Nevertheless . . ."

I *liked* Ricky. He's a master sleight-of-hand artist. You stand two feet away and you can't catch a thing. And he's written some wonderful books about the great magicians.

I was proud of everybody's performance, but I almost went to the mat with Thomas Jane, who plays Dirk's friend Todd Parker. On the first day of rehearsal he was getting physical with people. When he put his martial arts moves on me I said, "Don't make the mistake of pushing me, because I push back."

He looked at me and laughed. "I think you're getting a little touchy," he said.

"Fuck you!" I quipped, and walked away.

John Lyons came to my trailer and said, "I know you don't like the guy, but can you please come back and finish the scene?"

"Yeah," I said. "I can finish it, but you're right: I don't like the guy."

THOUGH I'VE SEEN parts of *Boogie Nights*, I've never sat down and watched the whole thing. I asked family members not to see it and they didn't. A few of the jocks I know gave me grief about it, but it was all in fun. I think.

The picture got rave reviews and my performance was recognized with just about every award you could win, and people were predicting I'd win an Oscar. I sat next to Charley Durning at the ceremony. Best Supporting Actor is always the first award.

Just before the show went on the air, Charley said, "You wanna change seats with me so you can be on the outside?"

"No, what are you talking about?" I said.

"You're gonna get it tonight."

"Maybe. But who should I thank?" I was so excited my mind was empty.

"Thank *me*!" Charley said.

"That's a great idea," I said. "That's what I'll do, I'll thank *you*."

I changed seats with Charley so I was on the end of the row, all set to dash onto the stage to accept the golden statuette, when Mira Sorvino announced: "And the Oscar goes to . . . Robin Williams for *Good Will Hunting*."

I once said that I'd rather have a Heisman Trophy than an Oscar. I lied.

As Robin ran toward the stage, for some inexplicable reason I saluted him. He claimed I flipped him the bird.

Then I had to sit there for the next two hours with people patting me on the back and saying, "You should have won!" But Charley saved me. He grabbed my arm and said, "I made it through World War II. What the hell's this thing?"

That night I locked myself in my hotel room and shut off the phone to concentrate on feeling sorry for myself. Jon Voight called to commiserate, but per my instructions, the switchboard wouldn't put him through. Jon being Jon, he came to the hotel, borrowed a waiter's uniform, and carried a room service tray into the room. I was in bed with my face in a book and didn't notice him . . . until he threw himself on the bed and kissed me square on the mouth. It shocked me out of my funk and we spent the rest of the night laughing. Jon can always make me laugh.

Jocks

During my freshman year at Florida State, a teammate named Mercury Paskalakis told me he was going home to Tarpon Springs for the dive for the cross.

"What's that?" I said.

"A Greek Orthodox priest blesses the cross and throws it into Spring Bayou and about fifty guys dive for it," he said. "If you get the cross, you have good luck for a year."

"Can I go?" I said.

"Well, we'll have to tell them you're Greek," he said. "You can be my cousin, Buddy Paskalakis."

I mussed up my hair (I had enough of my own then to do that) so it looked curly and I did my best Robert Wagner imitation.

According to the rules we could dive as soon as the cross hit the water, but I figured if you did that you'd go past it, so I waited two seconds and then dove. I was underwater and saw it floating down. I grabbed it at the same time as another guy, but I was able to wrestle it away from him. Everybody congratulated me except the priest, who looked at me sideways. I think he suspected I wasn't Greek, but he didn't say anything. A few years later, when I began studying acting, I realized that Buddy Paskalakis had been my first role.

MAKING *THE LONGEST YARD* was a lot of fun. It was a treat to work with a bunch of guys who'd played pro ball: We had Sonny Sixkiller, a full-blooded Cherokee from Oklahoma who'd played in the WFL, and Joe Kapp, the former Minnesota Vikings quarterback. I loved Joe. You could hit him with a board and he'd just smile. He was great fun to be around and great fun to go out with if you didn't mind getting in trouble. Dino Washington was good, too. Big fullback for the Atlanta Falcons. Flashy. Terrific receiver. He made me look good when I threw passes that were by no means catchable . . . and he caught them.

Then there was Hall of Famer Ray Nitschke of the Green Bay Packers. Ray tried to make me cry. He hit me hard on every play. He liked to tackle me, take my head off, and run with it into the end zone. It didn't matter whether I had the ball or not. One time he tackled me on the way to my trailer. And you know that little round hole in the helmet that you're supposed to hear out of? I was looking out of it.

I said, "Ray, this isn't the Super Bowl."

"It is to me," he said.

I had a scene with Ray where I drop-kick the ball. Nobody had drop-kicked since Red Grange, so in the script he runs up and says, "What the hell is that?"

My line was "It was a dropkick, you stupid son of a bitch."

The first time we rehearsed the scene Ray said, "Don't call me that."

Ray took offense even though we were in character.

I went to Bob Aldrich and said, "Bob, I've got a situation here. I call Nitschke stupid in the scene, and I can't call him that because he doesn't like it."

"Don't say it in rehearsal," Bob said, "but say it in the take and then run."

That's exactly what I did. Ray chased me for twenty minutes.

THE THING YOU LEARN about Westerns: If the wrangler asks, "Do you ride, son?" you say, "No, sir. I've never been on a horse in my life," because if you say, "Like the wind," he goes, "Bring Fireball out."

The thing you have to learn when you play football in the movies is that you do not say, "I played college ball."

That's because there's a big difference between being a good athlete in high school or college and making it as a pro.

A few years after *The Longest Yard*, I made another football picture called *Semi-Tough* (1977) with Kris Kristofferson and Jill Clayburgh, directed by Michael Ritchie. On the first day I was getting five hundred pounds of tape and Kristofferson, who's a terrific actor and a hell of a guy, was getting taped up next to me and he said, "I think we can run against them. We're in the best shape of any forty-year-old actors in the world."

"Are you out of your mind?" I said. "Do you know who's out there on that field? Too Tall Jones, Hollywood Henderson, and the whole Dallas Cowboys defense, and they love to play a game called Kill the Actor."

"Nah," Kris said, "I think we can take 'em."

We went out and Too Tall came up to me and said, "You were great in *The Longest Yard*."

"Thank you, Too Tall," I said.

"You played at Florida State, right?" he said.

"No!" I said. "It was all bullshit! I was a drama major . . ."

That's when I heard Kris say, "I played at Pomona College."

I tried to get his attention to tell him to shut up, but he kept going.

"Went both ways. Wanted to play pro ball. Got a Rhodes Scholarship instead."

The first play was a sweep with me carrying the ball. When we broke the huddle, I looked up and there were nine guys on the line who had started in the Super Bowl. The center snapped the ball, the quarterback handed it off to me . . . and they all hit Kris!

They carried him off with two broken ribs. As he went by on the stretcher, I thought, Rhodes Scholar! We had to double him from then on. As it turned out, I had to practice every day and he didn't, so maybe he wasn't so dumb after all.

I WENT TO WIMBLEDON with Johnny Carson one year to watch Chris Evert in the semifinals. Afterward we all went out to dinner and everybody recognized Chris, but not Johnny. They didn't carry *The Tonight Show* in England. They'd tried it, but it didn't go over. Johnny claimed that he liked to travel because he wasn't recognized outside the United States, but I wasn't so sure. I think he was hurt that the show wasn't big over there.

A few months later I was at "21" and Chris was across the room with a girlfriend. The waiter came over and handed me a note from her: "You're staying at my hotel. Would you call me?" I sent back a note: "I didn't know you owned the hotel. But I shall call you tonight." I did and we started to go out and we had wonderful times together.

I played tennis with her once. I hadn't played growing up, but I was fast. I could make up for mistakes and run balls down. Everybody would laugh because I'd take the scenic route to the ball, but

I could get it back over the net, and after two games with Chris I was doing okay.

"I feel pretty good. I got three points," I said.

"Well," she said, "in that case I'll play you right-handed now."

I was furious. "How dare you do that to me?" I said.

"I thought you'd think it was fun," she said.

"It wasn't fun at all. I want you to play right-handed and I want you to play the best you can."

So she played right-handed, and I didn't win a point.

AT JUST UNDER SIX FEET and barely two hundred pounds, Rocky Marciano wasn't big for a heavyweight, but he was one of the greatest fighters who ever lived. He retired undefeated in 1956 with a perfect 49-0 record, including forty-three knockouts. I think he could have whipped every one of the heavyweights around today.

When I was fifteen, I met Rocky through an oilman in Palm Beach and we hit it off. He was great to talk to and a wonderful guy. I have no idea why he took an interest in me, but he did. Maybe it was because I was guileless. He started to talk about boxing and I said, "I'm sorry, but I don't know much about boxing, Rock, because I'm a football nut."

"That's okay, kid," he said. "Football's good. I'm sorry I never got to play it."

He got me into the Golden Gloves amateur boxing competition when I was sixteen. I'd read about it in the Miami papers and wanted to give it a try. He became my unofficial trainer. Before my first bout he said, "You box right-handed and you lead with your right, so he won't expect you to have a left. But you've got a great left hook, so just pepper 'im with your right and then bring that left out of nowhere. I guarantee you'll put 'im to sleep."

And that's exactly what happened! I had two more fights and scored two more knockouts with my phantom left. Then I quit. I knew it was only a matter of time before I got my ass whipped.

I asked Rocky and he said, "Yeah, kid, this would be a good time to retire."

Rocky lived in South Florida, and when I was older, we'd meet for a drink at Villa's restaurant in Fort Lauderdale. I went to the fights with him a couple of times and it was like going with Muhammad Ali. Everybody wanted to be around him.

Rocky had a high voice and short arms. I used to call him "alligator arms" . . . but not to his face. One night we were standing at the bar, and after I'd had a few vodka tonics, he didn't look so tough. I thought, His arms are so short . . . he's got that high voice . . . I could give him one shot and be champion of the world.

He narrowed his eyes and gave me a look that said, "Don't try it."

"How'd you know what I was thinking?" I said.

"I always know," he said.

Over the years I got to know Rocky's family, and I was happy to attend his daughter's confirmation party. We stayed friends until his death in 1969. He crashed in a small plane piloted by a guy who didn't know what he was doing. Rocky was only forty-five.

WHILE WE WERE SHOOTING *Hawk* in New York, there were so many fight scenes, we ran out of stuntmen, so they brought in a hairdresser they said was a great fighter. It turned out to be boxing champion Emile Griffith.

I'm not going to resolve the eternal debate over which sport has the best athletes, but I'll cast my vote for boxing. It takes the most stamina and endurance. If you don't believe it, try slugging a heavy bag for three minutes, take a minute off, and then repeat that sequence nine times and imagine someone punching you while you're doing it.

To be a good boxer you have to be agile enough to slip punches, you need great hand-eye coordination to be able to throw an accurate punch, you have to be durable enough to take a decent blow, and above all you have to have the nerve to get into the ring in the first place.

After the show I worked out with Emile at the gym and he gave me pointers.

And he told me his life story. Growing up fatherless in the Virgin Islands, he was sent to a reformatory, where he was sexually abused. He came to New York at the age of fifteen and was working in the garment district when he was discovered by the legendary trainer Gil Clancy, who made him a world champion.

Emile was a natural athlete and a fierce competitor, but he was also a sweet man, sensitive and childlike in many ways.

"I want to be an actor," he told me.

"Well, I want to be a fighter," I said.

I was ringside in Madison Square Garden the night Emile fought Benny "Kid" Paret. During the weigh-in before the fight, Paret called Emile *maricón*, Spanish slang for "fairy." Emile was gay but pretended otherwise, and he was humiliated. In the twelfth round he trapped Paret against the ropes and unloaded on him. They carried Paret out of the ring unconscious. Emile tried to visit him in the hospital, but they wouldn't let him in. Paret died a week later. Emile had nightmares about it, he got hate mail, and people spat at him on the street.

Emile kept boxing for another ten years, but he was never the same. Not long after he retired, he was diagnosed with pugilistic dementia and spent the rest of his life in a nursing home. But before he died he came to terms with his sexuality and made peace with Benny Paret's son. I hope he was at peace with himself.

Actors and
Movie Stars

Fred Astaire was the most elegant man I ever met. The first time I saw him in person he was wearing a necktie around his waist instead of a belt. I thought it looked terrific, so I did the same thing and a guy came up to me and said, "Here's twenty bucks, buy yourself a belt."

Fred and Gene Kelly were the two greatest dancers the movies ever had. Fred was all grace and class, Gene was athleticism personified. While Fred made it look easy, Gene made it look like a workout. But they were both great, and they were good friends. It's a shame they made only one picture together, *The Ziegfeld Follies* (1945).

Fred had a series of dance partners: Jane Powell, Cyd Charisse, Rita Hayworth, Judy Garland, Ann Miller, and Ginger Rogers, who I thought was the greatest. People said that he gave her class and she gave him sex appeal, and that she did everything just as well as he did, only backward and in high heels. They made some marvelous pictures together. *The Gay Divorcee* (1934), *Top Hat* (1935), *Swing Time* (1936), and *Carefree* (1938) are all classics, as far as I'm concerned.

Fred was a perfectionist who rehearsed forever, and it drove

Ginger crazy. She wanted to shoot it and move on, but he'd keep her working until she was ready to drop. He made her do one scene in *Swing Time* so many times her feet bled. Whenever Fred was shooting, people would come from every show at Metro to watch. By the time he finished rehearsing, they thought they could do the number themselves.

But off the set, the taskmaster was a pussycat. We met at Dinah's and became friends.

One night he called to ask if I would give him a ride to the Hotel Bel-Air.

"Sure!" I said.

"Great!" he said. "Could you pick me up at my sister Adele's? She's having a party and she's not too thrilled about my going anywhere."

When I got there, Adele cornered me and said, "Where are you taking him?"

"To the hotel," I said.

I glanced at him and he kind of gave me a look like "Don't say I'm meeting anybody," so I added, "We're just going to have a drink and talk."

"That's all?" Adele said.

"Yeah, that's all."

When we got in the car, Fred said, "Thank you!"

"You're welcome," I said. "But what's going on?"

"Well," he said, "I'm meeting a young lady my sister doesn't like."

I drove around to the back of the hotel and she came out. Fred brought her over and introduced us. It was Robyn Smith, who'd recently broken through as the first successful female jockey. She was kind of butch, but pretty. Fred was a horse-racing fan. One of the Vanderbilts had introduced him to Robyn, and he was smitten. But they had to meet secretly because Adele and the rest of Fred's family thought she was a gold digger. Fred and Robyn got married anyway and stayed together for seven years, until his death in 1987.

Maybe Adele and the family were right, because as Fred's widow, Robyn licensed his image for a Dirt Devil commercial. I was sorry about that. He was too classy for a vacuum cleaner ad.

IF ANTHONY PERKINS and Tony Curtis had a son, it would be George Hamilton. You're prepared not to like him because you think he's a prissy guy, but he's not that way at all. He has a fabulous sense of humor and he's great fun to be around. The key to George is that he doesn't take himself seriously. And he's a much better actor than he thinks he is.

That whole thing about George being wealthy was a farce. He was born in Memphis to Ann Potter Hamilton, a beautiful Southern belle he describes as a cross between Scarlett O'Hara and Blanche DuBois. She did her best to support him after his father, a bandleader named George "Spike" Hamilton, left when George was five. He grew up in Palm Beach in the midst of wealth but without any of it, but he pretended he did to the point of half believing it.

George went to Hollywood at the first opportunity. He rented a Rolls-Royce and drove it around Beverly Hills wearing a chauffeur's hat. He parked it in front of MGM and they noticed him, signed him to a contract, and put him in a bunch of films: *Where the Boys Are* (1960), *Home from the Hill* (1960), *All the Fine Young Cannibals* (1960), and the first movie I ever did, *Angel Baby* (1961).

George is the least athletic person I've ever met. When we shot a fight scene in *Angel Baby*, he could barely throw a punch. I'd have to grab his fist and steer it. And when he had to throw me into the bushes, he sort of lifted me up and I jumped, and that's exactly how it looks on the screen. I was in two pictures that year: *Angel Baby* with George, Salome Jens, Mercedes McCambridge, Joan Blondell, and my old friend Dudley Remus, and *Armored Command*, with Howard Keel, Tina Louise, and Earl Holliman. I played a rapist in both films. They were a double bill on 42nd Street and I only hoped the audience didn't think it was typecasting.

In the era of James Dean and Marlon Brando, with their ripped T-shirts and blue jeans, George was Mr. Elegance. I went shopping with him once when he was buying a suit: "I want the cuff a quarter-inch from the bottom of the heel, and I don't want any drape here . . ." He talked like a tailor.

Like Cary Grant, George invented a persona and grew into it. He cultivated the image of a Palm Beach millionaire playboy and decided that suntanning would work for him the way the blue suit did for Superman. *Health nut* is too mild to describe his obsession with what he calls wellness. He reads books with words in the title like *detox* and *colon cleanse*. I hate to think of what's hanging on his bathroom door.

For a long time George never got the one part that would showcase his talent. When he finally started doing comedy, people realized how good he is. He spoofed himself with *Love at First Bite* (1979) and then *Zorro: The Gay Blade* (1981). They were both successful, I think because he worked with the writers to polish the scripts until they had nothing but George Hamilton lines.

Women love him. He dated Imelda Marcos, Britt Ekland, Lynda Bird Johnson, and so many Miss Worlds and Miss Universes, he could have his own pageant. Keely Smith was down in Miami Beach doing her show and I was dating her for a while . . . until George swept her away from me. I never had a chance.

WHAT I LOVED most about *Riverboat* were the guest stars, especially Ricardo Montalbán, who became one of my closest friends.

Ricardo was the first big star in Hollywood who befriended me, and our friendship lasted for the rest of his life. I went on vacations with him and his wife, Georgiana, and he was the godfather to my son, Quinton.

At first I didn't know that Ricardo's right leg was partially paralyzed. Because of who he was and how much he worked out in the gym, he built up his strength so it just seemed like a distinctive walk. I thought, Gee, I'd like to walk like him, and I imitated it. I thought I was being clever. I didn't know that a horse had trampled him when he was making a Western in the early fifties. But of course Ricardo was gracious about it. He actually laughed when I did it.

He was born in Mexico City, where his family had emigrated from Spain. When he came to Hollywood in 1943, MGM put him under contract and wanted to change his name to Ricky Martin. He played mostly Indians at first, and later suave Latin lovers. Throughout his career Ricardo broke barriers for Hispanics. He was one of Hollywood's first Latin leading men and the first Hispanic to appear on the cover of *Life* magazine. In the 1970s he was the spokesman for the Chrysler Cordoba with its "fine Corinthian leather" interior. People will probably remember him best as Mr. Roarke in the TV series *Fantasy Island*, or as Khan Noonien Singh in the original *Star Trek* television series and the 1982 film *Star Trek II: The Wrath of Khan*.

Ricardo shattered stereotypes just by being himself. He created the Nosotros Foundation to promote Latino involvement in the arts and entertainment. He told me that he lost jobs because producers thought he was militant, which wasn't true. He just didn't like the negative way Hollywood portrayed Mexicans and other Hispanics.

At the end of his life he was confined to a wheelchair, but he kept working both as an actor and for his beloved cause. I always wished I could have the talent of Spencer Tracy or James Stewart and the class and charm of Ricardo Montalbán. I'm honored to have been his friend.

A LOT OF PEOPLE think Marlon Brando was the best American film actor ever. I wouldn't go that far (Spencer Tracy), but I think his early work was outstanding. In those first few films with Kazan, he was more interesting at his worst than other actors are at their best.

He was electrifying in *A Streetcar Named Desire* (1951) and *Viva Zapata!* (1952), and it was impossible to take your eyes off of him in *On the Waterfront* (1954). It's a flawless movie and he's stunning in every frame.

After that, with a few exceptions, I think he was just phoning it in. The first time I saw *Teahouse of the August Moon* (1956), I was in the balcony with friends and they were all raving about Marlon's performance.

"The one who's great is Glenn Ford," I said. "His comedy is terrific."

But I caught Marlon acting. And I thought the buckteeth he wore were a cruel stereotype of the Japanese.

Someone once said that intelligence gets in the way of great acting. Marlon certainly never let that happen, because I don't think he ever grew up. I believe that was the key to his acting, and to his problems off-camera. He abused his body, the instrument that made him great; he ate himself out of the frame . . . because he was bored. Acting was too easy for him and he came to despise it. He was embarrassed by his success, so he retreated to his tropical island and worked only when he ran out of money. He got millions for a film but didn't bother to learn his lines.

Some of Marlon's mannerisms were accidental. The pauses that everybody thought were so brave happened because he was looking for a cue card. He wasn't generous to fellow actors, who said working with him was like working with a blank wall. And the way he constantly denigrated acting was an insult to everyone in the profession.

I worked in television with his sister, Jocelyn. She would tell me how much I looked like him and I'd say, "Yes, I've been told that. Thank you, I guess." People used to follow me on the street thinking I was Brando. At first it got on my nerves, and then it flat pissed me off. It's the main reason I grew a mustache.

Marlon's problem with me went back to a *Twilight Zone* episode in which I did an imitation of him. I played an annoying Method actor who'd been a big hit in *A Streetcar Named Desire,* and Marlon didn't like it.

I'd known Rita Moreno long before we did *B.L. Stryker* on TV. There's no other way to say it: Rita is just a great broad. On the set she was a total pro, and after work she loved to go out and party. Nobody could keep up with her. And what a marvelous actor. She's one of only a handful of performers who've won an Oscar, an Emmy, a Tony, and a Grammy. I met Rita when I was still new in Hollywood. She was dating Brando and said he was curious about me. I was curious about him, too, so I let her talk me into going to a party at his house. When I finally met him, he was rude. He was sitting in a chair and didn't get up; he just kind of looked away and mumbled something. After about two minutes of small talk, he accused me of trying to capitalize on my resemblance to him.

"I'll tell you right now: I'm not having surgery because you don't like the way I look," I said. "But I promise not to get fat."

That ended the conversation, and we never spoke again.

GUNSMOKE BEGAN as a radio drama. When they were casting the TV version, Duke Wayne recommended Jim Arness for the lead and introduced him in a prologue to the first episode. The show was a big hit, and ten years in, they needed someone to replace Dennis Weaver—Chester. They looked at a bunch of guys, but for some reason Jim liked me, so I signed on as Quint Asper, the half-Comanche town blacksmith.

The two and a half years I spent on *Gunsmoke* were the best of times. I learned a lot about acting and about what it means to be a professional. The cast and crew were like a family. It all came from the star.

Earlier in his career Jim made a number of features, including the sci-fi films *The Thing from Another World* (1951)—he played the title role—and *Them!* (1954). But he'll always be remembered as Marshal Matt Dillon.

Jim called the shots on the show. At six-feet-seven, he was an imposing figure, but he never pulled rank, he never made unreasonable demands, and he was kind to everyone on the set, cast and crew. I learned things from him that came in handy when I did a series of my own later on.

Jim had no ego. He'd say, "We need a show for Kitty" or "We need a show for Doc." He made sure everybody in the cast had at least one show that was all about them. He was in constant pain from wounds he'd suffered in the Anzio invasion in World War II, but I never once heard him complain. It surprises people to learn that he had a fantastic sense of humor. In fact he was one of the funniest people I've ever met. He'd ruin take after take with wisecracks and little practical jokes.

I always wanted to get a ride in his car because everyone said, "He'll try to scare the shit out of you," and I thought that would be interesting. We were shooting on location, and at the first opportunity I asked him to give me a ride to my car.

"Yeah, jump in," he said.

I mean, he went *crazy*. I think he was trying to get me to open the door and dive out, but I didn't blink. Finally he roared up to my car, did a figure eight, and said, "I guess I'm not gonna get you to say uncle."

"Shit no! How 'bout letting *me* drive?"

"Fuck you! Get out!"

Gunsmoke ran on CBS from 1955 to 1975, and it's still on the air more than half a century later. The shows hold up because they're good stories, well produced, with terrific actors. I had a great time doing it because the people were just as nice as they could be. Amanda Blake was perfect as Miss Kitty and as sweet as she could be off-camera. Milburn Stone, who played Doc Adams, was like a father to me. When Millie started the show, he was fifty years old and they had to make him up to look old, but over the twenty seasons he aged into the part.

I met three actors on *Gunsmoke* who became lifelong friends of mine: James Hampton, Bruce Dern, and James Best.

Jim Hampton grew up in Dallas. He majored in theater arts at the University of North Texas. He was drafted into the army and served in F Troop of the 6th Cavalry, which is fitting, because one of his first television roles was Hannibal Dobbs, the inept bugler in ABC's *F Troop*. He did a lot of episodic TV in addition to *Gunsmoke*, including *The Doris Day Show*, *The Rockford Files*, and *Gomer Pyle, U.S.M.C.* Later on, Jim was a key member of the *Evening Shade* company. His Caretaker in *The Longest Yard* was the first good movie part he had, and he was terrific in it. I don't know how many pictures we've done together since. Every time there was a part I thought he could do, I pushed like hell to get him, and he was always terrific. We had fun together on the screen because we ad-libbed a lot. Jim and I also did four or five shows together on the Kenley circuit, a kind of summer-stock company that toured the Midwest, and we had a ball. He's a giving actor and great friend.

I liked Bruce Dern immediately. He had that quirky delivery, and he was funny as hell. But he couldn't ride a horse worth a damn and I kidded him about it.

"*You* can do it because you're a jock," he'd say.

"Being a jock has nothing to do with riding a horse," I'd say. "You should have learned how to ride by now."

Of course he's always been a jock. He was a speed skater growing up in Chicago and a record-holding half-miler at the University of Pennsylvania. He still runs every day . . . forever.

And of course he's an amazing actor. He can do it all, from comedy to drama, from *Support Your Local Sheriff* (1969) to *Coming Home* (1978). And he should have won the Oscar for his performance in *Nebraska* (2013).

Bruce once told me that in his book, the greatest accolade you can give someone is "He could play." Well, Bruce could *really* play. And he still can.

James Best and I stayed friends until his death in 2015. He was a true good ol' Southern boy from Powderly, Kentucky, who grew up during the Great Depression. He was born Jewel Franklin Guy to Lark and Lena Guy, but his mother died young and he was farmed out to an orphanage until he was adopted by Armen and Essa Best. He grew up in Indiana and served as a gunner on a B-17 during World War II. His first acting role was a bit part in a movie called *One Way Street* (1950), and he went on to make dozens of films and hundreds of television shows. People remember him as Sheriff Rosco P. Coltrane on *The Dukes of Hazzard*. After it stopped shooting, he and his wife Dorothy moved to Florida, where Jim taught acting at the University of Central Florida. Jimmy Best was a sweet man. He had a sense of humor about everything, and I can still hear his beautiful laugh.

In the middle of my third season on *Gunsmoke*, I knew I was in trouble when Ken Curtis came in as Festus. *I* was there to replace

Chester, and I thought, Boy, if ever in the world there was a replacement for Chester, it's Festus. So I moved on, but with no hard feelings. I loved *Gunsmoke* and I loved those people.

I THOUGHT Marcello Mastroianni was brilliant. His comedy was effortless. He could do more without words than anybody since silent films. He was a huge star in Europe, but I thought he was underrated in America. I know the Actors Studio people didn't like him. They didn't get that he was as good as Cary Grant. But then, they didn't like Cary Grant.

While I was shooting *Navajo Joe*, I was in the commissary at Cinecittà and Mastroianni was there. He waved me over and I almost fainted. I thought I'd done something wrong. But he only wanted me to join him for lunch. It was just the two of us. He had a wonderful sense of humor and he was so charming. He said in broken English—his English was a lot better than my Italian—that he liked my work and that "We must-a work-a together."

"I would kill to work with you!" I said.

"Oh, please-a do not," he said.

THE FIRST FILM COMEDY I did was *Sam Whiskey* (1969), with Angie Dickinson and Ossie Davis. We got along famously. Ossie was already a good friend, and as for Angie, well, she's one of the great women of all time. We had a nude scene together, but I wasn't ready for it. I went to her trailer and said, "I'm just a little bit worried about this."

"Just walk in completely naked and act normal," she said. "After a while they'll get used to you. It's like being married."

That didn't help, because I couldn't imagine getting used to seeing Angie Dickinson in the altogether, so I ignored her advice and wore my ratty little robe.

True to her word, Angie came in wearing only a pair of slippers and a smile.

She pulled the covers back and climbed into bed. I slithered out of my robe and got under the covers next to her. I looked up and there were thirty guys hanging off the grid. They'd come from every feature film and television show on the lot. And there were people standing around where you never see anybody, and no wonder: My God, Angie had one of the greatest bodies in the history of the world.

Angie was absolutely wonderful with me, but I got the giggles and kept ruining takes. But we finally got the scene done, to my everlasting relief. If our "audience" got used to it, they didn't show it. Not one of them left until the end.

Angie is one of those rare women you can take anywhere, from a prizefight to a presidential dinner. She's always the same: she's just Angie. I think we both felt it was unlucky that she and I were never single at the same time. I think we would have been a great couple: We both liked the same things and we could make each other laugh. To me, that's at the top of the list.

I MADE A FILM with Raquel Welch and Jim Brown called *100 Rifles* (1969). I had third billing. It was a controversial film because Raquel kissed Jim in one of Hollywood's first interracial love scenes. That's probably the most memorable thing about the picture.

Jim and I were fast friends, but Raquel is another story. During production she said things to me that weren't particularly nice, and I said things back to her that were even worse, so we didn't part friends. But we made another movie together, *Fuzz* (1972), and I had top billing, which pissed her off. She told the producer, "I will not work with him. I will not be on the same stage." So I'd come to work and Raquel's double would have her back to the camera and I'd say my lines to her and they'd say, "Cut." I'd get back in the car, and as I was driving out the gate, the guard would pick up the phone and say, "He's leaving now" and Raquel would come in and say her lines to *my* double. If you see the movie, it's never us together. It was the only time I've ever had to work like that.

About ten years later Raquel was in a movie called *Cannery Row* (1982) based on the Steinbeck novel. It was an important role for her, a chance to show she could handle serious material. In a strange way I was happy for her because she'd been publicized as a sex symbol who couldn't act and I identified with that. In the course of her career she'd taken a lot of crap along those lines, and I was impressed by her courage.

They fired her from *Cannery Row* for being "unprofessional."

Tell you what: Raquel's a lot of things, but she isn't unprofessional. When we worked together she was always on time and always knew her lines. When I heard she was suing the studio, I called her agent and said I wanted to testify for her.

The jury was 90 percent Latino. A lot of people don't know that Raquel was born Jo Raquel Tejada to a Bolivian father and an American mother. During the trial she sounded like Carmen Miranda.

I got on the witness stand and said, "This is not right. Raquel Welch is very professional and anyone would be crazy to think otherwise." Long story short, she won the case and got $10 million. She thanked me for my help, but we still don't send Christmas cards.

I MET LIZA MINNELLI on *Lucky Lady* (1975), with Gene Hackman and Robby Benson. She's not the easiest person in the world to act with. She's never quite with you. It's like she's reading something somewhere off-camera. Yet she's amazing as a live performer. The entire audience is standing at the end of the show. She gives everything she has, just like her mother, Judy Garland, did.

I went backstage before one of Liza's shows and she grabbed my arm and whispered, "I think I'll sing one of Mama's songs tonight." About a year later I went to another performance and she said, "I'm going to sing one of Mama's songs."

I wanted to say, "Hey, you said that last time!"

I met Judy a few times, and I'll never forget her Carnegie Hall concerts in the early sixties. She did things that should be in a time capsule. She'd walk out on the runway, sit down, and tear out your heart. Judy was a tortured soul. You couldn't be with her ten minutes before you were thinking, This is going to end badly. But at the same time, I was surprised by how funny she was. That's why we got along. The first time I met her she told Liza, "Now, that's a funny guy. That's the kind of guy you should be with."

Liza and I never dated, though. I couldn't handle the drama. She was convinced that there was always something horrible about to happen, and she kept trying until it did. It got to the point where I felt protective. I wanted to put my arms around her and say, "What can I do?" or "Who can I keep away from you?" That was her M.O. Then I realized that she does the same thing with a whole audience. Just like Mama did.

Gene Hackman is a good actor. He's tough, and Liza is so *boop oopy doop*, it didn't sit well with him. Every once in a while he'd go, "Liza, shut the fuck up!" We'd all have to walk off the set until he cooled off. Gene's not a bad guy, but he allowed Liza to distract him. Gene wasn't the easiest to work with either. You'd do the rehearsal one way, and when you got to the take, he'd say, "You're not gonna do it that way, are you?"

He'd do that to Liza, and she'd fall apart.

I didn't let it bother me, and Gene and I parted on good terms.

I thought Robby Benson was a terrific young man and a good actor. He was having a hard time on the picture. I don't know whether he and the director, Stanley Donen, weren't communicating or what. And like all actors, he needed the director to tell him he was doing a good job and Donen wasn't. But Robby showed a lot of maturity and made the best of it.

Robby is an athlete, and when we played pickup basketball between takes, he ran circles around Hackman, who got pissed off and tried to rough him up. But Robby kept his cool. He's blossomed into a damn good actor-director and a wonderful teacher at NYU's Tisch School of the Arts, among other universities. He's written a bestselling novel (*Who Stole the Funny? A Novel of Hollywood*, 2007) and an off-Broadway play (*Open Heart*, 2004). We've stayed friends over the years and I think the world of him.

I LOVED WORKING with Goldie Hawn in *Best Friends* (1982). Of all my leading ladies, she was the most professional, the funniest, the sharpest, and the easiest to work with. You couldn't throw her no matter what you did. She was terrific and I was crazy about her. I first met Goldie on *The Tonight Show*. We went for drinks afterward and I thought she was terrific. I still do.

Goldie's boyfriend Kurt Russell was not crazy about me. I dated her for a while before they met, and, Goldie being Goldie, she talked about what a nice man I was, and Kurt didn't like it. Whenever I saw him, he was rude as hell to me, but we never had a confrontation, because I took the high road for Goldie's sake.

I ADORED Dolly Parton from her early days at the Grand Ole Opry, when I told an interviewer that I thought she would be a big star. Dolly wrote me a one-word note: "When?"

Working with her in *The Best Little Whorehouse in Texas* (1982) was a delight. The only problem was, we laughed too much and blew too much of the studio's money on retakes. You won't find anybody more fun to work with, and yes, she's sexy as hell, though I liked it better when she was more zaftig.

Dolly is so talented as a singer-songwriter-actor, and she turned out to be a sharp businesswoman, too: She made a big success of her theme park, Dollywood. It's beautiful. Every little place you go there—you throw darts at balloons or whatever—the guy's name is Wood. There must be a hundred Woods working there.

Dolly is very self-deprecating, at least in public, and it's part of her charm. She's smart about that, like when she says, "It costs a lot of money to look this cheap." I'm crazy about her.

RYAN O'NEAL was dating Farrah Fawcett and I had a crush on her. I have to admit that I was kind of hoping they would break up. When they did and I finally went out with her, I turned into Inspector Clouseau.

Hal had a brand-new Ferrari convertible, and when I mentioned my date with Farrah, he said, "Take the Ferrari!"

"Great idea!" I said, even though I'd never driven one before.

When I went out to the car, I couldn't get the door open. Fortunately the top was down, so I climbed over and got in the driver's seat. Then I couldn't figure out how to start the damn thing. I couldn't find a key or an ignition switch. I turned everything I could turn or click or pop, and the car finally started. Once I was in third gear, I couldn't figure out how to get back into first, so I drove in third all the way to Farrah's house.

When I got there she was outside watering the flowers.

"Hi!" I said.

"Hi!" she said. "Why don't you come in the house for a minute while I get my purse?"

Aw shit! I thought. I'll have to get out of the car. I climbed on the seat and sort of hopped out, trying to look cool. "It's a Ferrari," I said, stating the obvious.

"That's great!" she said. "I love Ferraris." She got her purse and we went back out to the car, and luckily she opened her own door.

I went around to the driver's side and stood there, hoping she'd reach over and open mine, as some gals do.

No such luck.

"Wanna open the door for me?" I said.

"Uh, sure," she said.

I got in and went through the machinations of getting the thing started. Again, I could only find third gear, and the car gasped its way down the driveway and stayed in third all the way to the restaurant.

Over dinner I confessed everything about the car, and Farrah thought it was hilarious.

After dinner the valet guy drove the Ferrari up and left it running, with the transmission in neutral. I fumbled around with it and somehow managed to get into . . . third gear. We drove that way all the way back to her house, and it must have been a sight: Farrah Fawcett and Burt Reynolds in a shiny new Ferrari, lurching from one stoplight to the next. Farrah and I went out a few more times, but I was never able to top that first date.

JOHNNY CARSON had a great rapport with Doc Severinsen and the *Tonight Show* orchestra, which I think was one of the finest bands ever. I liked Doc and had a lot of fun with him. I've always had an affinity for musicians. I met a lot of them through Dinah and liked them all. They have a sense of humor all their own, but you have to be around them for a while before you get it. It's hard to explain. It's like what Louis Armstrong said about jazz: If you have to ask what it is, you'll never know.

I used to hang out with Doc in a bar across the street from NBC in Burbank called Chadney's. My God, in those days the guy could drink. There was no way I could keep up with him, so I'd fake it. People would come in from the other NBC shows and they'd end up sitting with us. That's where I met a lot of actors, like the cast from *Hollywood Squares*. There was Paul Lynde, who was mean as a snake when he drank, but funny; Cliff Arquette, who played Charley Weaver; Johnny Winters; Rose Marie; Rich Little (you never knew who he was going to be that day); and Betty White. I'm absolutely crazy about Betty. We've been friends forever.

Hollywood Squares taped five shows in a day, usually two before they broke for "lunch." The producers had a hard time getting the talent back to the set, but the shows they did after the break were much funnier.

Bert Convy and I developed a game show called *Win, Lose or Draw*. We'd played it at my house all the time and we were just having fun, but Bert said, "Let's see if we can get this thing on TV." In those days game shows and soap operas were the most profitable shows, and we did get it on the air and it was a hit. But some people didn't get it. Agnes Moorehead, who could be a little bitchy, said, "Why on earth do you do that silly show?" and I said, "Because I like it and it's fun." She looked at me like I was crazy. It's just like Hollywood that people couldn't figure it out, when the simple answer was, I enjoyed it.

DOM DELUISE was one of the sweetest people on the planet. He was a loyal friend, and God, did he make me laugh, sometimes so hard I couldn't stand up. But I could make him laugh, too, so both of us together in front of a camera was a catastrophe. When *he* got the giggles, *I* got the giggles, and vice versa. Directors would try to make us shape up, but they could never get control because the crew was all laughing, too. We ruined take after take until the director gave up and called a wrap. We never did it on purpose. We just were so close, we liked each other so much, that it was easy to do something silly that set us off.

Dom was born in Brooklyn, the youngest of three kids of Italian immigrant parents. He made his acting debut in a school play when he was eight, in the part of a penny that rolled under the bed in the first act and stayed there until the last scene. Dom said that lying there quietly, out of the limelight, was the hardest thing he ever had to do on a stage.

He graduated from the High School of Performing Arts in Manhattan and Tufts University. He met his wife, the Broadway actress Carol Arthur, in 1964, while they were both doing summer stock in Provincetown. They married and had three sons, Peter, Michael, and David, who all became actors.

Dom was one of the great clowns. He couldn't help being a scene-stealer, but you didn't mind because he was so funny. He made a bunch of films with Mel Brooks, beginning with *The Twelve Chairs* (1970). He went on to do *Blazing Saddles* (1974), *Silent Movie* (1976, with Marty Feldman, Sid Caesar, and me), *Spaceballs* (1987), and *Robin Hood: Men in Tights* (1993). Mel said that whenever Dom was in the cast he scheduled an extra two days, "just for laughter."

Dom always said that he became a comic when they laughed at his serious acting, but he was more versatile than he let on. His film debut was a dramatic role in *Fail Safe* (1964), a grim drama about nuclear war starring Henry Fonda.

Dom created a character called Dominick the Great, a bumbling magician ("No applause please, save-a to the end") who was a regular on Garry Moore's variety show and then on *The Dean Martin Show*. From then on he was always working, whether on the stage, in movies, or on television. He was a lifelong opera fan who was thrilled to perform at the Met in nonsinging roles. He got rave reviews for his performances as Frosch in *Die Fledermaus*, and for the role of L'Opinion Publique (in drag) for the Los Angeles Opera's production of Offenbach's *Orpheus in the Underworld*.

I worked with Dom a lot during the 1970s and '80s, in *The Cannonball Run* and *Cannonball Run II*, *Smokey and the Bandit II*, *The End*, and *The Best Little Whorehouse in Texas*. Dom did voices in a bunch of animated films and we got to work together on one of the better ones, *All Dogs Go to Heaven* (1989). Voice actors usually work separately, but I wanted to be in the studio at the same time with Dom, so I asked them to let us try it and they loved it, I guess because we managed to behave ourselves (for once).

In his spare time Dom made himself into a gourmet chef. He loved to go on the morning TV shows and whip up his favorite recipes, and he wrote a bestselling cookbook. He also loved to eat, and his weight was a problem since boyhood. Whenever he was sick or depressed, his mother would say, "Here, eat something! It'll make you feel better." He starred in a movie about that, *Fatso* (1980), written and directed by Anne Bancroft.

Dom didn't get serious about losing weight until he needed hip surgery and the doctor refused to do the operation unless he lost a hundred pounds. But by then it was too late. He had high blood pressure and diabetes and was diagnosed with cancer. He died in 2009 at seventy-five. There will never be anyone like Dom. I miss him every day. And I smile whenever I think of him.

I'VE BEEN a movie fan all my life. When I was ten, there were three theaters in West Palm Beach: the Palace, which was nice; the Florida, which was nicer; and the Arcade, which was a bit rundown. I didn't care, because in those days it usually had a double feature and a serial.

I got there for the first show on Saturday morning and stayed all day. I had my allowance for the week—thirty-five cents—and after I paid the nine-cent admission there was enough left for popcorn, a candy bar, and a Coke. I loved every minute of it: the features, serials, cartoons, newsreels, and coming attractions. At the end of the day I caught the city bus back to Riviera Beach and got home after dark.

My earliest movie memories are of Westerns with Roy Rogers, Gene Autry, Wild Bill Elliott as Red Ryder, and the Durango Kid, played by Charles Starrett, whom I loved because his outfit was all black. He had a kind of Humphrey Bogart quality. I also liked Bob Steele. He was a terrific horseman and his fight scenes were always good.

EARLY IN MY FILM CAREER I started playing what I call the Movie Game. You name an actor and the other player has to name a picture he or she is in. So if I say Errol Flynn, you might say *Captain Blood*. Then I have to name someone else in *Captain Blood* beside Flynn. If I say Basil Rathbone, you have to name a Basil Rathbone movie, and it goes on like that until one of us can't come up with an answer, and gets a strike. Three strikes and you're out.

I used to play the Movie Game with fellow actors while sitting around waiting for the one line I had in the picture. A lot of times, when the assistant director would come over and say, "Okay, Reynolds, you're up," I'd be annoyed because we were right in the middle of a game.

Not all actors are movie fans. It shocks me how little some of them know about their profession, especially the actors who came before them. I could never understand it when an actor couldn't name three Bette Davis movies. And I don't understand directors who have no interest in the old black-and-white films from the 1930s and '40s. When I'm channel-surfing late at night I always stop when I come upon a black-and-white movie on Turner Classic Movies. Some of them are better than color films, the way some things are better on radio than on television. Certain stories seem more real in black and white. You can give them as much color as you like . . . in your mind.

MARILYN MONROE and I were walking down Broadway on our way to the Actors Studio. She was wearing slacks, an old football jersey, and no makeup. As we passed Childs Restaurant, I said, "I don't understand it: We've walked three blocks and nobody's bothered you."

"Want to see her?" Marilyn said. All she did was change her posture, and within twenty feet we were mobbed.

It took five cops to get us out of there.

That's a movie star. You can't fake it. You either have it or you don't.

Spencer Tracy, Bette Davis, James Cagney, Robert Mitchum, Gary Cooper, James Stewart, Mae West, Cary Grant, John Wayne— they all had it. They don't become the character, the character becomes them.

A journeyman actor looks at a script and says, "How can I

serve this material?" A movie star says, "How can I make this material work for me?" And that's the way it should be. If you go to a movie with Duke Wayne in it, by golly, that's who you want to see.

Duke was a force of nature. When he walked into a room, it got quiet. And he could persuade you to do anything. In addition to that walk of his, he had the most distinctive gestures of anybody: that way of shooting his arm out to point at something, of wrinkling his forehead, and of losing his breath when he talked. "We're . . . gonna . . . go over . . . there."

Even though Duke won a Best Actor Oscar for *True Grit* (1969), I don't think he got the respect he deserved. He made a lot of Westerns and war movies, and some of them were stinkers, but he was so powerful in *The Searchers* (1956) and so touching in his last film, *The Shootist* (1976). I went to a meeting of the Screen Actors Guild where someone said, "I think we should do something to celebrate Duke Wayne's career," and people laughed. They didn't understand! It made me angry and it soured me on the Screen Actors Guild for a long time.

ROBERT MITCHUM'S younger brother John played the cook on *Riverboat*, and we got to be friends. John was talented in his own right. In addition to his acting—he's probably remembered best as Inspector Frank DiGiorgio in the Dirty Harry films—he was a singer, guitarist, and something of a poet.

John and Mitch (everybody called Robert Mitchum "Mitch") grew up in Connecticut. Instead of finishing high school they jumped a freight, came to Hollywood, and got themselves into the movies.

John was tough. Whenever Mitch got in a fight the bartenders couldn't stop, they'd call John, who'd come in, slug him, and carry him out.

I never worked with Mitch, but I drank with him. There was a joint called the Keys across the street from Universal and he was always there, on his same old park bench at the bar. I'd go over whenever I could to sit with him.

He did something one night that I wanted to put in a picture. A guy came over and started badgering him. "You think you're tough, don'tcha?" he said, while poking Mitch in the chest. He kept it up until Mitch, who had the biggest hands I've ever seen, put one of them behind the guy's head and slammed his face down on the bar. As he slithered to the floor, Mitch said to the bartender, "This man has fainted."

Mitchum told anybody who'd listen, "I'm not an actor. I have two emotions: on a horse and off a horse." I'm sorry I never got to work with him, because in spite of what he said, he was a terrific actor. He knew that the best acting is not acting, it's behaving. The only time he'd even come close to making a false move was when he tried to do comedy. He wasn't good at anything that made him look clumsy, even if it got a laugh. He knew that and stayed away from it. That's what movies stars do.

MAE WEST'S PICTURES were vehicles for the Diamond Lil persona that she brought to every role. Her character managed to be a sex symbol and a parody of a sex symbol at the same time.

In the 1930s, films like *She Done Him Wrong*, *I'm No Angel*, and *Belle of the Nineties* made her one of the biggest stars in Hollywood. She wrote or rewrote most of her own dialogue, and lines like "Is that a pistol in your pocket, or are you just happy to see me?" and "Beulah, peel me a grape" became part of the language.

When I was still new in town I went to a party and she was

across the room with a bunch of people around her. Somebody came up and said, "Miss West would like to meet you."

I went over, and she looked me up and down like I was a piece of meat. "You lift weights, don't you?" she said.

"Not really," I said.

"Oh come on, I know you do. I like men who work out. Do you like apartments?"

"Uh, sure . . . I guess."

"I have an apartment. You'll like it."

She'd lived in the same building for twenty years, a great art deco thing in Hancock Park called the Ravenswood. When I got off the elevator an ape-shaped guy was standing guard. (Obviously a weight lifter.)

"Follow me," he said.

"Anything you say," I said.

He escorted me to the apartment and rang the bell. Another ape-shape opened the door.

"Come with me," he said.

"Yes, sir," I said. I followed him to a large bedroom in the back of the apartment, and there she was, sitting up in a round bed.

She looked up at me, and without changing the blank expression on her face, she said, "Pull up a bed."

I sat down beside her and we started talking like old friends. She was funny and fascinating. I couldn't get over her hands. They looked so young and so smooth, it didn't seem possible, and I almost looked to see if there was someone under the bed doing her hands for her.

I must have visited her ten times after that. Always a lot of laughs, and I loved hearing about the old days. I asked her the story of how she "discovered" Cary Grant and she said, "Yeah, it's true. I was in the head of Paramount's office and I saw him walking across the yard and I said, 'If that guy can talk, I want him.'"

That was the start of his career. She was talking to Cary when she said, "Why don't you come up sometime and see me?" in *She Done Him Wrong* (1933).

I asked if it was true that she didn't get along with W. C. Fields and she told me that they did all those pictures together without ever speaking off-camera.

"I thought he was kind of an asshole," she said.

Mae broke all kinds of barriers in terms of what you could get away with on the screen. She slipped in what was then considered risqué material. She made the movies grow up a little, but I don't think she got enough credit for that.

She knew how the movie business operated and how to pull the levers. She was in her late seventies when she stood in a receiving line at the premiere of *Myra Breckinridge* (1970). A parade of Hollywood heavyweights went by and they all came away saying, "Boy, she's still sharp and she really knows what's going on." Later somebody asked how she managed to make such an impression and she said, "It's simple, I said the same thing to everyone: 'Loved your movie.'"

CARY GRANT always said that Archie Leach created a character called Cary Grant and became that character. It was the man he wanted to be. If you look at the early movies, especially the ones with Mae West, he's still Archie Leach, with a thick Cockney accent. It took him a while to "discover" Cary Grant. When he did, everybody loved him.

Cary told me he'd patterned himself after men he thought were elegant and sophisticated, like Noël Coward and a character actor named Jack Buchanan. He also admired and copied Douglas Fairbanks and Cole Porter. But Cary wasn't just debonair, he was a good actor. People recognize his brilliance at comedy, but he was also wonderful in dramatic roles. He didn't get to play them because everybody loved him so much as Cary Grant, but he had the talent to play anything. And I never caught him acting, I only caught him being Cary Grant, which is what he wanted. I see so many actors trying so desperately, but Cary made everything look easy while seeming to enjoy it all.

He had the reputation of being a little tight with a dollar. When I was at Universal doing *Riverboat*, his dressing room, the biggest on the lot, was across the street from mine. Every day when the mail arrived, he'd come out and hold the envelopes up to the sun. If they contained money (from fans sending a few bucks in cash to cover postage for an autographed picture), he'd take it out, put it in his pocket, and throw the rest away.

Cary invited me to join him at the races one day. There were a bunch of people in his party and he collected two dollars from each of us for a pool. I thought, Two dollars is ridiculous, and without telling anyone I gave the runner an extra hundred bucks to bet. Wouldn't you know it, our horse won. When the runner came back with ten times what we should have collected, Cary happily divided the winnings without asking questions.

After the sixth race I told Cary, "I've got to pee, but I hate to walk through the crowd."

"Do you want me to take you?" he said.

"Great," I said, "nobody would ever recognize *you*."

"Trust me," he said.

He was right. People were so in awe of him they froze as we walked by.

Cary was a gracious man and very encouraging to a young actor. He seemed to believe in me, and he gave me a piece of advice. "Burty," he said, "everybody loves you, so be yourself and have a good time. But when it stops being fun, walk away."

Directors

I'd been acting ten years before I started to think about how I might have blocked a scene or read a line differently. That's when I began to imagine I could direct. When you get enough power in the movie business, you can get damn near anything you want. (Which is one of the things wrong with the movie business.) So when I finally said, "I want to direct!" I got my chance.

I've now directed five feature films: *Gator* (1976), *The End* (1978), *Sharky's Machine* (1981), *Stick* (1985), and *The Last Producer* (2000)—and I loved every minute of it. I enjoyed communicating with the actors and had definite ideas about what I wanted. The producers were happy because I always finished on time.

People ask if it's hard to both act and direct at the same time, and I say that it isn't as hard as you might think. When you've done as much bad television as I have, you become your own director anyway, because most early TV directors had no idea what they were doing. You didn't get anything from them beyond "Turn right at the chair." As a director, you have to know the big picture. But a good actor will know that, too, so it's not a big leap from acting to directing.

I wanted to be an actor's director, someone who works *with* actors rather than trying to control them. That means respecting them and not playing games. I hate any sort of manipulation a director uses to get a performance out of an actor. Elia Kazan was famous for that.

In 1968, I was in a film called *Fade-In* (aka *The Iron Cowboy*) with Kazan's wife, Barbara Loden. *Fade-In*'s only distinction is being the first release ever directed by Alan Smithee, the pseudonym used when control is taken away from a director by the studio, and the director no longer wants to be publicly associated with the film. In this case the actual director, Jud Taylor, didn't want his name in the credits after Paramount recut the picture without him.

Barbara and I were next door to each other in a little motel in Moab, Utah. When Gadge (I still don't know why they called him that) came to stay for a week, I met him one morning for breakfast.

I'd heard that as soon as anyone starts talking with him, they tell him their life story. I thought, I'll be damned if I'll tell him *my* life story! But two minutes after we sat down I heard myself saying, "Well, my father was chief of police in Riviera Beach, Florida . . ."

Kazan could squeeze every drop out of you because he pretended it was the most fascinating thing he ever heard. No wonder he dominated actors; he mesmerized them. And pitted them against each other. He had all these little tricks to put an actor in the mood he wanted for a character.

When Kazan was making *Baby Doll* (1956), Eli Wallach told me that Kazan took him aside and said, "Have you heard the things Karl Malden's been saying about you?" That was typical, and I didn't like it. I didn't want to be a puppet, and I resented how easy it was for him to control me in casual conversation. Looking back, though I admire his films, I can't say I'm sorry I never worked with him.

As an actor I look on the director as a collaborator. I feel I have something in me that hasn't been tapped yet, so I want us to try to find it together. Let's talk about the script and figure out what the writer intended for the character. Once we've settled on that, I promise to give everything I have. Unfortunately, some directors hate actors.

ROBERT ALDRICH was born into power and money. His grandfather was a U.S. senator, and his cousin, Nelson Rockefeller, was the governor of New York and a presidential candidate. Bob would have inherited a piece of the Chase bank, but his family disowned him when he dropped out of college to go to Hollywood. He started as a production clerk at RKO and climbed the ladder to become one of the top directors in Hollywood, with credits like *Vera Cruz* (1954), *What Ever Happened to Baby Jane?* (1962), and *The Dirty Dozen* (1967). I made two films with Bob, *The Longest Yard* (1974) and *Hustle* (1975).

The Longest Yard has a simple plot: The prisoners in a tough penitentiary form a football team and play the guards. We wanted to shoot at Georgia's Reidsville State Prison, so Al Ruddy, Bob Aldrich, and I went to see Governor Jimmy Carter for permission. The governor was gracious. "That's a pretty rough place," he told me with a grin, "but if you get taken hostage, I'll personally come down and take your place."

I turned to Bob and said, "This man lies so damn well, I think he's going to be president someday."

Governor Carter laughed, thank God.

I'd filmed in prisons before, and I knew it was essential to have the inmates on your side, so in addition to building a football field complete with bleachers, we had six basketball courts installed on the yard. I also knew from experience that every prison has its inmate leadership, so I went to the top man and made him my stand-in. His name was Ringo. He looked like a Brahma bull with glasses and he was serving ninety-nine years for manslaughter and kidnapping.

Six months later I was in Nashville shooting *W.W. and the Dixie Dancekings* when who should appear at my trailer door but Ringo. There were a couple of state troopers guarding me, and I was afraid of bloodshed if they knew who he was, so I sent him to James Hampton's trailer. Ringo told Jimmy that he'd decided "to take a vacation." The next time I saw Ringo, he was leaning against a wall watching us shoot a scene. A week or so later I heard that he was back at Reidsville, in solitary confinement. (Jimmy still hasn't forgiven me.)

I played a former pro quarterback in *Longest Yard*. He's a sleaze, a kept man who sold out his teammates. But prison changes him. A bunch of convicts teach him that there are more important things than winning. I loved making that movie, and it was very successful.

At the previews I attended, people were cheering and ripping up the seats. It was the first picture I'd done since *Deliverance* that takes the audience on an emotional ride, and that's what movies are supposed to do. And I think *The Longest Yard* still holds up. In my un-humble opinion, it's one of the best football movies ever made.

Unfortunately the remake wasn't in the same league. Ninety-nine percent of remakes aren't as good as the original. They never seem to recapture the magic. But Hollywood keeps making them because studio executives think they're the safe way to go.

Before shooting started on the remake, Adam Sandler asked if I had any advice.

"Just one thing," I said. "Get a walk. Pretend you're a motorcycle cop striding up to some poor guy's car. He knows he's in trouble before he rolls the window down."

I'm not sure if he took my advice, but if he did, it didn't help.

I WANTED TO WORK with Bob Aldrich again, and I optioned a screenplay by Steve Shagan about a burned-out detective who falls in love with a high-class call girl. Bob and I flew to Paris and managed to persuade Catherine Deneuve to come to Hollywood.

Catherine is one of the most beautiful women in the world. The camera loves her, and she's even more breathtaking in person than on the screen. I'd catch myself staring whenever we were together. She was elegant, intelligent, and independent. She dressed like a fashion model, she had a good sense of humor, and she could discuss any subject—in six languages. Catherine had children without being married before that was acceptable, and she became a feminist icon without sacrificing her femininity. The first day of shooting, there were twenty secretaries on the set. I thought they were there to watch me until I realized they'd come from offices all over the studio lot to see Catherine.

Bob treated Catherine a little rough and I felt bad about it, but not to the point of confronting him, I'm ashamed to say. Bob was a strange man, God love him. He was wonderful with men—*The Dirty Dozen* and that kind of action movie—but I noticed that he didn't seem to like any of the women on the set. Catherine handled it well, but I should have stepped up and protected her.

I'd read somewhere that the French love picnics, so one day I got a boxed lunch for two and a bottle of wine and drove with Catherine to right up under the Hollywood sign. She was wearing high heels and slacks and a beautiful silk scarf. When I complimented her on it, she took it off and gave it to me. We sat on a blanket, looking down on the city. It was a clear day and the view was magnificent.

"Do you like this?" I said.

"Non!" she said.

There was nothing to do but pack up and leave.

I thought I'd blown it big-time, but a few days later, out of no-where, she said, "Why don't we go and park?"

"What?"

"Park? I hear people do that here."

We drove down to the lake and she said, "What happens now?"

What happened? As much as possible under the circumstances. But it didn't go any further. I knew the next move was mine, but I didn't go there. I was intimidated. I didn't think I was in her league.

ONE DAY between setups on the set of *Hustle*, Bob said, out of nowhere, "You know, you're not the only one who ever played football."

"What?" I said.

"You're not the only one who ever played football, for Christ's sake."

"I never said I was, Bob . . ."

Before I could finish he turned and walked away.

The next day I tried to talk to him, but he was too busy, and from then on he was never available to me. I still don't know where it came from. Maybe it was the pressures of directing a movie. Or maybe somebody who was jealous of my relationship with Bob, or what they thought it was, said something to him about me, and he believed it. I didn't want to think that Bob considered me an obstacle or that he wanted me to be a puppet. And I know I wasn't being difficult. I thought he knew what I could do and that I had always delivered for him.

But I'll never know, because we didn't discuss it again and never communicated beyond what was necessary to shoot the picture. I've often thought that we might have straightened things out if we could have sat down and cleared the air.

But I got along great with Bob's wife Sibylle, who was a sports fan. "Bob changes on me," I told her. "One day he's pitching soft-balls that I can knock out of the park, and the next day he's throwing at my head. What the hell should I do?"

"That's him," she said. "Don't worry about it. I know he likes you."

"Really?" I said. "I'd hate to see it if he didn't like me."

All I know is that we'd had enormous success with *The Longest Yard*, and that should have been a plus, but he turned on me and I didn't know why. I was fond of him, and it still bothers me that we were never able to reconnect.

Hustle got good reviews but lost money, because my character dies at the end. It wasn't in the script. Bob changed it at the last minute, and I couldn't talk him out of it.

It was my fault because I'd ignored Duke Wayne's advice: "Never play a rapist and never die in a movie," he said. "People don't like to see their leading men die."

I MADE A PICTURE in Mexico with Samuel Fuller called *Shark!* (1969). It was a terrible film and Sam was tough, but I loved him. Know what he did instead of saying "Action"? He shot a gun off. There I was with my arms around the gorgeous Mexican star Silvia Pinal ready to do a tender love scene, and all of a sudden, BAM!

"Sam," I pleaded, "can't you just say, 'Action'?"

He puffed on his cigar and said, "No."

FRANK CAPRA is one of my favorite directors. He made some truly great pictures: *It Happened One Night* (1934), *Mr. Smith Goes to Washington* (1939), *Meet John Doe* (1941), *It's a Wonderful*

Life (1946). Some people think they're schmaltzy, but I love them. They're touching and beautifully made.

I once sat in a restaurant with Woody Allen and picked ten movies we'd want on a desert island. Woody didn't take a single Capra picture and I took two. Woody took three Ingmar Bergman films. I'd rather be shot in the leg than watch a Bergman film. Though the actors are wonderful, I find his films depressing. I didn't say anything to Woody, but I thought, Bergman? You're shipwrecked on an island! Why would you want to be more miserable than you already are?

I made one picture with Woody, *Everything You Always Wanted to Know About Sex * But Were Afraid to Ask* (1972). It was just a little cameo: Tony Randall and I played sperms. Woody never said anything to us. We had fun and he was very nice, but he never gave us direction.

I don't think he has a very high opinion of his own talent as a director, even though he's made some wonderful films. If there has ever been an independent filmmaker, it's Woody. He's actually made a picture a year since the 1970s without ever having to beg for money or take script notes from studio execs or check with anyone on casting, because he finances them privately. He takes three months to write a film, three months to shoot, and three months to edit. And he always has final cut. He's unique in the industry.

PETER BOGDANOVICH has made some terrific films, especially the first two, *The Last Picture Show* (1971), and *Paper Moon* (1973). When I worked with him in *At Long Last Love* (1975), with Cybill Shepherd and Madeline Kahn, he was writing and directing, and I don't think writing is his strong suit.

Peter was living with Cybill at the time and they were wrapped up in each other. The movie was a showcase for her and he wasn't interested in anything else. I could have fallen down and bloodied my nose, but if she was good in the scene, he would have printed it. I felt like the two of them were making a movie and I was along for the ride.

Cybill has been criticized for her acting, but she can be good. Her work was a little uneven in those days, and though I don't like to do a lot of takes, I think the film would have benefited from a few more in some places. The problem was that neither of us could sing, and it was the first time anyone had tried to record live musical numbers in a feature film since 1932. The orchestra was right there on the set with us. And Cole Porter, no less! Dinah told me that his songs are the toughest in the world to sing. Yet Peter wanted us to do them in one take, and if a truck rumbled by outside the sound stage, we'd have to do it over. I kept telling him, "You know, I can't sing," but he kept saying, "Yes, you can." So I kept trying. I must have been out of my mind. Maybe if we'd had a little thing at the bottom of the screen that said, "THIS WAS DONE LIVE," we might have gotten *some* credit.

The only bright spot was Madeline Kahn. She pulled me through. Especially the singing. She encouraged me and practically held my hand in rehearsals. Then she confessed to me that she couldn't sing either.

I told her that was ridiculous. "You've sung opera!" I said. "You've sung on Broadway, for God's sake!"

"Only because I was playing someone who could sing," she said.

What a wonderful answer.

Madeline was both sexy and funny, and I had a terrible crush on her. I think it was mutual, but we never did anything about it. She was a lovely woman and a huge talent.

Peter had done something unusual: He went from being a film critic to a successful director, and the other critics hated him for it. And he does like to pontificate. He's brilliant when he talks about films, but you can't talk a scene. You have to know what you want and how to get it from the actor. But he just talked and talked and talked. That's how we spent most of our time on the set, listening to him talk. And he loved to give line readings. It drove me crazy, but I'd just smile and say, "I don't know if I can do it that badly, but I'll try."

JOHN AVILDSEN was a polarizing director. No, that's too wishy-washy: He was an arrogant prick and the biggest asshole I ever had the misfortune to work with. He was good technically, but there he was in Nashville shooting W.W. and the Dixie Dancekings (1975) surrounded by the best country musicians in the world, including Mel Tillis, and he hadn't done his homework. He didn't understand the South. Just had no idea who these people were.

Mel is a sweet man. He was in the Grand Ole Opry for years and years and had a huge recording career. He's been a stutterer all his life. The only times he doesn't stutter is when he sings or when he's drunk.

One night after a take, Avildsen turned to Mel and said, "Cut the stutter."

"What?" I said.

"Cut the stutter," he said. "It isn't working for me."

"Let's go outside, John. I need to talk to you," I said.

We were shooting in a gas station and we went around back. It took everything I had not to strangle him. I got up close and said, "You don't know anything about the people you're working with! How can you tell Mel Tillis to 'cut the stutter'? He has a speech impediment!"

While we were having our little discussion, Mel had got hold of a fifth of brandy and chugged it, so by the time we got back on the set, he was no longer stuttering. We did one more take and he said his lines perfectly. Avildsen looked at me like I was some kind of maniac, and gave me a wide berth for the rest of the shoot.

ONE DAY MEL BROOKS called and said, "I want you to do a little part in my next picture." He went on to describe *Silent Movie* (1976), his tribute to the great silent comedies of the 1920s. I said I'd be happy to do it, especially since Dom DeLuise was in the cast.

Mel wanted me to ride around in a wheelchair and do all kinds of funny things, but I said, "Look, the thing I have the most fun doing is kidding myself, so make me a movie star with his name on top of his house who can't pass a mirror without spending five minutes in front of it."

Mel loved the idea. In my scene, three guys surprise me in the shower: Mel, Dom, and Marty Feldman, whose one eye goes east and the other goes west. Shooting it was one of the funniest days of my life.

I liked Mel and thought he was very clever. But he could be cruel. He has a nasty sense of humor that's hysterical if you're not the brunt of it. I think he considered himself a tough guy. I don't know where he got that idea. Maybe because his father died when he was a baby and he grew up fending for himself in a tough Brooklyn neighborhood. He was proud of the fact that he'd been a drummer. He told me that Buddy Rich, another "tough guy," had taught him how to play. We'd kid around. Mel would warn me not to fuck with drummers, and I'd say, "You don't wanna know how many drummers I've whipped."

It seems silly now, but we went back and forth like that on different things. One night I was at his house for dinner and he suggested I do a movie with his wife, Anne Bancroft.

"That's a great idea," I said.

"Yeah," he said, "you'll bring them into the theater and she'll keep them there."

That cut me to the quick, and I didn't talk to Mel for a long time afterward. We got to be friends again, but it was never the same.

HAL NEEDHAM was the first stuntman to make the leap into directing. Beginning with *Smokey and the Bandit,* he directed ten features, and every one was successful. He was a good director. He knew when to leave the actors alone. But he would watch, and when he noticed something that wasn't right, he knew how to fix it. He was always open to suggestions on line readings and blocking, but he never needed advice on car chases. And he didn't give a shit about your "tertiary motivation."

I want to walk away when I hear the word *motivation.* All I need to know is whether I'm on the right track with the character, and if there's anything the director wants different: bigger, smaller, whatever. But when they start talking about motivation, I pretend to listen and then do what I want.

All of Hal's pictures made money, but the critics panned every one. He got so disgusted he decided to put an ad in *Variety* with quotes from his worst reviews and a picture of him sitting in a wheelbarrow full of money. I thought it would be a big mistake, and I tried to talk him out of it. I told him point-blank: "This is not a good idea, Hal. It'll only piss them off more."

Of course he didn't listen and of course that's what happened. They were *really* mad. If he'd been anybody else, he never would have worked again, but Hal got away with it.

MY CHARACTER in *Starting Over* (1979) is me. He's the closest I've ever come to playing myself in a film, and I approached every scene as if it was me in that situation. Because of my wisecracking playboy image, I had to campaign like hell to get the part. My own agent said that audiences wouldn't accept me as a divorced guy living in a Greenwich Village loft, struggling in the singles world. But I had dinner with the director, Alan Pakula, and he finally said, "Let's do a test."

I liked Alan a lot. He was a gentleman, and a different kind of director than I've ever worked with. He made some wonderful films as a writer-producer-director, from *To Kill a Mockingbird* (1962) to *All the President's Men* (1976). On the set he was slow to make up his mind, but once he did, he was firm. I always felt welcome to voice my opinion about a scene, and he often took my suggestions.

I also had a terrific time working with Candice Bergen and Jill Clayburgh. Jill was a wonderful actor and a lovely woman. It's a tragedy that we lost her so soon. I loved Candice. She's a great wit, and one of the most intelligent and well-educated people I've ever met, but without a hit of pretentiousness. I was happy to work with her again in *Stick* (1985).

She sings in one scene and said, "God, what do I do? I'm supposed to sound lousy."

"Candy," I said, "just sing the best you can, honey."

I was afraid she'd be insulted by that, but she laughed. She's very special.

I saw *Starting Over* recently and was bowled over. I think it captures the spirit of the times: The swinging sixties were over and we were still dealing with the hangover. There's a scene where I have a panic attack in Bloomingdale's. I say, "Does anybody have a Valium?" and thirty-five people throw them on the counter.

I MET DAVID STEINBERG at a party and I liked him instantly. I'd thought he was funny as a stand-up comic and I loved the way he skewered the people and things he thought were phony. I'd heard that David had stuck up for me with people who were putting me down and I thanked him for it. "Nah," he said, "it was nothing." But it meant a lot to me.

We became good friends, and a year or two later, when I had the chance to pick the director I wanted for *Paternity* (1981), I chose David, even though he hadn't directed a movie before. I knew he could do it because I'd watched him direct television skits. He knew how to work with actors and he was always right about where the joke was.

I made the right choice. David did a hell of a job on *Paternity*. I'm sure he could've had a big career as a film director. He just didn't take the ball and run with it. He had his reasons, I suppose, and I respect that.

I NEVER HAD the privilege of working with him, but Orson Welles was a dear friend. He had more talent than any ten directors combined. He had such a strong and original style. Everything he did was fresh, even the credits.

Orson was a natural and he learned fast. When he came to Hollywood at the age of twenty-five to make his first movie, *Citizen Kane*, he had a secretary write him a little manual with all the terminology and the different camera shots. He used it to communicate with his cameraman, Gregg Toland.

I was in awe of him. He did everything in a big way. One day I watched him polish off a breakfast of a dozen eggs and a couple of steaks, then consume ten Cuban cigars and twenty cups of coffee before dinner.

Orson was curious about everything, including things you might not expect, like football. He'd say, "Tell me about football. Tell me why you love it." And I would go on and on about it and he'd listen intently and be enthusiastic and finally say, "Yes, I understand! It's like boxing, isn't it?"

"Well," I'd say, "in some ways, maybe . . ."

Orson and I talked about everything. We talked about the Mercury Theatre, that wonderful radio ensemble he brought with him to films: Joseph Cotten, Ruth Warrick, Everett Sloane, Paul Stewart, Agnes Moorehead, Ray Collins.

"I notice you use Ray Collins a lot," I said.

"Yes," he said, "he's a director's actor because he does everything you ask and he does it perfectly." I never thought Ray Collins was a great actor, but Orson was right, he gave just the performance needed.

It's a shame we didn't get the work we might have from Orson. I think a lot of it had to do with his insistence on total control over his pictures, which the studios refused to give him. He didn't help himself, either. He wouldn't kowtow, and his reputation for not being able to finish a picture was a curse he couldn't overcome.

Orson got to be kind of a joke toward the end of his life. It was those damn wine commercials as much as anything else. ("We will sell no wine before its time.") It bothered me, because I idolized him as an actor, as a director, and as a man. He was always generous with compliments and showered goodwill on people he liked. He never gave me advice, but he would visit the set when I was directing and whisper encouragement. He was always patting me on the back. What a thrill it was to get an "attaboy" from Orson Welles!

Students

John D. MacArthur made two fortunes, one in the insurance business and the other in Florida real estate, especially in Palm Beach County, where my dad worked for him building houses. I think Mr. MacArthur is best remembered as a great philanthropist. His foundation supports Public Television and awards MacArthur Fellowships, the "genius grants," to encourage creativity in America. Though he was one of the richest men in the country, you never knew it. Instead of buying Bermuda shorts, he'd cut down old trousers. He drove a beat-up Lincoln and lived at the seedy Colonnades Hotel in Palm Beach Shores, where he conducted business from a booth in the bar. I got to know him through my dad and he gave me business advice over the years. One of the things he said was "Never open a restaurant or a theater."

I did both. In the same place.

My dream of having my own theater came true in 1979, when I opened the Burt Reynolds Dinner Theatre in Jupiter, Florida. I wanted to give something back to the community where I grew up, and I wanted an alternative to the snooty and expensive Palm Beach Playhouse. I wanted a theater for people who'd never seen live actors on a stage, at prices they could afford. (I imagined half the audience climbing down out of pickups.) I wanted a place where actors could come and have fun without having to worry about being clobbered by the New York critics, and where apprentices could earn their Equity cards. I spent two million dollars to build it.

Dinner theater had a bit of a stink to it. It got laughs on *The Golden Girls* and other shows, and before we opened people wanted to know what kind of plays we were going to do—"Smokey and the Bandit IV"? But the first season was a sellout even before Sally Field, Tyne Daly, and Gail Strickland started rehearsing for our first production, *Vanities*.

It was wonderful to see film or television actors who'd never been on the stage before come there and fall in love with theater. Farrah Fawcett made her stage debut in *Butterflies Are Free* and proved she could do wonderful work in the right vehicle. Robert Urich was a sensation in *The Hasty Heart,* and we took the production to Washington, D.C. Julie Harris in *Death of a Salesman* and Charley Durning in *Mass Appeal* both won Florida Drama Awards. Ossie Davis did *I'm Not Rappaport.* Sally and I did *The Rainmaker.*

But it wasn't ALL sweetness and light. Jim Nabors came down to do *The Music Man,* and it was a disaster. He sat there with tears in his eyes and I said, "Jim, you can either quit and go home, or you can stay and try to make it work." He had the guts to stay and it did get better. He realized that you're not an actor until you've been on the stage. Jim has that magnificent singing voice. That's the surprise: You think you're getting Gomer Pyle and all of a sudden he breaks into one of those wonderful songs.

He came back the following year in another show and it sold out. They were out there screaming and hollering for him, and he loved every minute of it.

We were able to attract the likes of Martin Sheen, Vincent Gardenia, Elliott Gould, Ned Beatty. If they were reluctant—the singers wanted to act and the actors wanted to sing—I'd ask, "What's your favorite play?"

Carol Burnett has been a pal for a long time. Her comedy show on CBS ran for ten years with that marvelous ensemble—Harvey Korman, Tim Conway, Vicki Lawrence, and Lyle Waggoner. I had a ball guesting on an episode where I played the Lavender Pimpernel and sang "As Time Goes By." Carol returned the favor by coming to Jupiter and doing *Same Time Next Year* with me, directed by Dom DeLuise.

I was asked by a reporter who I'd like to take on a deserted island and I said, "Carol Burnett." It got back to Carol and she sent me a picture of herself in a bathing suit. On the back of the picture she wrote: "When?" I sent her a box of candy and she took a bite out of each piece and sent them back. I sent her flowers and she kept them for two weeks and returned them with a note: "Your flowers died."

We did a revival of *Mister Roberts* with Josh Logan directing and Marty Sheen in the title role. Josh later said that Marty was as good as Henry Fonda, who'd created the role on Broadway, and we also had the original captain, William Harrigan. It was quite an evening at the theater, and I could have run it for a year. It was way above other dinner theaters.

We had problems with audiences until we got tough. I'd told the ushers, "Look, we'll have people who'll talk over the actors, put their feet up on the back of the seat in front of them, and generally act like they're home watching TV. You'll have to hush 'em up and make 'em behave, or make 'em leave." It worked. The audience learned how to behave themselves.

We didn't pay the actors a lot, but we treated them royally and I think they had a good time. We kept ticket prices low, so we had to fill the theater to break even. We were able to do that in the winter, but attendance dropped off in the summer. Even though we kept the overhead as low as possible, we almost never turned a profit. Anybody who's been around the theater knows that you don't do it for money, you do it to feel good and to sharpen your craft. Hal Holbrook took three months off of *Evening Shade* to do *King Lear*, and the money he was paid didn't cover half his hotel bill. (When Hal came back to the show, I said, "Now you're gonna get to work for a *good* writer.")

WE HAD WONDERFUL people who worked without pay because they loved the theater. There was a lovely lady named Barbara— very classy-looking, with short snow-white hair—who volunteered for everything. She was always asking if we needed help at a party. She'd cook and do just about anything we asked.

One day she said, "I have a son who's an actor."

"Oh God," I said, "this has been such a great relationship until now . . ."

"No," she said, "I think you'll like him."

"What's his name?" I said.

"Jon Voight."

I fell over.

She never told me or anyone else that she was Jon's mother, even though she knew that Jon and I had been friends since *Deliverance*. I should have spotted it, because you could see Jon's face in hers. Jon had no idea of the connection either, and when I told him his mother had been working anonymously for us, he almost fainted.

Sally Jo Wagner was the matriarch of the theater and my hero, not just because she worked tirelessly for us. I've never met anyone braver than that little lady. She had a serious spinal condition, but I never once heard her complain. She never asked for anything, and if you did something for her, she'd turn around and do something twice as nice for you. She went all over Jupiter with the flags flying on her wheelchair. Friends would bring her to the house and we'd sit and talk for hours. She was my psychiatrist! Everyone loved Sally Jo, but no one more than I.

I STARTED the nonprofit Burt Reynolds Institute for Film & Theatre when the dinner theater opened in 1979. Acting has been the one constant in my life since I was nineteen years old. Looking back, I see an unbroken line from the day Watson Duncan told me I was going to be an actor until now, and one of the reasons I teach acting is to pay Mr. Duncan back. I wanted a drama class for aspiring actors who couldn't otherwise afford training. Charles used to say that everything goes in circles, and it's strange that our classes are held in the Mirror Ballroom, the big auditorium in Lake Park. There are ghosts there. It's where I first took the stage in *Outward Bound.*

I'VE KNOWN Frank Eberling since he was a young journalism student at Palm Beach Junior College. That's when his mother heard that "an actor from *Gunsmoke*" would be speaking at the college and suggested he interview me, and he did. I remember his reel-to-reel "portable" tape recorder. Not long ago he reminded me that even then I was talking about starting an acting school.

Frank is an accomplished author, teacher, and filmmaker. He made a wonderful documentary about Watson Duncan, *Good Night, Sweet Prince*, and I was honored to be part of it along with another of Professor Duncan's "discoveries," Monte Markham, who also narrated the film.

Over the years Frank has done a lot to help my students learn about film acting technique—camera angles and movement, lighting, master shots, close-ups. If the camera is the most important "person" on the set, the cameraman is a close second. I always tell the kids to make friends with him. (I call all my students "kids," even the old ones.) "I don't care if the other actors think you're sucking up to the cameraman," I say. "I don't care what they think, and you can't care what they think. It's important that both the camera *and* the cameraman like you."

MY STUDENTS are enthusiastic, and I've had success with all kinds of people, from cops to schoolteachers to business executives. I watch them become actors before my eyes.

When we take a break, they'll ask about my early days in New York, and as I tell them stories, I think to myself, My God, was I that brave?

It may seem like a contradiction, but a lot of actors are shy. They don't seem to be because they have two different personalities: the real human being and the actor. They discover that they're more comfortable as the actor, so they never go back to the shy individual they really are. They figure the actor is a better person than they are, and a lot of them are right.

Peter Sellers was like that, to an extreme. Liza Minnelli told me she had a date with him once, and over the course of the evening he was three or four different people. It drove her nuts.

"Didn't you find him amusing?" I said.

"No," she said. "There was nothing amusing about him. He was scary."

Peter was so talented. The only character he couldn't play was himself.

Some characters are easier because they're closer to home. I had no problem playing detectives. I think I did decent work on TV as Dan August, though it was pretty basic. Dan had two expressions: mean and meaner. It was a gritty show. A lot of our guest actors were in Broadway shows, so they weren't available until eleven at night. We wanted a noir look anyway, and you could do anything you wanted in New York at three a.m., so we filmed all night and never saw the light of day.

Hawk was an Iroquois detective in the big city. We shot it in Harlem. I used to drive up there, and one night I was circling the block looking for a parking space when a couple of guys came over and said, "You da Hawk?"

"Yeah," I said, "I'm da Hawk."

"We like da Hawk. Just leave your car here and we'll watch it."

They watched that car like it was theirs. I never had to worry about it. I tried to give them money, but they wouldn't take it. They were insulted.

B.L. Stryker is an ex-cop who lives on a broken-down houseboat in West Palm Beach. The boat was just a shell, no heart, no guts—just like Hollywood. We named the guy B.L. Stryker for my first initials, Burton Leon. (Leon is my middle name, after my grandpa.) My dad didn't like war pictures, but he liked Duke Wayne, and Stryker is the name of the character Duke played in *Sands of Iwo Jima* (1949).

It was easy to slide into those detective parts because I was playing my father. All actors are thieves. I'm no exception. I often used Big Burt's walk, his gestures, his speech patterns.

I LOVE TEACHING, but I couldn't do it without the skill and dedication of certain people.

Todd Vittum was a student of mine before he came to work for me. He's competent and personable, and knows how to handle himself in a pinch. Todd is also a good teacher, especially with people who are just starting. His improv class helps them develop muscles they never knew they had. When he decides that a beginning student is ready, we boost them up to my class. Todd's a good man. I'm lucky to have him in my corner.

Carmen Magri is our unofficial historian. At eighty-five, she's a bundle of energy. While most people slow down at that age, she's speeding up. She just got back from her annual European vacation. Until recently she owned a jaguar (the cat, not the car) and rode an Indian motorcycle. A year or two ago Todd finally got Carmen on the stage for the first time, and she loved it.

Jim Lynch was a student who became an assistant director. He was a movie encyclopedia. We'd be talking about who was in this film, who was in that one, and he'd go all the way through the cast. Our mutual love of films was a great bond. He was shy, but we finally got him up on the stage and he was terrific. Jim wasn't much past forty when he passed away, God love him, but I think the last few years of his life were happy.

I'VE REACHED the point where I teach "master" classes, even though I'm still learning myself. New actors ask me where the land mines are because they know I've stepped on them all. I can tell them where they are, but they'll probably step on them anyway, so I take a different approach. Rather than tell them what *not* to do, I try to keep the advice positive, with a single exception. The one piece of advice I give again and again is from Spencer Tracy: "Never let them catch you acting."

An actor's confidence is fragile. It's easy for a teacher to bruise a young actor with the wrong words. I tell my students, "Don't act; behave." When I catch them acting, I say as gently as I can, "Let's start again, and don't let me catch you acting. You're too good for that."

Dudley Remus and I go way back, to a little theater in Delray Beach. Dudley is a terrific actor, but he never had the guts to go to

Hollywood or New York. I tried to talk him into it more than once, but he was afraid he'd get his ass kicked. "I'm not that good," he'd say, and I could never convince him otherwise. He didn't understand that you gain confidence by venturing into the most dangerous places. Every time you take a risk as an actor it makes you better. Besides talent and a so-called look, you need the courage to try in the first place. And you have to hang in when you're told to quit and get a real job. Actors have to learn to be kind to themselves. They're going to get beat up enough when they go to New York or L.A.

I tell my students to try to work with actors who are better than they are and try to figure out *why* they're better. And to think of themselves as part of a community. In Hollywood you're only as good as your last picture, but in France you're as good as your best picture, and I've been treated warmly by French audiences, critics, and especially actors. On my first trip to Paris I went to a club with a bunch of French actors and they were wonderful to me. I don't speak French and most of them didn't speak much English, but it didn't matter, because actors are the same everywhere. We talked for hours and had a lot of laughs (I'd do a bad imitation of some famous actor and they'd be hysterical). The camaraderie was glorious. It was one of the highlights of my life.

There are three stages of an actor's career: young, old, and "You look good." My advice to older actors, which I haven't always followed myself, is to play your age. Leading men have a tendency to hang on too long. You can't hold your stomach in forever.

The man who's made the best transition is Clint Eastwood. He's done it with dignity and style. It's worse for women: Whoever said that "actors get older, actresses get old," was right.

Robin Williams once told a young comedian: "If you're gonna be a star, you'd better start acting like one. Do you think Burt Reynolds gets nervous? Of course he does."

Well, not really. I don't usually get nervous on the stage or a movie set. I don't see any reason for it. If a lot of time and money has been spent on a shot, that might make me a little tense, especially if it's the one that you just *have* to grab before the end of the day. Generally speaking, though, acting doesn't make me nervous.

I'm usually fine with public speaking, too, but once in a while I do get nervous talking in front of a group, and for a long time I couldn't figure out why. Then I realized that it depends on what's at stake. If the occasion is in honor of someone I love and respect—if I'm speaking at a testimonial dinner or an awards ceremony for a friend—I do get a little nervous. It isn't performance anxiety exactly; it's fear of letting someone else down. But it doesn't last. It's kind of like football: the nerves disappear after first contact.

I once gave a commencement address where I threw away my prepared speech. I started out trying to be whomever they thought they were getting that year, but found I couldn't do it, so I put the speech away and said, "Do you mind if we just talk?"

They applauded and that put me at ease.

Listening is everything for an actor, and one of the first things I say to a class is "I don't want to teach you how to act, I want to teach you how to listen. If you can really listen, they won't even see the other actor." Spencer Tracy did that better than anybody.

I run *Father of the Bride* (1950) for my class. It stars Tracy with some good actors, including Joan Bennett, Elizabeth Taylor, and Billie Burke. (I love to watch other actors with him. You can see it in their faces: *My God, I'm working with the master!*) I tell my students to watch Tracy. He owns the picture. In some scenes he doesn't have a laugh line, but he steals them anyway. He listens to the other actors, and they make him laugh, and when he laughs, we laugh. That's the power of listening, and it's Tracy at his best.

There's no secret to remembering lines. We all have our own system. But good writing helps. It's easier to remember dialogue that's truthful. If it's a good script, you can memorize a speech quickly and you won't have a problem with it. The trick is finding the heart of the watermelon. What's in the middle of the speech that you're trying to get to? What's your character trying to say? If I can figure that out, I'll coast through the rest of it. But getting there is tough if you're anxious about it. It also depends on the other actor. If I was working with Ossie Davis, I could talk all day because he always stayed right there. But when an actor drifts on me, I lose focus. I don't know whether it gets me angry or what, but it throws me.

There are basic notions about playing drunk. The idea is that you try to be sober. If you work hard at that, you look like you're drunk. That's the theory, anyway. I try to show my students how to sip a glass of fake whiskey in a convincing way. It's usually luke-warm tea without sugar, so it's bitter. I always drink like it's pretty awful at first. But the more you drink, the better it tastes, and you get into the swing.

The question comes up: "When you see an actor in a movie waking up, how do they get that look?" Charley Durning, God love him, would mash his head into the pillow. He'd start ten minutes before the take, and by the time the director said, "Action," he'd look like he'd been run over by a truck.

Students want to know about having to kiss a stranger in a scene. I always try to find something about the woman that I like and hope I can make her laugh before the scene. It's like a first date.

The big difference between making a TV show and a movie is that the budget is usually much higher on a movie, where you do two or three pages a day. You work much harder on a TV show. You're often shooting all night, and you'll do eight, twelve, sometimes fourteen pages. I like that pace rather than sitting around. In my experience stage actors generally behave better than movie actors when they make a film. No matter how big a star they were on Broadway, they don't pull rank on fellow actors and they're available to the director. Another difference: On the stage you use your body more than on film. You have to reach the back row, so you make gestures that wouldn't be seen in close-ups on film.

I love what old radio dramas used to do with just the spoken word, and lately I've been assigning parts to my students from shows like *Inner Sanctum*. I'll have the rest of the class turn their chairs around so they can't see the actors. I tell them they have to work without using their bodies because it won't mean anything to the listening audience.

It's said that all a film actor has to do is think it and the camera will pick it up, and I believe that's true of good actors.

In *The Snake Pit* (1948), Olivia de Havilland plays a sane woman who's committed to an asylum. She tries to convince them she's not crazy, but no one believes her. In one scene she collapses into a corner. She doesn't speak, but there's a look on her face of such despair, it says more than ten pages of dialogue.

Many actors went on the set and watched Gary Cooper, thinking, What's the big deal? He isn't doing anything. But on the screen there's a whole performance not seen in person. Good film actors don't do much because everybody around them is saying it and doing it for them. To illustrate that, one day in class, Wynn Handman showed us a film of three actors and asked us what we saw in their faces. Between close-ups of the actors' faces, there'd be a pitcher of ice water dripping with condensation. They'd cut back to one of the actors and you'd swear he was dying of thirst. They'd show a sexy woman and then cut to a guy looking at her and you'd see the most lascivious look on his face. What a pervert! The point is, when you act in movies, you don't have to do much because the film does it for you.

As a teacher, I try to use as much of my own experience as I can. Most beginners are scared to death of auditions, and understandably so: They're among the toughest things actors have to do. You look around and there are thirty-seven guys in the room who are taller and better-looking than you are. And they sound better, too. You think, What the hell am I doing here? I must have been crazy to think I had a chance. But actors have to get past that.

Screen tests aren't much fun either. I did one for a picture called *But Not for Me* (1959) with Clark Gable and Lilli Palmer. The other actor up for the part was named Barry Coe.

I tested first. When I was introduced to Gable, he said, "Do you duck-hunt?"

Trying to be funny I said, "No, I can't shoot anything since I saw *Bambi*."

He looked at me like I was crazy, and my test was a disaster.

I hung around to watch Barry Coe's test.

When Gable asked him if he hunted and Barry said, "Yeah, I've got a Browning over and under and I go duck-hunting all the time," I knew he had the part and I was out. Barry went on to play Mr. Goodwrench in a series of TV commercials. I never saw Gable again, except on the screen.

I'VE ALWAYS BEEN curious about people, no matter who they are or what they do, and I try not to be judgmental. I think that's important for any actor. How can you do justice to a character if you're looking down on him? I tell them that the old line is true: "Dying is easy, comedy is hard." What people dismiss as "light comedy" is tougher to play than deep drama, and I think it's easier to make a dramatic actor out of a comedian than vice versa. I tell my actors that if you're in a comedy, never beg for laughs, forget you're in a comedy, and just be real. If the laughs are there, they'll come. I tell them that no part is ever beneath them, and that no part is too small, as long as they bring something interesting to it. I tell them that acting isn't about *them*, it's about a gift they're giving to other people. And I repeat Spencer Tracy's advice: Never let them catch you acting.

Burt

I've done more than a hundred movies. I'm proud of maybe five of them. And I'll match my record of missed opportunities with anyone in the business. There's only one actor I can think of who can rival me in that department, but I have to go back pretty far. In 1941, George Raft passed on *The Maltese Falcon*, *High Sierra*, and *Casablanca*. Humphrey Bogart did them all, of course, and they made his career.

In a few cases I was unlucky, but it was mostly bad decisions. For a long time I took roles that would be the most fun, not the most challenging. In the process I missed out on some wonderful parts.

I backed away from the original *Batman* TV series (1966–68) because I doubted I could bring it off and didn't think it was a star-making part. I wouldn't have been nearly as good as Adam West, who was brilliant as Batman. But as it happened I was right: *Batman* didn't do much for his career.

I tested for *Rosemary's Baby* (1968), but Roman Polanski went with John Cassavetes.

Brian's Song (1971): The role of Brian Piccolo, the Chicago

Bears running back who was stricken with terminal cancer in the prime of his career, would have been perfect for me, but I lost out to James Caan. (It was perfect for him, too.)

I don't know if it was before or after both Warren Beatty and Jack Nicholson passed on the part of Michael Corleone in *The Godfather* (1972), but I was up for it. Someone told me that Marlon threatened to quit if I came in.

I was dying to do *Blume in Love* (1973) and *A Touch of Class* (1973), but George Segal got both.

In 1977, when I was the top box-office star, Francis Coppola said he wanted me for the title role in *Tucker,* about the visionary car designer who took on the Big Three automakers in the 1940s.

I flew to San Francisco, and over a long dinner we made plans for the film. I stayed the night, and the next morning Francis screened seven different endings of *Apocalypse Now* and asked me which one I liked. Then he showed home movies of Preston Tucker, who looked just like my dad. We talked in detail about how to make the picture and agreed on just about everything. I left that afternoon thinking I had the part.

A few days later someone called from Paramount saying that they wanted to make *Tucker* but not the five other pictures Francis had pitched them. It seems he tied all the projects, most of which he was only going to produce and not direct, to me! He was using me to bootstrap his other films. We never spoke again. (He made *Tucker* with Jeff Bridges ten years later.)

When Sean Connery held out for more money to play James Bond, Cubby Broccoli came to me and said, "We want you to play Bond!" and I said, in my infinite wisdom, "An American can't play him. The public won't accept it."

For a long time afterward I'd wake up in a cold sweat going, "Bond, James Bond!"

I was the first choice for the part of John McClane in *Die Hard* (1988), but I passed. That's okay. I don't regret turning down anything that Bruce Willis took.

I declined the Richard Gere role in *Pretty Woman* (1990). I saw it the other night and thought, Damn, Julia Roberts! What the hell was I thinking?

I turned down two parts that went to Jack Nicholson. I was Milos Forman's first choice for R. P. McMurphy in *One Flew Over the Cuckoo's Nest* (1975). Jack won the Oscar for it. But by far the dumbest thing I ever did was turn down the role of the dissipated ex-astronaut in *Terms of Endearment* (1983) because I was committed to make *Stroker Ace* (1983) with Hal. It never occurred to either of us that we could simply postpone it. Jack got another Oscar for it. He was so good in both roles, I can't imagine anyone else in them, including me.

I've been told I was considered for Trapper John in *M*A*S*H* (1970—Elliott Gould) and Travis Bickle in *Taxi Driver* (1976— Robert De Niro). I'd love to have done both.

I turned down the part of Han Solo in one of the *Star Wars* sequels. I guess it would have been nice to be part of film history, but I don't regret it.

I was in awe of Sally in many ways, not least for her ability to pick up a phone and ask a director to work with her. I could never do that. I wanted to call Peter Weir and ask to play the cop in *Witness* (1985), but couldn't bring myself to do it. Peter made a terrific movie with Harrison Ford.

Sidney Lumet wanted me for the lead in *Power* (1986) and I would have loved to work with him, but I had a serious ear infection and he cast Richard Gere instead.

I coveted the Nick Nolte character in Paul Mazursky's *Down and Out in Beverly Hills* (1986). At the time I felt like *I* was down and out in Beverly Hills, so it wouldn't have been a stretch.

I had to pass on the Kevin Kline part opposite Sally in *Soapdish* (1991) because Loni would have poisoned me.

Sylvester Stallone was parking cars when he wrote a script about a South Philly pug who gets a shot at the heavyweight championship. He took it to United Artists, who had three actors in mind for the title role: Ryan O'Neal, James Caan, and me. But Sly said he'd have never forgiven himself if the film was a hit without him playing Rocky.

The studio still wanted an established actor, so they offered him $300,000 for the script to make him go away. At the time he had $100 to his name, but he held out for the part and kept the rights to the character.

The rest is Hollywood history. Made for a little over $1 million, *Rocky* grossed $250 million, its five sequels have earned more than $1 billion, it won the 1976 Best Picture Oscar, and there's a statue of Sly as Rocky Balboa on the steps of the Philadelphia Museum of Art.

I DON'T HOLD GRUDGES. There are people who kicked me when I was down, but I don't want to get even. The only way you can get even with anyone in this business is by succeeding and hurting their pocketbook, or by smiling and not giving up. I'm living a happy and fulfilled life. It's the best revenge.

I've been lucky in terms of the people I've met professionally and how loyal they've been to me, like Jon Voight. I don't see Jon as often as I'd like, but we talk on the phone and send each other little notes. I got a card from him the other day that said: "Dear Burtram, I'm gonna find a film for you."

I see George Hamilton and Joe Namath because they both live in Florida, and I have dozens of colleagues all over the world whom I stay in touch with. I've known my manager, Erik Kritzer, since he was Sue Mengers's assistant at an agency in the 1990s.

I have a diverse group of people outside of show business who keep me on the straight and narrow. Jess Moody is more than a spiritual adviser, he's a dear friend. Mo Mustaine is my lifelong pal of sixty years and counting. We share so many memories, we finish each other's sentences.

HAVE I DONE it my way? Yeah, I think so, even when it wasn't the best way. If I had it to do over, are there things I'd change? Of course. For one thing, I'd be nicer to certain people. I was too rough around the edges in some situations. And there were people I wish I'd gotten to know better who were friendly toward me, but I just moved on. Especially actors I respected who'd been big stars but were reduced to smaller parts later in life. There was an actor named John Bromfield who was an ex-jock and a great-looking guy. He made feature films after World War II and then a TV series called *Sheriff of Cochise* in the fifties that lasted a few years. Then he moved down to playing heavies. John was a real gentleman and we liked each other. I would love to have had the benefit of his experience in the business. I've always regretted not making the effort to know him better.

Like everybody, I've had my ups and downs. Well, maybe not everybody: The chart of my career looks like a heart attack. I've been through every career phase imaginable, some more than once. I was number one at the box office five years in a row, which I don't think anybody has done since. In 1978, I had four movies at once playing nationwide. If I met you then, I'm sorry. I was flying through life trying to take a bite of everything. My only excuse is that I was on top of the mountain, where the air is thin. How can you smell the roses when you can't breathe?

When you're on top, you're surrounded by people telling you what they think you want to hear. All you have to do is say, "I'd like a Diet Coke," and forty-eight people run to get it for you. If I'd wanted, I could have had three people pulling up my zipper in the john. It's easy to lose touch with reality and believe your own publicity. It's hard to explain what it's like to be number one. It's even harder to explain what it's like to go from number one to number sixty-eight. When you're on top you know there's only one way to go, but you can't prepare yourself for it, in the same way you know your mother and father are going to die but it still comes as a shock when it happens.

By 1980 I'd done a string of car chase movies—*White Lightning, Gator, Smokey and the Bandit I* and *II*, and *Hooper*. I wanted to try other genres and swore that I wouldn't drive a car over the speed limit in another movie. Then Hal and the automotive writer Brock Yates came up with *The Cannonball Run*, a script based on an illegal cross-country car race. It sounded like so much fun I couldn't resist, and I was paid $5 million to make it. (I was told that set a record at the time.) A year later I couldn't get my phone calls returned. I'd chosen too many films because I liked the location ("Jamaica? I'll take it!"). Or the leading lady. Or because I'd be working with friends. If the script was crap, I rationalized that I could make it better, and I usually did, but it was just better crap. I didn't open myself to new writers or risky parts because I wasn't interested in challenging myself as an actor, I was interested in having a good time. As a result, I missed a lot of opportunities to show I could play "serious" roles. By the time I finally woke up and tried to get it right, nobody would give me a chance. I'm not bitter about it. It happens to a lot of actors. I feel my best performance is still ahead of me. I'd love the chance to give it, but it won't kill me if I don't.

Teaching is the most important thing in my professional life now. I love sharing the knowledge I've gained over the years, but

I'm also still curious. (If you want to learn, teach!) Maybe that's one of the secrets of staying young. If I had to choose, I'd take being a good teacher over being a good actor, and if I have a legacy, it's the actors I've taught.

I'VE BEEN RICH and I've been poor . . . and miserable both times. Rich and miserable is better. I don't know how much money I've made and spent, and I don't want to know.

I'm not proud of the fact that I haven't always handled it well. But money was never at the top of my list. I just wanted enough so I didn't have to worry about it. My biggest mistake was trusting people who took advantage of me. I went through bankruptcy, and it's not pleasant. People treat you like a leper. They think their money will disappear if they touch you.

I didn't save my money like some people. (A lot of those people never pick up a check, so maybe that's the secret.) I've owned big houses, a ranch, boats, private jets, helicopters . . . and I enjoyed them all. But I don't miss them. I feel like a man whose house was blown away in a hurricane. His possessions are gone, but he's thankful to be alive. He realizes that objects aren't important.

I cannot put into words my gratitude and love for my niece, Nancy Lee Hess. Nancy Lee's brother, Rick, runs the feed store in Jupiter Farms near what was once my ranch. They both inherited the best qualities of my sister, Nancy Ann.

I had some lawyers, accountants, and real estate advisers who didn't have my best interests at heart. When it all started unraveling, I asked Nancy Lee to help straighten things out for me. She had just retired from the phone company and was planning on doing some traveling, but she dropped everything and said yes. She's done an amazing job. I know she's been under a great deal of pressure and lost a lot of sleep in order to help me through some very stress-ful issues. I almost think of her like a stuntwoman taking the falls for me in the business world. I dedicated this book to her in grati-tude for all that hard work, and because I love her so much.

I LOVED DOING STUNTS, and I did as many as I could without the studio tying my hands and feet. Now I'm paying the price. My body is a wreck. A while ago I was invited to a party given by the kids I teach, but I couldn't go. I hurt too much. Sometimes I think ego made me do those stunts. Well, maybe it wasn't all ego—maybe it was part perfectionism. I didn't want the scene to look phony.

Now, when my body hurts somewhere, I can name the movie. "Ooh, that's *Hooper*," or "Ahh, *The Longest Yard*." I did my own stunts for most of my television shows, too. In one episode of *Dan August*, I had to run into a burning building and rescue an infant, but it was so hot in there that the prop baby melted into a glob of plastic and the door was on fire. I had no choice but to jump through a window, and I messed up my shoulder. That was fifty years ago, but I can still feel it. But aside from the aches and pains, I'm healthier than I've been in twenty years. A while back the doc-tors overhauled my coronary arteries, so I can eat anything I want now. (If my cardiologist is reading this, just kidding, Doc.)

AT FIRST, acting was a great way to make a living and meet girls and be around interesting people. When I started, I was faking it, and I hid my fear behind cockiness. The ambition came later. It wasn't until I was close to forty that I wanted to be respected as an actor and began to think I might be good if I really worked at it. I don't know if I ever reached that point, but I think I did get better.

I may not be the best actor in the world, but I'm the best Burt Reynolds in the world.

I'VE HAD TO REINVENT myself four or five times. And I'm now working on the most challenging reinvention: survivor. (Speaking of survival, my hair will probably outlive everyone. They'll find a skull with a perfect haircut.) I hate self-pity. I believe it damages you and the people who care about you. They want to hear that you're happy. Well, I am happy! I live every day to the fullest, and I try to experience new things. People kept telling me about *Archer*, an animated spy comedy where the main character has seen all my films, even *At Long Last Love*. I tuned in and liked it, though I was surprised at what they get away with. The scripts are funny and it looks terrific on the screen, especially the car chases. I was delighted when the show's creator and head writer, Adam Reed, wrote an episode for me, "The Man from Jupiter," and I had nothing but fun doing it. And I recently attended the Wizard World show in Philadelphia. I thought it was about time to find out what those conventions are all about, and I'm glad I did. I enjoyed talking with the fans and seeing what's going on in their world.

AS I LOOK BACK, I'm proud of my accomplishments and disappointed by my failures. I always wanted to experience everything and go down swinging. Well, so far so good. I know I'm old, but I feel young. And there's one thing they can never take away: Nobody had more fun than I did.

Credits

TEAM REYNOLDS	Erik Kritzer
	Ryan Bundra
	Todd Vittum
BURT'S LITERARY AGENT	Katherine Latshaw
JON'S LITERARY AGENT	Paul Bresnick
PENGUIN PRESIDENT	Madeline McIntosh
PUTNAM PUBLISHER	Ivan Held
ASSOCIATE PUBLISHER	Christine Ball
EXECUTIVE EDITOR	Kerri Kolen
EDITORIAL ASSISTANT	Sofie Brooks
EDITORIAL ASSISTANT	Alise Hofacre
DIRECTOR OF PUBLICITY	Alexis Welby
ASSISTANT DIRECTOR OF PUBLICITY	Katie Grinch
MARKETING DIRECTOR	Ashley McClay
MARKETING DIRECTOR	Carrie Swetonic
PRODUCTION MANAGER	Denise Boyd
PRODUCTION EDITOR	Claire Winecoff
COPYEDITOR	Nancy Inglis
JACKET DESIGNER	Kaitlin Kall
PHOTO RESEARCHER	Helene Demeestere
MANAGING EDITOR	Meredith Dros

Index